Microsoft Dynamics 365™

for
dummies®
A Wiley Brand

Microsoft® Dynamics 365™

by Renato Bellu

A Wiley Brand

Microsoft® Dynamics 365™ For Dummies®

Published by: **John Wiley & Sons, Inc.,** 111 River Street, Hoboken, NJ 07030-5774, www.wiley.com

Copyright © 2018 by John Wiley & Sons, Inc., Hoboken, New Jersey

Published simultaneously in Canada

For general information on our other products and services, please contact our Customer Care Department within the U.S. at 877-762-2974, outside the U.S. at 317-572-3993, or fax 317-572-4002. For technical support, please visit https://hub.wiley.com/community/support/dummies.

Wiley publishes in a variety of print and electronic formats and by print-on-demand. Some material included with standard print versions of this book may not be included in e-books or in print-on-demand. If this book refers to media such as a CD or DVD that is not included in the version you purchased, you may download this material at http://booksupport.wiley.com. For more information about Wiley products, visit www.wiley.com.

Library of Congress Control Number: 2018955085

ISBN: 978-1-119-50886-1; ISBN: 978-1-119-50888-5 (ebk); ISBN: 978-1-119-50889-2 (ebk)

Manufactured in the United States of America

VWEP41657X_092718

Contents at a Glance

Table of Contents

Introduction

Welcome to an exciting new software offering from Microsoft that is destined to change the lives of millions of people all over the globe. As with Office 365, Dynamics 365 is a major release of cloud-based business software from Microsoft that is sure to have a huge impact on the IT industry. It may even profoundly affect your company, your job, and your opportunities for career advancement.

Dynamics 365 is a major release from a major player, Microsoft, which has set the standard in business software for decades and will continue to gain a massive following as it successfully competes with Salesforce.com, SAP, Oracle, NetSuite, and other CRM and ERP (accounting software) developers. Businesses are now increasingly making their inevitable transformation from "on premise" software that you own to online subscription-based "software as a service" that you rent. Dynamics 365 is a topic you need to get acquainted with ASAP so that whenever you come across it in your business career, you can talk intelligently about it and understand how you can prosper from it

Who Should Buy This Book

This book is targeted toward four kinds of people like you:

>> You are using Dynamics 365 and want to take advantage of its core features, customization options, and workflow and reporting tools, such as Power Apps, Flow, and Power BI, which are included as part of the offering.

>> You are tasked with evaluating whether Dynamics 365 is right for your company or your clients.

>> Your company or your client has already or is about to migrate to Dynamics 365, and you need to quickly come up to speed on what this software has to offer.

>> You are an existing user of "on premise" Microsoft CRM or Microsoft ERP (such as Dynamics AX or Dynamics NAV), and you are eager to learn about the new cloud versions, which have been rebranded and are now part of Dynamics 365.

About This Book

This book can help you safely and quickly navigate the turbulent and confusing bundle of software that falls under the umbrella of Microsoft Dynamics 365. This software is a bewildering mixture of repackaged products that are already used by millions of users but have only recently been moved to the cloud, as well as a whole host of powerful brand-new applications, tools, and technologies. This book dispels the mysteries surrounding Dynamics 365 — mysteries that cannot be unraveled by reading online reviews or marketing hype, but rather can be cleared up only by a concise, easy-to-understand guide that provides an unbiased picture of what truly comprises Dynamics 365 and what it can do (or can't do) for you and your business.

I've organized this book into five parts.

Part 1: Doing Great Things with Microsoft Dynamics 365

Part 1 is all about how Dynamics 365 is so much more than just CRM and ERP software. I discuss the benefits of cloud computing, integration with Microsoft Office 365, as well as Power BI (for business intelligence reporting), PowerApps (for point-and-click configuration of custom mobile apps), and Microsoft Flow (for creating cross-application workflows).

Part 2: Customer Engagement (formerly Dynamics CRM Online)

Part 2 explores the applications that were formerly part of Dynamics CRM Online and now comprise most of Dynamics 365 for Customer Engagement. You will learn how Microsoft has expanded, enhanced, and revamped the Microsoft CRM Online applications for Dynamics 365. Applications discussed include Sales, Customer Service, Project Service Automation, Marketing, and Field Service.

Part 3: Business Central ERP (formerly Dynamics NAV)

Part 3 is an overview of Business Central, one of two ERP offerings that fall under the Dynamics 365 umbrella. Business Central is geared toward small to mid-sized organizations.

Part 4: Finance and Operations ERP (formerly Dynamics AX)

Part 4 is an overview of Dynamics 365 for Finance and Operations, the more complex of the two ERP offerings that fall under the Dynamics 365 umbrella. Finance and Operations is geared toward enterprise clients and mid-market organizations.

Part 5: The Part of Tens

The first chapter in Part 5 provides information about the most exciting capabilities in Dynamics 365. The second dispels common myths associated with cloud computing, business software, and ERP implementations.

Foolish Assumptions

This book can be read by beginners to Dynamics 365, and it is geared toward the layperson rather than as a guide suitable only for professional computer programmers or business software consultants. Nonetheless, I had to make certain assumptions about you as the reader:

>> You are generally familiar with the Microsoft Windows operating system and related Microsoft Office applications such as Excel, Outlook, and Word.

>> You are a Microsoft Dynamics 365 user or are interested in becoming one, or in assessing this software for your company or for a client or an associate.

>> You are involved in business in some capacity, and you have a general understanding of business terminology, such as customer service and accounts payable.

Icons Used in This Book

You'll find icons in all *For Dummies* books, and this one is no exception. Each one is a little picture in the margin that lets you know something special about the paragraph it sits next to.

TIP

A Tip provides the extra tidbit of information that expands on the topic under discussion, making a useful Dynamics 365 feature even more powerful.

REMEMBER

The Remember icon is there to remind you of important points and considerations that may have already been touched on earlier in the chapter.

WARNING

Take note of the Warning icon when you see it. It's there to alert you to potential pitfalls you may encounter when using, configuring, or assessing the Dynamics 365 software.

TECHNICAL STUFF

Don't let the Technical Stuff icon scare you away from reading this extra information that is of a slightly more technical nature. That being said, if you're in more of a rush, you can safely skip these sections.

Beyond the Book

In addition to what you're reading right now, this product comes with a handy Cheat Sheet associated with this title. To get the Cheat Sheet, simply go to www.dummies.com and search for **Microsoft Dynamics 365 For Dummies cheat sheet** in the Search box.

1

Doing Great Things with Microsoft Dynamics 365

Chapter 1

Floating on a Secure Cloud

When electricity was first used commercially, a factory that wanted to run electric motors had to build its own power plant on the premises of the factory grounds. Each factory had its own power plant. There were no public utilities for electricity. Nicola Tesla pioneered the first large, centralized, electrical utility company at Niagara Falls, using the force of the falling water for power and converting it to electricity, which would then travel long distances over copper wires to customers using the alternating current (AC) system he devised. Creating a centralized electric utility using alternating current that could travel large distances, instead of Thomas Edison's direct current (DC) system, which was limited to short distances of a few miles, was revolutionary at the time. Companies quickly realized that it made much more sense to simply pay for electricity with a monthly utility bill rather than bother with the trouble and expense of having to maintain their own on-premise equipment for generating electricity.

The same type of revolution is taking place within the computer industry today, where computing power is rapidly becoming a utility that you pay for monthly, and you no longer have to maintain your own local, on-premise computer servers. Rather than buy your own hardware equipment, you pay for a service, and the "utility company" (in this case, Microsoft, IBM, Oracle, Google, Amazon, or Alibaba, to name the major players) takes care of the physical hardware computer equipment for you at its centralized locations. You connect to its centralized server farms by way of an Internet connection. (A *server farm* is a collection of interconnected computer servers housed together in a single physical location to provide massive computing power for large numbers of offsite users.)

These service providers not only provide disk space for you to save your files but also hosts applications. The hosted applications are installed and upgraded by the centralized provider, so you no longer need to install and upgrade your software; instead, you create user accounts on its system and then simply log in by way of a web page. These hosted applications are referred to as Software as a Service (SaaS) rather than the software products. SaaS is software you rent rather than buy.

Furthermore, you don't need to buy a new computer if you run out of disk space or database space; you simply ask for more space, and it can be quickly partitioned for your use — for a price, of course. Your data is stored on the cloud provider's computer system in communal computers, but separated by software that partitions your data into a separate area that is referred to as your *tenant* or your *instance*. The term *tenant* is now common usage because the SaaS software is rented rather than owned.

This list describes some of the benefits of the SaaS/cloud computing model:

>> **You always have the latest software.** The hosted application is continuously upgraded by the SaaS provider. You avoid costly upgrades — and the dreaded problem of falling too far behind in application version.

>> **You can add more capacity and increase performance incrementally.** This way, you don't have to purchase, install, configure, and maintain any additional hardware computer equipment.

>> **Your data is backed up for you by the cloud computing provider.** Your IT staff doesn't have to purchase backup equipment and configure backup software and backup plans.

>> **Your data is more secure from hackers.** Though many company executives worried at first about the security of their data in the cloud, nowadays the prevailing wisdom is that the opposite is true: It may be easier for hackers to attack your data if you're trying to safeguard it by yourself on your own small network rather than relying on the sophisticated security safeguards put in place by large corporations such as IBM, Amazon, Microsoft, and Oracle.

>> **Your employees can connect to the cloud applications using an Internet connection from anywhere in the world.** They aren't restricted to getting on a virtual private network (VPN) connection. Most often, cloud applications are mobile enabled so that employees can use them on their smartphones and tablets as well.

Microsoft's cloud service, Azure, is a leader in cloud computing. Public companies such as Microsoft and Amazon don't always break out their revenue numbers in consistent and comparable categories when reporting financial results, so it's hard to tell exactly who is in the lead at any given time. Nonetheless, Microsoft is typically listed in the top three of cloud providers, with IBM and Amazon. As a leader in providing cloud services, with Azure, Microsoft has a powerful and extensive cloud hosting environment. In other words, it has massive computing resources in data centers throughout the globe. When you get Dynamics 365 for ERP (enterprise resource planning) and CRM (customer relationship management), you also get the scalability, performance, security, and tight integration with other Microsoft cloud technologies that comes with Azure. Also, because Microsoft has its own cloud service infrastructure with Azure, it isn't dependent on another company to provide it — and so it isn't affected by another company catching it off guard and changing the rates or technology. That decreases your risk of a compatibility problem between the hosting company and the application development company. With Dynamics 365, the cloud provider is also the app developer.

Getting Under the Dynamics 365 Umbrella

Microsoft Office is the name of the suite of common business productivity applications that includes Word for word processing, Excel for spreadsheets, Outlook for email and scheduling, PowerPoint for presentations, and SharePoint for document management, among other applications. This suite of applications has become a common standard: Most people in the business world now use at least some part of Microsoft Office — especially Outlook — every day, 365 days a year. Microsoft has migrated Office to the cloud, as a subscription-based online Software as a Service suite of applications, and has branded it Office 365.

This move of Microsoft Office from *on premise* to *in the cloud* has proven to be extremely popular, as many organizations have now already transitioned their users from the desktop version of Office to Office 365. The computer network managers at most organizations prefer the online version because it's much easier to manage a link to a website than to install and troubleshoot applications on the individual desktop PCs and laptops of users.

As a follow-up to Office 365, Microsoft came out with a cloud version of its ERP (again, enterprise resource management), which is financial, accounting, and operational software, and combined it with its CRM (again, customer relationship management), which is sales, marketing, and customer service software. It has branded this combination of ERP and CRM in the cloud as Dynamics 365.

The 365 in Dynamics 365 emphasizes that the software plays nicely with Office 365, and it sure does — it's highly compatible and integrated with Excel, Outlook, and SharePoint, especially. Of course, 365 is the number of days in a typical year, so the name also imparts the constant availability of the software, every single day (even on the 366th day of a leap year).

Gaining a little historical perspective

The *Dynamics* part of the name Dynamics 365 has quite an interesting history. Once upon a time, two college buddies, Steve Ballmer and Doug Burgum, were roommates at Stanford University. Steve went on to become the CEO of Microsoft, replacing Bill Gates, and Doug founded his own accounting software company in North Dakota called Great Plains. Doug would eventually become the governor of North Dakota. Great Plains started out with a popular character-based (in other words, *nongraphical*) version that ran on IBM compatible PCs on the old DOS operating system. When the Windows operating system was first introduced in the early 1990s, Great Plains created a new software called Dynamics, which was a graphical-based software (you used a mouse and clicked graphical icons) that ran on Windows and, believe it or not, also on Apple Macintosh at the time. (Today's version no longer runs on Apple.)

TECHNICAL STUFF

The original Great Plains Dynamics was written in a proprietary computer language invented by the Great Plains developers called Dexterity. Dexterity was written in the C programming language and was invented to speed up the creation of Dynamics. As it turned out, Dexterity was never used for anything other than Great Plains Dynamics and add-on products designed specifically for Great Plains Dynamics. Therefore, Microsoft has no future plans to continue developing new products using it.

Years later, Great Plains was acquired by Microsoft for over a billion dollars. When Microsoft acquired Great Plains, it picked up Solomon, another popular accounting package. Solomon, well regarded for its project accounting and job costing features, had been previously acquired by Great Plains, before Microsoft acquired Great Plains. Acquiring Great Plains along with Solomon gave Microsoft a strong domestic presence in the ERP market in the United States.

To gain a foothold in the ERP market in Europe, Microsoft acquired Navision, a highly modifiable ERP package with strong manufacturing features. Navision, founded in Denmark, had previously acquired Axapta, another more robust ERP package, also with extensive manufacturing features, from Damgaard, another Danish software developer.

Microsoft's marketing department, which was quite fond of the Dynamics brand name, extended the brand to other Microsoft software products, including Microsoft's CRM package, originally called Microsoft CRM, and later rebranded as Dynamics CRM. This CRM package wasn't acquired from another company, but rather was developed by Microsoft internally. Microsoft CRM was one of the first packages that Microsoft migrated to the cloud, calling it CRM Online, in order to stay competitive with Salesforce.com, its main CRM rival. Microsoft CRM has captured a large share of the CRM market and is a successful and widely used product.

Microsoft's marketing folks kept using the Dynamics name, eventually rebranding as Dynamics the other three ERP packages that the company acquired and adding a short acronym to distinguish among them.

Microsoft ended up with these four ERP packages — and one CRM:

» Dynamics GP (formerly, Great Plains) ERP – not moved to 365

» Dynamics SL (formerly, Solomon) ERP – not moved to 365

» Dynamics NAV (formerly, Navision) ERP – Business edition in 365

» Dynamics AX (formerly, Axapta) ERP – Enterprise edition in 365

» Dynamics CRM (formerly, CRM Online) – Sales/Service/more in 365

Microsoft realized that maintaining four separate ERP packages with four separate programming code bases, and a CRM package that didn't natively talk to any of the four ERP packages didn't make a whole lot of sense, and certainly didn't provide for a long-term roadmap. Something would have to be done to simplify and unify its business software offerings. To make matters worse, most of the components in these ERP packages weren't web-based applications, but rather were the old-style client/server applications, which don't run on web pages, and instead either need to be installed on each user's computer or else require the users to log in to remote desktops or Citrix sessions, which is rather inconvenient and cumbersome to maintain for the IT department. The Microsoft ERP software needed to be migrated from client/server to web based. Fortunately, Microsoft CRM had been built from the ground up as a web-based application, so at least that didn't need as much revision as the ERP software.

Reading the roadmap for Microsoft ERP and CRM

Microsoft needed to come up with a strategy for their business software solutions that would address the problem of having four unrelated, redundant, on-premise ERP offerings, with insufficient interoperability between their CRM and ERP solutions to boot. To address these problems Microsoft devised a fourfold strategy:

1. **Move to the cloud because everybody is moving to the cloud, for many compelling advantages, especially the easier start-up.**

   Customers want the ease of setting up and maintaining a software infrastructure for their ERP and CRM systems, and of course it's much easier if the software vendor — in this case, Microsoft — handles all that for them. In other words, the systems are hosted by Microsoft, so you just surf to a web page, which is so much easier than buying servers, configuring them, installing software, creating backup plans, and on and on. Customers also prefer to rent instead of buy the software, because they can avoid having to shell out lots of money up front, even if it may end up costing them more money in the long run, which isn't necessarily the case, either.

2. **Modify several existing Microsoft applications to be web enabled rather than client/server, if they weren't already web enabled, and then combine them into a large, unified offering with a common look and feel, and a common brand name, Dynamics 365.**

   Microsoft already had several good applications, so rewriting an ERP and CRM from scratch would have been reinventing the wheel (not to mention that it would be impractical to do so). ERP and CRM systems are so packed with features and capabilities that they take many years, even decades, to develop and evolve to the level where they can address the needs of complex organizations.

3. **Provide a simplified license that allows you to get all (or at least, most of) this combined software for one combined cost per user, as a subscription SaaS offering.**

   The advantage to Microsoft here is that subscription-based revenue is preferred by stockholders because it tends to even out the revenue, providing steady and reliable profits year after year. The advantage to customers, dealers, and Microsoft is that obtaining Dynamics 365 involves less upfront cost and avoids the complexity of customers and dealers having to pick through a confusing menu of available modules to determine a price. Instead, a few basic plans include almost all the software.

4. **Program these applications to have tight integration to other, more general Microsoft applications, tools, and technologies, such as Microsoft Office 365, Power BI, PowerApps, Common Data Service, and the like.**

Doing so increases the usefulness of the software and makes it more appealing to customers who already have a large investment in Microsoft products.

Asking what's in the Dynamics 365 "sausage"

Microsoft's solution to its CRM/ERP roadmap problem was to create a SaaS subscription-based offering, available exclusively on Microsoft's cloud service, Azure. It combines CRM with ERP along with tight integration to Office applications such as Excel, Outlook, and SharePoint as well as a few other applications, plus other, newer Microsoft tools and technologies such as PowerApps for building mobile and web apps, and Power BI for business intelligence reporting.

REMEMBER

Dynamics 365 is a true SaaS solution; in other words, it's not available on-premise; you can only run it in the cloud, just like Salesforce.com, Workday, Oracle's NetSuite, and many other, newer competing CRM and ERP choices now prevalent in the marketplace.

In an effort to be all things to all people, Microsoft has jam-packed the capabilities that are included under the Dynamics 365 umbrella, extending the reach from ERP and CRM to FSA, PSA, HR, and POS.

See Table 1-1 for a clarification of what all this alphabet soup of acronyms actually means.

TABLE 1-1 ## Acronyms Related to Dynamics 365

Acronym	Stands For	Represents
ERP	Enterprise Resource Planning	Accounting software
CRM	Customer Relationship Management	Sales and customer service
FSA	Field Service Automation	Field technicians management
PSA	Professional Service Automation	Timing and billing/Project accounting
HR	Human Resources	Employee onboarding
POS	Point of Sale	Retail store software

Dynamics 365 is composed of the following major pieces:

- >> **Dynamics AX ERP:** Rebranded as Dynamics 365 for Finance and Operations, Enterprise edition (for larger organizations)

    Or, alternatively, for ERP you can choose a simplified version of Dynamics NAV ERP, rebranded as Dynamics 365 Finance and Operations Business edition (for smaller organizations)

- >> **Dynamics CRM:** Rebranded as Dynamics 365 for Sales, including Sales Force Automation, Customer Service, and Marketing

- >> **FieldOne:** A CRM add-on that was acquired by Microsoft and became CRM Field Service and CRM Resource Scheduling

- >> **Project Service:** Another CRM module that is a project accounting/time-and-billing application

- >> **Talent:** A separate application that is human resources (HR) software for employee onboarding and has a self-service portal, employee benefits management, and so on

- >> **Retail:** Another separate application that is a point-of-sale (POS) system used for retail store operations

Dynamics 365 also has tight integration with a whole host of Microsoft technologies, including SharePoint, Excel, Outlook, PowerApps, Power BI, and the Common Data Service.

Dynamics GP (formerly Great Plains) and Dynamics SL (formerly Solomon) are both widely adopted ERP packages, especially in the United States. Microsoft is still maintaining, and to some limited degree, enhancing these products due to continued customer demand. Though it's true that many customers do not want to migrate from these products because of the large investment of time and money spent in the complex configuration and modifications they have made to the core systems, Microsoft's R&D dollars and focus are clearly skewed toward favoring Dynamics AX (now Dynamics 365 Finance and Operations Enterprise editions). Microsoft's vision is that AX is the future product to compete with its main rivals, such as Oracle and SAP. GP and SL are sometimes referred to as *sunset* products because they will eventually be phased out by Microsoft. However, the ERP world moves at a glacial pace because of the complexity and the mission-critical nature of the beast. In all likelihood, GP and SL will be around for many years to come, because of customers refusing to migrate.

Microsoft keeps rebranding its business software, and frankly, that can become confusing to the consumer. Of course, the seemingly endless rounds of renaming are for the purpose of staying current with buzzwords and trends, and are an honest attempt to clarify what the software is designed to do. To help you see clearly through this foggy haze, I have created Table 1-2, which lists the major software applications that have evolved into Dynamics 365.

TABLE 1-2   **The Move to Dynamics 365**

Type	Original Developer	What It Is	Rebranded as Dynamics 365
ERP	Damgaard	Dynamics AX (Axapta)	Finance and Operations Enterprise edition
ERP	Navision	Dynamics NAV	Business Central
CRM	Microsoft	Sales Force Automation	Sales
CRM	Microsoft	Customer Service	Service
CRM	Microsoft	Marketing Automation	Marketing
FSA	FieldOne	Field Service Automation	Field Service
PSA	Microsoft	Project Service Automation	Project Service
FSA	FieldOne	Technician Scheduling	Resource Scheduling
HR	Microsoft	Human Resources	Talent
POS	Microsoft	Point of Sale	Retail

Standardizing the tools and terminology

As the software that comprises the origin of Dynamics 365, such as Damgaard Axapta, has evolved over decades, and eventually became part of Dynamics 365, Microsoft has spent a tremendous amount of time, effort, and money to modernize it on the one hand and to standardize it to fit into the overall Microsoft environment of operating systems, databases, and development tools on the other so that Microsoft offerings would have a consistent look and feel. The work of thousands of software engineers has transformed the software to a point where it's barely recognizable from what it started out as.

For example, Axapta (which become Dynamics AX) is customized using a proprietary tool unique to AX called the Application Object Tree (referred to as the AOT). Mastering the AOT was essential to becoming skilled in the customization of Dynamics AX. In Dynamics 365, the proprietary AOT has been done away with. Instead, Microsoft has substituted a more mainstream standard Microsoft tool — namely, Visual Studio. In Dynamics 365, you use the Application Explorer in Visual Studio to look under the hood of AX and manipulate the programming objects that make up the new Dynamics 365 cloud-enabled version of AX, Dynamics 365 for

Finance and Operations Enterprise edition. Microsoft has changed the proprietary terminology of the AOT to the standard terminology of Visual Studio, the application used by programmers to code computer programs using Microsoft programming languages, such as .NET. In other words, as Microsoft has taken existing applications, such as Dynamics AX, and transitioned them into Dynamics 365 components, the applications have been made to conform to overall Microsoft terminology and technology standards.

Table 1-3 lists the terminology standardizations Microsoft made when migrating the Dynamics AX Application Object Tree (AOT) from AX to Dynamics 365 Finance and Operations Enterprise edition.

TABLE 1-3   ## Moving from Dynamics AX to Dynamics 365

Dynamics AX Application Object Tree	Visual Studio Application Explorer
Data Dictionary	Data Model or Data Types
Classes	Code
Macros	Code
Forms	User Interface
Menus	User Interface
Other GUI Elements	User Interface
Business Intelligence Components	Analytics

Transitioning to the Cloud

If you're an existing user of one of the software packages that has been incorporated into Dynamics 365, you may be wondering how the release of Dynamics 365 will affect you and your organization. Clearly, it's Microsoft's goal to retain you as a customer, and also to encourage you to migrate to Dynamics 365 as soon as possible. Microsoft's long-term ERP/CRM strategy is to focus its research-and-development efforts on its cloud offering, which is what it will use to compete against archrivals Oracle and SAP. The sooner its customers move to the cloud offering (Dynamics 365, in other words), the less effort and expense needs to be diverted to maintaining older, *sunset* products, and the better the cloud offering will become. (The unspoken assumption here is that, yes, the better the offering, the more it can gain market share against Oracle, SAP, and newer rivals such as Workday and Salesforce.com.)

Many customers of earlier Dynamics versions — the ones that predate Dynamics 365 — are *midmarket* organizations: They have hundreds, if not thousands, of employees, and hundreds of millions of dollars in annual revenue or budget, if not billions. These large organizations — which may be privately held or publicly traded for-profit companies, not-for-profit charities, or city, state, or federal government public sector agencies — are sometimes referred to as *enterprise* clients. Smaller companies, charities, and government agencies are sometimes referred to as *SMB* clients — short for *small* and *medium-size businesses*. These clients are said to fall within the SMB space, as opposed to the enterprise space.

Implementations of pre-365 Microsoft CRM or AX or NAV ERP at enterprise clients typically include extensive modifications to the out-of-the-box screens, lots of customized reports, and complex custom integrations that were added to electronically import or export transactions into or out of Dynamics from or to external applications. Big organizations have complex ERP and CRM configurations. Migrating these to the Dynamics 365 cloud isn't a simple matter, and it won't happen overnight.

Microsoft certainly cares about these big enterprise clients who, after all, have high user counts and therefore mean big money to Microsoft. Given that fact, it makes sense that Microsoft encourages migration to the cloud, but won't force it on its customers. The transition in the enterprise space will be piecemeal, and will happen over the course of several years. Transitioning to the cloud in the SMB space will be easier because SMB implementations have fewer customizations — but then again, SMB organizations have fewer human resources and less financial wherewithal to deploy toward changing their IT systems than enterprise organizations do. Either way, transitioning your Dynamics system to the Dynamics 365 cloud will take careful planning and plenty of patience.

REMEMBER

Microsoft CRM Online is now part of Dynamics 365, and because Microsoft CRM was always a web-based product from day one, and because it was the first major business application of Microsoft's to be transitioned to a SaaS cloud solution, the transition from CRM Online to Dynamics 365 is easier than transitioning an on-premise installation of Dynamics AX ERP to the cloud. Transitioning CRM Online to Dynamics 365 is primarily a matter of switching your user licenses.

Understanding the difference between hosted client/server and true SaaS

Dynamics GP, Microsoft's sunset ERP package, is a client/server application, not a web-based SaaS offering. However, for many years now, application service providers, or ASPs (an older term meaning cloud providers), have been offering hosted environments for Dynamics GP and other non-SaaS applications. What they do is install the client/server application on their own remote server farms on application servers. They will use *virtualization* as well, in which the servers aren't necessarily physical boxes, but rather only virtually simulated physical computer servers. You then log in from your organization to the application service provider's remote server to run your ERP application. The SQL database is likewise on a virtual server on the application service provider's system. This hosted application setup is very common and has many of the same benefits of a true SaaS solution; however, it's not true SaaS, as will soon become clear. To make matters even more confusing, these non-SaaS applications, such as Dynamics GP, are sometimes hosted on the Microsoft Azure cloud. To make matters yet more confusing, the Azure cloud provider can be Microsoft itself, or another IT company that is renting space on Azure from Microsoft.

Most of the application service providers (ASPs) offer the same kind of subscription models that involve a monthly user fee, instead of having to purchase the software up front. So in that sense, the hosted client/server software is like SaaS. Also, the ASP takes care of backups and database maintenance and owns the actual hardware (or perhaps rents space on another company's hardware). Though an ASP-hosted application seems like a true SaaS application, it is not, because the software application itself wasn't initially designed to run over the Internet, nor was it designed to have multiple unrelated organizations using the same version of the software at the same time, in a similar way to different renters or tenants living in the same apartment building. In the case of a hosted client/server application, the implementation of it is still your own separate install of the application, which is different and totally disconnected from the installations of other organizations that the ASP is also hosting. Old-school client/server-style applications that predate the cloud, but are now being hosted in the cloud, weren't designed from the ground up as a true multi-tenant architecture, and so, unfortunately, they still need to be upgraded independently.

True SaaS software is typically software that was built for being rented by several tenants, and was designed to be run over the Internet and on mobile Internet devices, rather than an older style client/server application that is running on a remote server. True multi-tenant SaaS software is upgraded by the cloud application provider, and all tenants gain the benefits of the new version automatically at the same time. As shown in Figure 1-1, the separate companies, as well as their separate environment tiers, are treated as tenants within the same application building. To use an analogy, if an apartment building gets a new furnace, for example, all the tenants receive the benefit of improved heating right away.

TIP

Best practices for changing any IT system recommends using different environments, sometimes referred to as *tiers*. Ideally, your organization has at least three tiers for your CRM or ERP system.

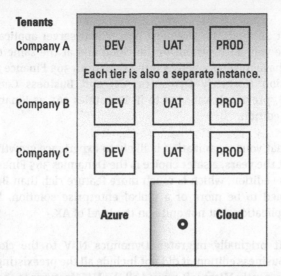

Tenants

Company A

| DEV | UAT | PROD |

Each tier is also a separate instance.

Company B

| DEV | UAT | PROD |

Company C

| DEV | UAT | PROD |

Azure   **Cloud**

FIGURE 1-1:
True SaaS
software is
typically a
multi-tenant
architecture.

Typical CRM/ERP environment tiers are described in this list:

>> **DEV (Development):** Where the programmers play

>> **UAT (User Acceptance Testing):** Where the users test the system

>> **PROD (Production):** The actual live system

The UAT tier or DEV tier is sometimes referred to as a *sandbox,* or a place to play around with scenarios without corrupting the live production system. Sometimes the sandbox is loaded with demo data rather than a copy of your organization's data so that you can work with an unmodified, out-of-the-box version of the software for testing purposes. Software training may be accomplished using the UAT tier, or perhaps you may have an additional tier called TRAIN. Also, sometimes there's a tier called PRE-PROD, which is a last stop of IT system testing before promotion to PROD.

Dynamics 365 is a true SaaS solution, even though all the pieces, such as Dynamics AX (formerly Axapta) didn't start out that way. Microsoft has taken the trouble to rewrite the code so it works in a true multi-tenant SaaS environment. Microsoft can provide as many tiers as your organization requires so that you can develop, test, train, and run your application safely.

Migrating from Dynamics GP or SL to Dynamics 365

Dynamics GP (formerly known as Great Plains) and Dynamics SL (formerly known as Solomon) aren't part of Dynamics 365. If your organization is running

Dynamics GP or SL (both, for the most part, client/server applications) and you want to migrate your ERP system to the cloud and at the same time stick with Microsoft, you have to choose between the Dynamics 365 Finance and Operations Enterprise edition (formerly Dynamics AX) and Business Central (formerly Dynamics NAV), previously referred to in Dynamics 365 as Finance and Operations, Business edition.

If you believe that your organization is likely to experience growth and increased complexity over the years, a safer choice is the Dynamics 365 Finance and Operations, Enterprise edition, which is much more feature rich than Business Central and was designed to be more of a global enterprise solution. NAV itself is a feature-rich application, but not quite on the level of AX.

When Microsoft originally migrated Dynamics NAV to the cloud to become Dynamics 365 Business edition, it did not include all the preexisting NAV features; however, more recently Microsoft moved all the NAV features to the cloud version, when rebranding it as Business Central. At one point, it was unclear how much of NAV would eventually make its way to the cloud. It seemed that Microsoft may have been intending to keep the Business edition relatively clean and simple, a bit more like QuickBooks than a full-blown NAV, so that it could satisfy the SMB (small to midsize business) requirements and be easy to implement. But Business Central isn't just another QuickBooks Online, nor is it trying to be like SAP, a huge global ERP for the Fortune 500. Business Central is a good middle ground in the ERP landscape.

Dynamics GP and Dynamics SL tend to get fairly complex, but Business Central may be able to handle your ERP requirements. It all depends on what modules and features you're using in GP or SL. If you have complex ERP requirements that demand a global enterprise solution, the Finance and Operations Enterprise edition (formerly Dynamics AX) is probably the way to go.

REMEMBER

Whatever edition you choose, if you plan to migrate from GP or SL to Dynamics 365, it would be prudent to consider such a project to be, in essence, complete ERP reimplementation of a new ERP package rather than an upgrade or simple migration that can be accomplished using a wizard application. Though it's true that Microsoft has created some data migration wizards that can be useful for the data conversion aspect of the project, data conversion is only one part of the ERP implementation puzzle. There is custom reporting, module configuration, screen customizations, process and workflow re-engineering, integrations, and more to consider. You will most likely need the assistance of a consulting firm that is an authorized partner for Dynamics 365, who can propose an implementation plan, and provide an estimated budget and timeline to complete the project. It's very unrealistic to think you can just click a few buttons and move from GP or SL to Dynamics 365; rather, you will be looking at a full blown ERP implementation project.

Migrating from Dynamics CRM or CRM Online to Dynamics 365

If you're an existing customer of Dynamics CRM Online and you want to keep using Microsoft's CRM software, you won't have a choice about whether to migrate to Dynamics 365; you will have to do it. Because you're already in the cloud, your software is continuously being upgraded by the cloud provider — in this case, Microsoft. Microsoft has, in essence, upgraded CRM Online to Dynamics 365. Your CRM Online subscription will expire, and for you to be able to continue using the software, you will need to switch to a Dynamics 365 license. If you don't switch to a Dynamics 365 license, your CRM Online will eventually be disabled by Microsoft. However, there's no reason not to switch licenses because, after all, you will want to be on the latest version, and benefit from the newer user interface, expanded features, and improved integration with Microsoft Office.

REMEMBER

Microsoft Dynamics CRM Online is pretty much already Dynamics 365, in the sense that CRM Online is cloud based. This is the easiest of all the Dynamics 365 migrations, and it's primarily a license change. To make the transition even easier, Microsoft has created a wizard to switch your user license plans, called the Switch Plans Wizard.

To migrate your license from Dynamics CRM Online to Dynamics 365, using the Switch Plans wizard, follow these steps:

1. **Sign in to Office 365 at office.com with the account that has admin permissions.**

2. **Click the app launcher icon in the upper-left and click to select the Admin tile.**

   The Admin tile appears only to people who have Office 365 admin permissions. If you don't see the tile, then you don't have permissions to access the admin center for your organization.

3. **Click Billing.**

   A drop-down menu appears.

4. **Choose Subscriptions.**

5. **Select the plan you want to renew, and click the Switch Plans button.**

6. **Click the Buy Now button on the plan you want to buy.**

   Talk with your Dynamics 365 authorized partner to learn about the various plans, and decide which plan is right for you.

After the license change, you will notice that the software looks slightly different. Menus and buttons are in different places, and some items may use different terminology. There's definitely a learning curve involved in getting up to speed on Dynamics 365.

You will want to make the license change in a lower tier (development or testing) environment. If your organization has access to a user acceptance testing (UAT) environment, the license change can be applied there first. Users can train and test on the software before actual cut over, when the license is applied in the PROD (production) live tier.

TIP

If you're running an earlier version of Dynamics CRM, one that is perhaps an on-premise version, your CRM software is (unfortunately) not already cloud based. The migration to Dynamics 365 will involve more steps. Confer with your Dynamics 365 authorized partner on developing an upgrade plan.

Migrating from Dynamics AX to Dynamics 365 Enterprise edition

Dynamics AX (formerly known as Axapta) has evolved into Dynamics 365 for Finance and Operations Enterprise edition. However, that doesn't mean you can simply upgrade your software license as you can with Microsoft CRM Online, to migrate your existing AX software to the Microsoft Azure cloud. Unlike CRM, AX wasn't originally developed as a web-based application, and unlike CRM, AX wasn't previously migrated by Microsoft to an online version. In other words, there was never an AX Online, like there was a CRM Online. Furthermore, AX is a much more complicated application than CRM, because it's a full-featured accounting and financial system that has a much broader depth of functionality, encompassing accounts payable, accounts receivable, inventory, supply chain, financial reporting, general ledger, warehouse management, manufacturing, and so much more.

In migrating AX to 365, you will need to plan for a full-blown ERP implementation project, not a simple upgrade. That being said, Microsoft, in some of its literature, does refer to the migration of AX to Dynamics 365 for Finance and Operations Enterprise edition as an upgrade or as an upgrade path. Keep in mind that it isn't an upgrade in the sense of running an upgrade wizard application, but rather a complicated series of steps that will require analysis, decision making, and, most likely, some level of redesign.

Microsoft is justified in referring to the migration of Dynamics AX 2012 as an upgrade path, although a complicated one, because it does provide automated programs to migrate the data. Data upgrade is accomplished using a deployable package, which is similar to the mechanism used to deploy new code from one environment (tier) to another.

TIP

Fortunately, Microsoft has provided extensive tools and documentation designed to assist you and your Dynamics AX authorized partner in migrating your Dynamics AX ERP to Dynamics 365 for Finance and Operations Enterprise edition in the Azure cloud. These tools include an upgrade analyzer tool, a code upgrade estimation tool, and a project methodology. Ask your authorized partner about how to access and deploy these tools.

TECHNICAL STUFF

In order to help clients map out a transition plan, Microsoft has come up with Dynamics Lifecycle Services (LCS, for short. With LCS, Microsoft has designed project methodologies for various Dynamics-related projects. A project methodology called Upgrade AX 2012 to Dynamics 365 for Finance and Operations describes the three phases (analyze, validate, and execute) that are recommended by Microsoft, and it provides links to the applicable documentation.

The *upgrade analyzer* is a tool that you can run against your existing AX 2012 environment. The output of the upgrade analyzer tool provides information about these options:

>> Data Cleanup

>> SQL Configuration

>> Deprecated Features

The upgrade analyzer provides information that may be useful in planning your upgrade, but it doesn't actually upgrade anything. Also note that it points out *deprecated* features — features that were available in Dynamics AX but are no longer available in Dynamics 365. Microsoft is discontinuing some functionality from AX, so it may be impossible to migrate all your AX data, because some of the database tables will not even exist in the cloud. Nonetheless, it's still a good idea to migrate to the cloud because, although your setup may lose some features, it will be sure to gain many new features and have tighter and more standardized integration with other Microsoft technologies — and it will be taking advantage of all the benefits of multi-tenant cloud computing.

Migrating from Dynamics NAV to Dynamics 365 Business edition

Dynamics NAV (formerly known Navision) is a full-featured ERP package, deployed by customers mostly as an on-premise solution. Dynamics NAV is more widely adopted in Europe than in the United States. It's generally believed that

Dynamics NAV has a better manufacturing capability than Dynamics GP or Dynamics SL, and that it's easier to customize than GP or SL because it has more flexible and user-friendly customization tools.

NAV, unlike GP and SL, has been ported to the cloud and has been rebranded as Business Central, though it's also referred to as Dynamics 365 for Finance and Operations Business edition. Though the marketing folks at Microsoft have been making product name changes that are hard to keep up with, to clarify this one, just think of the baby ERP as Navision and the big boy ERP as AX. The baby ERP isn't the full-blown NAV because NAV is a fairly complex application with loads of features. NAV has been reduced to the most essential features before being ported to the cloud to become Business Central. Whether Microsoft will continue to add features and capabilities to Business Central to bring it on par with NAV isn't yet known; it may choose to keep it relatively simple.

Unlike AX, Microsoft has not touted an upgrade path from the on-premise Dynamics NAV to the cloud Business Central. This may be because Business Central is a stripped-down version of NAV, so it's not really possible to migrate most of it anyway. The rule of thumb is that if you have an extensive implementation of on-premise Dynamics NAV and you want to migrate your ERP to the cloud, you should probably consider a full-blown ERP implementation of Dynamics 365 for Finance and Operations Enterprise edition (in other words, move to AX in the cloud). Enterprise edition will have the manufacturing features or other complex features you may be looking for. Consult with your authorized Dynamics partner for more information on migrating from NAV to Dynamics 365.

IN THIS CHAPTER

» **Managing users, subscriptions, and passwords in the Admin Center**

» **Emailing within Dynamics 365 using Outlook integration**

» **Working with spreadsheets within Dynamics 365 using Excel integration**

» **Organizing documents within Dynamics 365 with SharePoint and OneDrive**

» **Handling messaging with Skype for Business**

Chapter **2**

Extending Your Reach with Office 365

I f your organization is considering purchasing subscriptions for Microsoft Dynamics 365, you should also consider Microsoft Office 365. Chances are good that your organization already has migrated to Office 365, before implementing Dynamics 365. In any case, ideally, your users have both subscriptions — Office 365 and Dynamics 365 — because the integration between them is extensive and powerful. The subscriptions are separate, but the software is very much connected.

Working with the Admin Center

One of the greatest selling points for signing on to both Microsoft Dynamics 365 and Microsoft Office 365 is the method that Microsoft has devised for administrators to manage Dynamics users — namely, by logging in to the Office 365 Admin

Center. In other words, Microsoft already had an Admin Center for Office 365 designed and coded, so that same mechanism was simply used as the way to manage Dynamics 365 users. In this way, the code base was reduced, and having less code to manage means less buggy code. As an added benefit, you get more standardized software. After you know how to manage users in Office 365, you'll already know how to manage them in Dynamics 365, because you'll use the same interface. The standardization between the various Microsoft products makes learning and mastering the software much easier because the terminology, the look and feel, and the menu navigation are more consistent.

Having your ERP and CRM in the cloud is great, but if your email (Outlook), spreadsheets (Excel), and document sharing (SharePoint and OneDrive) are also in the cloud, and on the same highly integrated cloud environment (Microsoft Azure), you will gain maximum interoperability. (*Interoperability* is a fancy word for indicating that all your software plays nice together.) For example, you can print a financial statement in Finance and Operations and automatically generate a link on SharePoint as a way to distribute the report to users, or you can respond to a customer complaint on a customer service case with an email that you send directly from within the Dynamics 365 Service application — without having to toggle to Outlook, cut-and-paste data, or manually add attachments to the email.

Managing users

For people in your organization to be able to access Dynamics 365 applications, they first need to be set up as users in the Office 365 Admin Center. After a person has been set up as a Dynamics user, you will be able to assign licenses and security privileges as needed.

To add a user to Dynamics 365, follow these steps:

1. Using your Microsoft username and password, log on to the Office 365 Admin Center.

The URL is https://portal.office.com/AdminPortal/#/homepage.

2. Choose Users from the navigation menu located at the far left of the page.

A pull-down menu appears.

You can expand or collapse the navigation menu by clicking on the left arrow (<) to collapse it, and on the right arrow (>) to expand it.

3. Choose Active Users from the pull-down menu.

A view of users appears, showing you the active users.

4. **Click the Add a User button.**

The New User window appears, as shown in Figure 2-1.

5. **Fill out the appropriate information.**

The display name and username are required. If the user needs administrative access, you need to change their role.

Most users are fine with the default, which is User (no administrator access).

6. **Still in the New User window, click the Product Licenses link.**

A pull-down menu appears. By default the licenses are turned off.

7. **To turn on (and yes, use up) a license, click anywhere on the On–Off slider to toggle the control on or off.**

The number of licenses still available for each type of license you're subscribed to is shown underneath each license type. For example, you may see the message "20 of 25 licenses available."

8. **Click the Add button to add the user to Dynamics 365.**

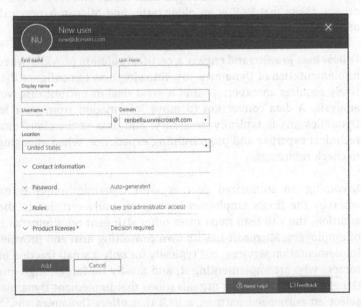

FIGURE 2-1:
The Office 365
Admin Center
New User
window.

If your organization has dozens of users, create a custom view to filter the user list. This helps you manage your users more effectively. Click Views, and a drop-down list appears, displaying all available built-in views. At the bottom of the list, you'll find a choice for custom views. Click the Add Custom Views option, and the Custom View window appears. Fill out the requested data to create a custom view.

Purchasing and managing subscriptions

Because Dynamics 365 is a Software as a Service (SaaS) offering, you cannot purchase the software outright, as you can with an on-premise application that you install on your own computers. With SaaS, you pay a monthly amount per user. Dynamics 365 exists in the cloud and is accessed by logging on over the Internet using a web browser or, in some cases, a mobile app on your tablet or smartphone.

Microsoft's Dynamics products are typically purchased via authorized partners who are dealers of the software. These partners add value by helping you configure the software, train users, and develop custom reports, integrations, and modifications to the user interface. A firm that's authorized to sell ERP and CRM packages such as Dynamics is sometimes referred to as a *value-added reseller (VAR)*. The collection of value-added resellers for Dynamics is often referred to as the *Dynamics VAR channel*. Microsoft relies on the VAR channel to sell and to implement its products out in the real world. The VAR receives a small percentage of the price of the subscription from Microsoft, but most of the VARs' revenue typically comes from consulting services, which they bill directly to their clients. You can find hundreds of VARs, some larger than others and some more experienced than others. (Note that *VAR* is an older term, and Microsoft now calls these dealers *authorized partners* or *solution providers*.)

TIP

Follow best practice and engage a certified solution provider when considering an implementation of Dynamics 365. Knowing how to configure the software effectively requires an expert — and a great deal of upfront discovery and business analysis. A data conversion to move information from your legacy system to Dynamics 365 is typically necessary, and data conversions most often require technical expertise and programming experience. When engaging a VAR, be sure to check references.

Becoming an authorized partner with Dynamics requires extensive testing whereby the firm's employees become officially certified in these products. In addition, the VAR firm must meet other stringent requirements, such as number of employees. Microsoft has its own consulting arm and provides Dynamics 365 implementation services, but typically for only a small fraction of the many customers who are implementing it, and mostly for larger, high-profile customers. Generally speaking, most organizations that implement Dynamics 365 must first select an authorized partner, a VAR that offers Dynamics 365. Your authorized partner then guides you through the purchase of subscriptions for Dynamics 365. Often, the cost of the subscription is included in the VAR's proposal for its implementation services.

Knowing which subscription to purchase isn't always clear-cut. Again, you need the expertise of the authorized partner to sort it out, because the subscriptions are bundles of various applications that fall under the Dynamics 365 umbrella. Also, the names of the applications have changed over the years, and understanding the functionality of the applications is necessary to know which ones should be included in your subscription. Knowing how many licenses you'll need is, generally speaking, more straightforward: You simply need to know how many users will need access to the software.

To log on to Dynamics 365, you need to purchase a subscription from Microsoft. The subscription contains a number of licenses and is priced per user per month or, in a few cases, per instance per month. You can purchase a subscription in the Office 365 Admin Center. Your authorized partner receives credit for your subscription because it is — you guessed it — your authorized partner. You can work with multiple firms when purchasing implementation services for Dynamics 365, but you can have only one authorized partner who receives a margin on your Dynamics 365 subscription. If you're unhappy with your authorized partner, you can talk to Microsoft at any time about making a change.

TECHNICAL STUFF

Older on-premise Dynamics products such as Dynamics GP (Great Plains) are sold using *concurrent* licenses, so if you have five concurrent licenses, five users can be in the system at the same time. You're free to create as many users in the system as you want; they just can't log in at the same time. However, Dynamics 365 is sold using a *named* user: You purchase a subscription that has a certain number of active named users allowed; each time you create a user, and activate that user, you use up one of your active named user licenses. Therefore, you need in your subscription a user license count that's sufficient to buy a license for all users who need to get on the system, regardless of whether they all log in at one time. Otherwise, you would need to keep deactivating licenses to allow other people to enter the system, which is both inconvenient and impractical.

To view your Dynamics 365 licenses, follow these steps:

1. **Using your Microsoft username and password, log on to the Office 365 Admin Center.**

   The URL is https://portal.office.com/AdminPortal/#/homepage.

2. **Choose Billing in the navigation menu at the far left.**

   A pull-down menu appears.

3. **Choose Licenses.**

   A view of licenses appears, showing you valid, expired, and assigned licenses for each of your subscriptions. (By examining the counts in this view, you can see whether you're running out of licenses and need to purchase more.)

To purchase subscriptions for Dynamics 365, follow these steps:

1. **Log on to the Office 365 Admin Center.**

The URL is https://portal.office.com/AdminPortal/#/homepage.

2. **Choose Billing in the navigation menu at the far left.**

A pull-down menu appears.

3. **Choose Purchase Services.**

Offers appear for subscriptions to Office 365 Enterprise Suite, Dynamics 365 Suite, Small Business Suite, Other Plans, and Add-On Subscriptions.

4. **If the blue arrow to the right of Dynamics 365 Suite is pointing downward, click it to view the subscription offers.**

The blue arrow then points upward, and the subscription offers become visible.

5. **Hover the mouse over the bottom of the offer tile.**

A blue Buy Now button appears.

6. **Click Buy Now.**

The Checkout window appears.

7. **Fill out your purchase address and click Next.**

For the purpose of sales tax calculation, this should be the main address of your organization, such as its headquarters, or wherever the purchase occurs.

8. **Enter the number of user licenses you want to purchase for this subscription in the User text box, and then press Tab to move out of that field.**

The extended price is displayed. If you have a promo code, click the Have a Promo or Discount Code? link, fill out the promo code, and then click Apply.

9. **Select whether to pay annually or monthly by clicking either radio button: Pay by the Year or Pay by the Month.**

10. **Select a payment method from the drop-down list, or click New Credit Card to add a payment method.**

To set up a payment method ahead of time, find the Payment Methods option under the Billing menu.

Setting the password expiration

The use of passwords is vital to security in Dynamics 365. Managing them improperly could enable unauthorized persons to access your mission-critical customer and accounting data. Dynamics 365 provides the ability to autogenerate passwords. Doing so is recommended because an autogenerated password is typically more random, and thereby secure, than ones that humans devise, such as password123. When resetting passwords in Dynamics 365, you can choose to make users change their passwords when they first sign in. This option is especially important if you haven't used an autogenerated password, and instead have set your own, generic initial password and assigned that same initial password to multiple users. You want to ensure that users are forced to change to a password that only they know, so this option to force the user to change their password when they first sign in is highly recommended.

To reset a password for a user of Dynamics 365, follow these steps:

1. **Log on to the Office 365 Admin Center.**

   The URL is https://portal.office.com/AdminPortal/#/homepage.

2. **Choose Users in the navigation menu located at the far left.**

   A pull-down menu appears.

3. **Choose Active Users.**

   A view of users appears, displaying all active users. Keep in mind that if you don't see the user you're looking for, you can search for that person in the Search Users text box, located above the list of users.

4. **Click the name of the user whose password you want to reset.**

   This step selects the check box to the left of the name, and the Edit User window appears to the right.

5. **Click the Reset Password button located near the top of the window, under the user's name and login name.**

   The Reset Password window appears, as shown in Figure 2-2.

6. **Make your selections and then click the Reset button.**

   Doing so resets the user's password. The changes take place immediately.

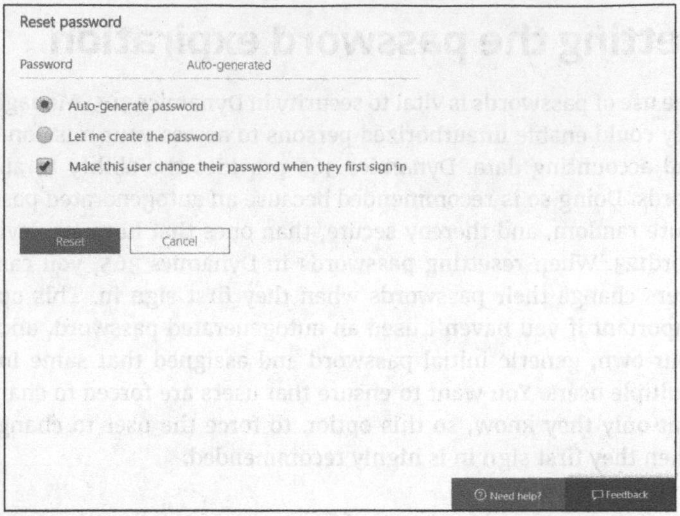

FIGURE 2-2:
The Reset
Password window
in the Office 365
Admin Center.

Integrating Dynamics 365 with Outlook Email

Microsoft takes seriously the integration between Outlook and its other applications, and Dynamics 365 is certainly no exception. After all, most business users respond to emails all day long. The emails you receive often dictate which tasks you focus on. The way you communicate with co-workers and customers alike is mostly by email. So if your email system is separate from your front-office CRM (sales force automation and customer service) and back-office ERP (finance and operations), you'll toggle between disconnected applications, cut and paste data, laboriously download file attachments, browse to find those files, and then make new file attachments. Contacts in your CRM or ERP system will have to be manually added to your email contacts, or email addresses will have to be cut-and-pasted back and forth. Clearly, not having tight integration between your mission-critical front-office, back-office, and email applications is inefficient, error-prone, and time consuming.

Microsoft's answer to Outlook email integration with Dynamics 365 is Dynamics 365 App for Outlook. This app, which is a Microsoft Office add-in, is the preferred app, especially if you're running Dynamics 365 on mobile devices.

TECHNICAL STUFF

Previously, an application called Dynamics 365 for Outlook (the old name doesn't contain the word *app*) was the go-to integration provided by Microsoft. The older application (sometimes called the Dynamics 365 for Outlook *client*) is still available for reasons of backward compatibility.

The following newer features are included in Dynamics 365 App for Outlook, but were missing from Dynamics 365 for Outlook:

» Allows for one-click ability to set a regarding record (in other words, to link a record in Dynamics 365, such as a customer account, to an Outlook email).

» Displays a summary of information from Dynamics 365 for email recipients in Outlook.

» Displays the Regarding Record summary in the email or appointment.

» Compatible with the Outlook Web App.

» Compatible with Outlook for the Mac.

» Compatible with smartphones and tablets.

» Ability to track sent emails.

» Ability to create Word mail-merge documents.

Fortunately, regardless of which version of Outlook you're using, Dynamics 365 App for Outlook is available for recent releases for all of these Outlook versions:

» Outlook for the Desktop

» Outlook Web App (included with Office 365)

» Outlook Mobile App (for smartphones and tablets)

When Dynamics 365 App for Outlook is installed, a Dynamics 365 pane appears to the right of your email message; this same pane appears whenever you're setting up a meeting. With a single click, you can link an email message to a Dynamics 365 record, such as a case in Dynamics 365 Customer Service. The linked email becomes an activity on the case automatically. In other words, the email is now part of a customer service case, and is therefore visible in both applications. (See Figure 2-3.) (Note that an integration type that allows the transfer of data in both directions is called a *bidirectional integration* or *synchronization*.)

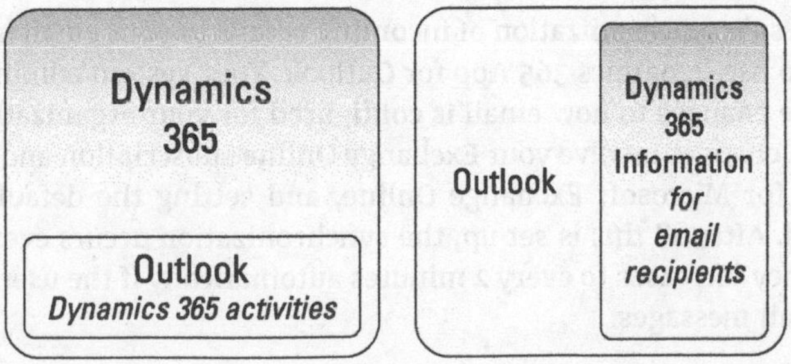

FIGURE 2-3:
Bidirectional
Outlook
Integration with
Dynamics 365.

To launch the Dynamics 365 pane within Outlook, click the Dynamics 365 icon —
that funky logo consisting of two triangles and one trapezoid. (See Figure 2-4).
Get to know this logo because it signifies Dynamics 365 Finance and Operations
(Enterprise ERP system) and because it often appears in other applications where
an integration with Dynamics 365 is available.

FIGURE 2-4:
The Dynamics
365 logo.

Using the features available in Dynamics 365 App for Outlook, you can

>> See information about your Dynamics 365 contacts and leads while you're
viewing emails, meetings, or appointments in Outlook.

>> Link email messages, meetings, and appointments to an account (customer), a
sales opportunity, a case, or any custom entity you have created in
Dynamics 365.

>> Open Dynamics 365 accounts (customers), opportunities, or cases directly
from Outlook.

>> Add activities (in other words, phone calls, tasks, or appointments) to
Dynamics 365 directly from Outlook.

>> Include, when creating an email or an appointment, knowledge articles and
sales literature from Dynamics 365 in your Outlook email or appointment.

>> Track Outlook contacts directly in Dynamics 365.

REMEMBER

Server-side synchronization of incoming emails to your email inbox is required in
order to use Dynamics 365 App for Outlook. Your system administrator may need
to make changes to how email is configured for your organization. These configuration changes involve your Exchange Online subscription and your Email Server
Profile for Microsoft Exchange Online, and setting the default synchronization
method. After all this is set up, the synchronization occurs every 5 minutes. This
frequency increases to every 2 minutes automatically if the user has many incoming email messages.

To link an email message to a Dynamics 365 account, follow these steps:

1. **Click the Dynamics 365 button in the email pane.**

The Preview window appears.

2. **Click the Set Regarding/Link icon (the two overlapping ovals that look like links in a chain).**

A search box appears.

3. **Enter your search text and click the magnifying glass icon.**

A list of accounts and other records that match your search criteria text appears below it. You can limit the list of records to only accounts by clicking the Accounts button, which is above the list of records.

4. **To link the email, click the account you want to link it to.**

REMEMBER

You can also track without regarding, which means that the email is tracked within Dynamics 365 but isn't associated with (linked to) a particular account, contact, or other entity within Dynamics 365. The email shows up in Dynamics 365 on your list of tracked emails, but doesn't pop up in association with viewing a particular record.

REMEMBER

The terms used by Microsoft to describe this functionality are *tracked*, *linked*, and *set regarding*. These three terms are used fairly interchangeably to describe emails that are integrated between Outlook and Dynamics 365.

A useful feature of Dynamics 365 App for Outlook is the ability to automatically add a contact or lead to the Dynamics 365 Customer Engagement system (in other words, CRM) based on an email you have received. Doing so saves keystrokes, avoiding the need to toggle between applications, to cut-and-paste data, or, worse, to rekey the same data multiple times.

To add a contact to Dynamics 365 from an email recipient in Outlook using Dynamics 365 App for Outlook, follow these steps:

1. **In the Dynamics 365 pane that appears in Outlook, click the plus sign (+).**

In the menu that appears, you are given a choice between Contact or Lead.

2. **Choose Contact.**

The contact is added to the Dynamics 365 Customer Engagement application.

You can create a task, an appointment, or a phone call from within the Dynamics 365 pane. In other words, you don't need to navigate, toggle, or switch applications. The Dynamics 365 pane is embedded directly in Outlook; it's part of Outlook, yet you're adding new records into Dynamics 365 CRM. (This is a *deep* integration.)

To add a phone call reminder from within Outlook to Dynamics 365 Customer Engagement (CRM), using the Dynamics 365 pane of Dynamics 365 App for Outlook, follow these steps:

1. **Open an email message in Outlook as you normally would.**

2. **Click the Dynamics 365 icon.**

   The Dynamics 365 pane appears within Outlook to the right of the window.

3. **Track the email (if it isn't already tracked).**

4. **Set Regarding to link the email to a particular contact in Dynamics 365.**

5. **Click the blue plus sign in the circle located in the lower right corner of the Regarding Contact window.**

   A drop-down menu appears, with the choices Task, Appointment, and Phone Call listed.

6. **Choose Phone Call.**

   The Create Phone Call window appears.

7. **Set the priority and due date.**

   These fields are optional. Required fields are preceded by a red asterisk.

   The due date includes a time, so make sure to set the time of day you plan to call this contact, if a specific time was prearranged.

8. **The Subject field, which is a required field, automatically populates with the subject of the email message as a default.**

   You may overwrite the subject.

9. **Call From and Call To automatically populate with your username (Call From) and the contact's name (Call To).**

10. **Click the Save button.**

    A message appears (in green), saying that the phone call was created successfully. The phone call be associated with the contact in Dynamics 365, and you'll be reminded within Dynamics 365 to follow up and make the phone call on the due date at the appointed time.

Adding the Excel Add-In for Finance and Operations

Finance and Excel go hand in hand. Accountants live and breathe Excel spreadsheets. Without an extensive, efficient, and easy to use Excel integration, the value of your financial software is seriously limited. To get the most out of your ERP system, you need to be able to extract data from your ERP system into Excel at the touch of a button. You need to be able to create journal entries in an Excel template and load them into your ERP system with the click of a mouse. You need live links between Excel workbooks and records within your ERP system so that when a record is updated by someone in your organization, your Excel spreadsheet reflects that change as soon as you refresh the link. These days, having the ability to pump stale data extracts from your ERP into Excel isn't sufficient. Fortunately, the Excel Add-in for Finance and Operations provides robust integration between Dynamics 365 and Excel for Office 365.

WARNING

The Dynamics 365 integration works only with a recent version of Excel; ideally, you should be using Office 365 along with Dynamics 365, both cloud-based versions. Make sure that your version of Excel is at least 16.0.6868.2060. To see the version number, start Excel, choose Account from the File menu, and then choose About Excel. The version number appears in the upper left corner of the About window.

The way that Excel works with Dynamics 365 for Finance and Operations is by way of an Excel add-in. An Excel *add-in* is a program you install that extends the functionality of Excel. These add-in programs are designed specifically for Excel, and they do not run outside of Excel; rather, they increase what Excel can do. Some of the ways that add-ins extend Excel is by including these items:

>> **Web-based task panes and content panes:** Display and allow you to interact with data from another application that's related to data in your Excel spreadsheet

>> **Custom menu items and ribbon buttons:** Provide you with more features and functionality

>> **Dialog windows:** Allow you to provide additional information or verify processes before running them

The add-in you need in order to integrate Excel with Dynamics 365 is the Microsoft Dynamics Office Add-in. To install it, follow these steps:

1. **Start Microsoft Excel.**

2. **On the Insert tab, click the Store button in the Add-ins group. Alternatively, if you're running the Excel Online version, click the Office Add-ins button and then the Store button in the Office Add-ins window that appears.**

   The Office Store opens.

   Check out Figures 2-5 and 2-6 to see the different menu navigation methods to the Add-ins button in the online versus the full Excel versions.

3. **In the Store's Search text box, type** Dynamics **and press Enter.**

4. **From the results, click the Microsoft Dynamics Office Add-in link.**

5. **Click the Add button.**

6. **In the dialog box that appears, select the Trust This Add-in option.**

   You need to specify that you trust the add-in only the first time you run it, not every time.

7. **Enter the URL of your Finance and Operations tenant instance.**

   You can copy-and-paste it into the Server URL field.

   Delete everything after the hostname.

REMEMBER

   The resulting URL should have only the hostname, as in https://xxx.dynamics.com, where xxx stands for your hostname.

8. **Select OK and then select Yes to confirm the change.**

   The add-in restarts.

   Metadata (the lists of tables and available fields that you can edit in Excel) is loaded.

   The Design button is now enabled. The Design button allows you or your IT department to specify the touch points between Excel and entities (types of records) within Dynamics 365 for Finance and Operations, such as customers, vendors, and purchase orders.

REMEMBER

You can switch from Excel Online to the full (installed) version of Excel (assuming that you have it installed) by clicking the Edit In Excel button in Excel Online on the top menu bar.

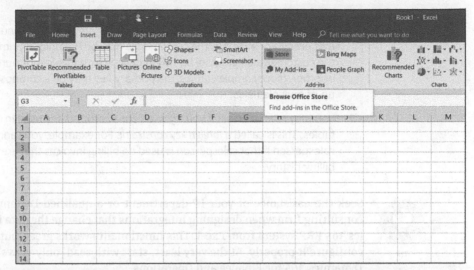

FIGURE 2-5:
Store button
used to find the
Excel add-in.

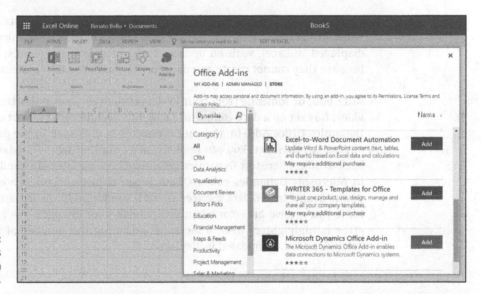

FIGURE 2-6:
Office Add-ins
button found in
Excel Online.

Adding, deleting, and updating entity data (such as vendors, customers, invoices, and sales orders) is normally done within the screens of the ERP system itself, not in Excel. The add-in, however, does let you create, update, or delete ERP entity data records from Excel, though this isn't a simple matter to set up for a whole host of reasons, including these:

>> You cannot add records without ensuring that you have included all required fields.

>> You need to specify the field that is the primary key (unique ID number) for that entity. For example, the customer ID may be the unique primary key of the customer master table, but when dealing with invoices or purchase orders or other, more complex tables, the primary key may be a composite key made up of multiple fields.

>> You may receive errors if you try to delete a record that's used in other related tables. This is called a *foreign key constraint.* For example, you cannot delete a salesperson if that salesperson is used on billing invoices that are part of your billing history.

TIP

Seek the assistance of your IT department or a qualified Dynamics 365 partner consulting firm when designing integrations that change the data in your Dynamics 365 ERP system from Excel. This functionality works great, but an expert must configure it properly. At the very least, start with read-only views of Excel data in Dynamics 365 for Finance and Operations.

If you do not have any experts to help you, you may wish to start with creating Excel integrations that are merely read-only views of Dynamics 365 ERP data displayed in Excel, with no update, insert or delete commands; these are safer because they cannot create any data corruption in the ERP system.

After you, or someone from your IT department or your authorized solution provider, has set up a data connector using the Designer that is part of the Microsoft Dynamics Office Add-in, the data connector is displayed in the pane to the right of your spreadsheet. You can publish (save, in other words) updates to your data back to your Microsoft Dynamics systems. These updates are handled by a feature in Microsoft Dynamics called OData (open data protocol) services. Only touch points available in OData services are now supported in the Dynamics Office Add-in. If you receive an error when you publish your changes, the row that had an error is highlighted. Also, a message indicating the number of rows that were deleted, added, or updated is displayed.

Organizing Documents with SharePoint and OneDrive

Back in the bad old days, in order to collaborate with your co-workers, it worked well enough to simply save a document in a folder on a network drive. Other users on the computer network would be able to open, view, update, and edit the document, as long as they had rights to that folder. A problem that arose from this method of document collaboration occurred whenever users would change a document and you had no record of who made the changes (in other words, who messed up the document). This would result in a lot of finger pointing and no way to prove anything. Another problem was not being able to search the documents easily, by title, by date, or by the actual content of the document. Enter Microsoft SharePoint, a document repository where users check in and check out documents, leaving an audit trail of who changed what, and where it's much easier to control much more carefully who has access to documents. You can think of SharePoint as a file folder system on steroids.

Nowadays, as workers travel around using mobile devices such as tablets and smartphones and expect to be connected to not only the Internet but also their files at work and at home, cloud services such as Dropbox have sprung up everywhere. Dropbox, a company based in San Francisco, California, has over half a billion registered users worldwide. You simply go to its website, log in, and drop your files onto a web page. Your files are stored securely, and you can access them from anywhere as long as you have an Internet connection.

The original Microsoft SharePoint, on the other hand, was not as easy to use as services like Dropbox. SharePoint was installed on your organization's network, so you would need a VPN connection to your organization's network to connect to it while on the road. You couldn't simply plop files onto it, either. Generally speaking, the combined navigation and complexity of using SharePoint was a challenge. Furthermore, the difficulty of installing and configuring it, and the overhead of maintaining it, plus the license cost, made SharePoint a daunting proposition. The original SharePoint was an on-premise software solution, not a cloud service, either. Of course, many organizations rely on their on-premise SharePoint environments, and these will take time to be transitioned to the cloud.

Enter Microsoft OneDrive (previously called SkyDrive, Windows Live SkyDrive, and Windows Live Folders). OneDrive is Microsoft's answer to Dropbox and similar cloud file-sharing and -storage solutions; these services are geared toward home users, not businesses or other large organizations. On the other hand, OneDrive for Business (which replaced SharePoint Workspace) is an enterprise file synchronization and sharing (EFSS) platform. OneDrive and OneDrive for Business are different applications. *Enterprise* means "large organization." *File synchronization* (or *sync,* as it's sometimes called) refers to refreshing a local copy of a document with a copy stored on a network. *File sharing* relates to the features needed to collaborate with a group of people on a document, such as check in / check out, auditing, and create, read, update, and delete (CRUD) privileges.

With OneDrive for Business, you can

>> Store and share your files from anywhere that you can access the Internet.

>> See your changes automatically synchronized in the cloud or work with them offline.

>> Have more than one person updating the same document at the same time in your most widely used desktop applications, such as Word and PowerPoint.

>> Use your favorite mobile device to view and edit files, regardless of whether it runs the Android, Apple, or Windows operating system.

>> Use the Office 365 Admin Center as your command post to configure rules for mobile devices, and even remotely wipe data from devices that have been lost or stolen.

>> See who has been sharing files — and with whom.

>> Allow each user in your organization to set permissions for the files they create and share or, alternatively, base permissions for file sharing on your organization's global settings.

With the advent of Office 365 and Dynamics 365, Microsoft has made its big move to the cloud. So now OneDrive for Business is part of the Office 365 family of applications. As an example of how integrated OneDrive for Business is with Office 365 (Office in the cloud), you can now navigate to the security settings for OneDrive for Business from within the Office 365 Admin Center. The good news is that you don't have to worry about the differences between SharePoint and OneDrive when talking about Dynamics 365, because Dynamics 365 is a cloud service and because Microsoft has added SharePoint file synchronization to OneDrive. Microsoft's goal is to consolidate its different document management applications into one unified platform so that it's transparent to the user whether SharePoint or OneDrive is storing the document. This consolidation is still under way, but Office 365 and Dynamics 365 are at the forefront of this consolidation process.

To use OneDrive for Business with Dynamics 365, the following requirements must be met:

>> **Server-based authentication with Dynamics 365 and SharePoint Online must be configured.** Talk to your system administrator.

>> **Each user must have their own license for OneDrive for Business or a SharePoint license.** Keep in mind that Office 365 subscriptions come with SharePoint Online licenses.

>> **OneDrive for Business must be accessed via the website itself, before trying to link to it in Dynamics 365.** The reason is that the site and additional information get created on the initial access; if you don't do this first, you can't configure Dynamics 365 for OneDrive for Business integration.

To better control access to OneDrive Office 365, you may want to limit sharing to internal employees — namely, only people in your organization. To do so, follow these steps:

1. **Browse to the Office 365 Admin Center.**

   The URL is https://portal.office.com/AdminPortal/Home#/homepage.

2. **Choose Admin Centers from the navigation menu located at the far left of the page. (You'll find it at the bottom of the menu).**

   A pull-out menu appears, as shown in Figure 2-7. It shows you all the other admin-related sites that you can go to in order to configure various settings for applications that fall under the Office 365 umbrella.

3. **Choose OneDrive from the pull-out menu.**

   Doing so launches another tab on your web browser, which takes you to the OneDrive Admin Center.

   The URL is https://admin.onedrive.com.

4. **Click Sharing on the OneDrive Admin Center tab.**

5. **In the Sharing section, click the radio button to the left of the option named Internal: Only People in Your Organization under the Links heading.**

6. **Scroll down to where the blue Save button is located and click Save.**

   Your security setting for file sharing is saved.

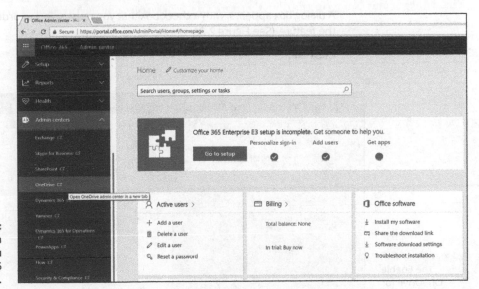

FIGURE 2-7:
The Admin Center's menu in Office 365 Admin Center.

To connect Dynamics 365 to SharePoint 365, follow these steps:

1. Click the down arrow located immediately to the left of the words Dynamics 365 in the upper left corner of the black band along the top of the screen.

A pull-out menu, known as the App Selector menu, appears on the left side of the screen.

REMEMBER

All applications listed on the App Selector menu operate on the same back-end database, so global settings that are made in one application affect them all.

2. Choose Customer Service from the menu.

The Service application displays.

3. Click the down arrow located immediately to the left of the word Service.

Another pull-down menu appears.

4. Click the Settings tile, which appears between the Service and Training tiles.

5. Under the Systems group, click the Document Management button.

Doing so displays the Document Management window.

6. Click Enable OneDrive for Business.

A dialog box appears, with a check box that you must select in order to enable the feature. (See Figure 2-8.)

7. Click OK.

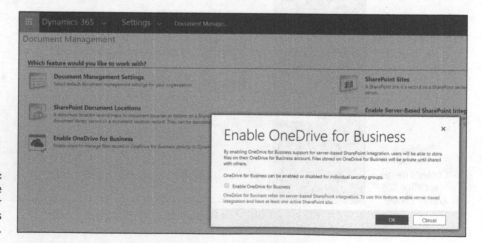

FIGURE 2-8:
The Enable OneDrive for Business dialog box.

Messaging with Skype for Business

Messaging and screen sharing have become more and more an essential aspect of business collaboration. Rather than dial a co-worker's extension, it's quicker to "IM" (instant-message) the co-worker, especially if all you need is a quick answer to a simple question. Instant messaging is a huge time-saver. Likewise, screen sharing is now common on conference calls, and is standard for technical support calls. Being able to see the computer screen of the people you're talking to is so much easier than trying to describe what you see verbally. Screen sharing is a huge time-saver as well. It's even more convenient when you can share your screen and hear the voices of the conference call participants from within the same application, without having to place a separate phone call. Wouldn't it be nice to simply click a link and be able to both hear and see what is happening in real-time? Well, you can do just that with Skype for Business integrated with Dynamics 365.

AOL Instant Messenger and Yahoo Messenger were two of the first and most popular instant messaging (IM) applications. These IM clients were used mostly for social media rather than for business communication. The popularity of IM started with social media, but soon businesses realized the value and potential of quicker communication. Microsoft's competing application to Yahoo Messenger and AOL IM was Windows Live Messenger. Live Messenger has since been phased out. Another instant messaging client from Microsoft was Lync (formerly Office Communication Server). Lync was more business oriented, but still more of an internal office communications tool than a way to reach out to people outside your organization. Microsoft has replaced Live Messenger and has rebranded Lync as Skype for Business.

Skype is an application, first developed in Europe, that originally gained popularity as a way for people to make long-distance phone calls over the Internet cheaply. Microsoft acquired Skype in 2011 for $8.5 billion in cash (which was, at the time, Microsoft's largest acquisition ever). Skype gives Microsoft an easy way to connect callers to traditional phone systems. Lync and Skype together have evolved into Skype for Business, and Skype for Business is integrated with Dynamics 365.

In Skype for Business, a feature called *presence* is a way to show your status online so that people can know whether you're available for a chat or a phone call or have simply stepped away from your desk for a moment.

REMEMBER

To enable the Skype for Business Presence (Status) feature, add https://*.dynamics.com to the web browser's list of trusted sites in Internet Explorer. Trusted sites can be found in Internet Options under the Security tab.

When you use Skype and Dynamics 365 together, you have the ability to activate the Skype click-to-call feature from within Dynamics 365. This feature is supported in all these devices and browsers:

>> Firefox (from Mozilla)

>> Chrome/Android devices (from Google)

>> Safari/iPad and iPhone (from Apple)

>> Internet Explorer and Edge (from Microsoft)

>> Windows tablets

TIP

Skype must be selected as the telephony provider on the General tab found under Settings ⇨ Administration ⇨ System Settings in Dynamics 365. In addition, each user must have the Skype for Windows desktop client or Skype for Windows app installed on their computer in order to use Skype with Dynamics 365.

To configure Skype for Business in Dynamics 365, follow these steps:

1. Sign in to the Office 365 Admin Center.

The URL for the Admin Center is

https://portal.office.com/AdminPortal/Home#/homepage.

You need to log in as an Office 365 Global administrator to configure the proper settings.

2. Choose Admin ⇨ Skype for Business from the navigation menu on the left.

The Skype for Business Admin Center window appears.

3. Click General.

The General section is where you should specify the Presence Privacy mode.

4. Click External Communications.

In the new window that appears, you'll find a check box to turn on communication with Skype users and users of other public IM service providers under the Public IM Connectivity heading. Select this check box.

After Skype is properly installed and configured, your Skype calls are automatically tracked as activities within Dynamics 365 Customer Engagement.

To call a contact in Dynamics 365 Customer Engagement using the Skype for Business Click-to-Call feature, follow these steps:

1. **On the navigation bar (the black band at the top of the screen), click the down arrow to the right of Dynamics 365 to switch to another app.**

   A pull-down menu of apps appears.

2. **Select Customer Service from the list of apps.**

3. **Click the down arrow to the right of Service to navigate to the Service tile.**

   Another pull-down menu appears, with the Service tile already selected.

4. **Click on Contacts, found under the Customer heading on the Service tile, to navigate to your default system views of contacts.**

   A list of contacts appears. Contact phone numbers are displayed as one of the columns in the list. You can simply click that phone number and Skype automatically launches and asks whether you're sure you want to call that number.

5. **Click Yes to call the contact using Skype.**

   Skype initiates a call with that contact.

   You can also click the phone number from the Contact window itself, not just from the view of contacts. Either way, Skype instantly launches and makes the call.

Chapter **3**

Powering Up Your Business Intelligence

I f you've worked in the business world long enough, you may be of the opinion that the term *business intelligence* is a self-contradiction because, most likely, over the years you've witnessed a lot of idiotic business practices. However, over my many years as a business management consultant performing countless business analysis engagements, I have come to believe that business processes tend to evolve into a rather elegant and efficient dance of duties, although they may appear at first glance to be chaotic or irrational. After all, people want to get their work done as soon as possible, go home, and have dinner — so they hate wasting time. When you study the workflow of a business process in sufficient depth, you tend to find that the devil is in the details and that what looked like sheer madness has a lot of meticulous methods baked into it. Users often have valid reasons for having to devise all the many steps they take. The lesson that's learned is that users aren't stupid — they're intelligent. And, if you give them tools to use their intelligence themselves to gather information from the huge store of data lying dormant in your organization's databases, they can become empowered to do a better job, by having better access to more instantaneous and accurate information.

A Little Pre-History

People have come a long way from getting most of their business information from hard copy printouts delivered on continuous-feed paper (as shown in Figure 3-1) noisily banged out on an ancient dot-matrix printer (though, surprisingly, office supply stores still stock that kind of paper — a clear indication that we have a long way to go in creating a paperless office).

FIGURE 3-1:
The old way
of reporting:
continuous-feed
computer paper
on dot matrix
printer.

Today, many reports are distributed via a link to a web page. You click the link (which may come in an email), and the report displays on the screen. The report is actually a read-only view of data, but you can sort, filter, and refresh the data or download it at the touch of a button to an Excel spreadsheet, where you can reformat it, add new columns with formulas, create pivot tables, and play with the data to your heart's content. (Try doing that with a piece of green-bar computer paper.) Many of these reporting links are available all the time, on web pages, or in Microsoft SharePoint, so users can run them whenever they want, without having to request them from the IT department. Self-service reporting empowers users and saves time.

Creating these interactive, web-based self-service reports, however, has still mostly been the providence of IT folks. Microsoft's primary report-writing software is SQL Server Reporting Services (SSRS). The SSRS service is part of the Microsoft stack, or the SQL Server database family of products: SQL Server database, SQL Server Reporting Services, SQL Server Integration Services, and SQL Server Analysis Services. SSRS reports are designed within Visual Studio, which is the same programming environment used by coders of .NET programs and other Windows-based applications. SSRS reports are not all that easy to create, especially when you have no programming skill or knowledge of computer languages, such as Visual Basic or Transact SQL (Structured Query Language). Also, SSRS was developed before the advent of cloud computing. Fortunately, now there is an easier way to write reports.

TIP

The rule of thumb for when to use SSRS as opposed to Power BI Desktop to create reports is this: Use SSRS for reports that need to be printed to precise specifications (such as invoices and contracts); use Power BI for reports that are graphical displays of information, as opposed to official documents.

Exploring Data through Power BI

Microsoft knew that it needed a user-friendly, cloud based, self-service ad hoc reporting tool that was geared toward end users rather than toward IT professionals. The solution it came up with is Microsoft Power BI. The BI in Power BI stands for *business intelligence*. BI is a hot buzzword. When information technology professionals talk about business reporting, you hear the terms *BI, data warehouse, data mart, big data, analytics, data mining,* and *key performance indicators (KPIs)*. Unless you're an IT salesperson, you may not ever need to understand the nuances of these terms, which are changing all the time anyway.

The bottom line is that, as an end user, you need a way to create interactive reports without having to understand low-level computer programming. Wouldn't it be great to be able to get access to data yourself, without having to be at the behest of your IT department (or, worse, expensive consultants) and present the data to yourself in easy-to-understand reports, displayed as dashboards of sortable, filterable lists and graphs on a web page, and be able to share your reports with others in your organization? And wouldn't it be great if the data you can access is the data in your all-important ERP and CRM systems (in other words, your prospects, customers, vendors, employees, inventory, quotes, sales orders, invoices, purchase orders, projects, and so on)? Well, with Microsoft Power BI integrated with Dynamics 365, you can do just that. You can create your own self-service ad hoc reports based on data in Dynamics 365 applications, such as Customer Engagement, Business Central, Finance and Operations, Retail, Talent, and more. Furthermore, you can share your reports with others by creating a dashboard that is accessible on the Power BI website, or embedded into Dynamics 365 itself.

As with many of Microsoft's products, *Power BI* is an umbrella term that encompasses several software products, including these:

» **Power BI Desktop:** This is the Windows application that you install on your desktop PC or laptop. Use this to create reports.

» **Power BI Service:** This is the website (cloud service) that you sign into to share your reports.

» **Power BI Premium:** This is a way to license BI for your entire enterprise without having to purchase per-user licenses (and it now includes the Power BI Report Server, so you can run in the cloud or on premise).

» **Power BI Mobile:** This is the Android and iOS (Apple) version for smartphones and tablets.

» **Power BI Embedded:** This allows you to build applications that can be used by end users who don't have access to Power BI itself.

» **Power BI Report Server:** This is an on-premise reporting infrastructure used to create, publish, and distribute Power BI reports (if you're not quite ready to move your reporting to the cloud).

The key components of Power BI (as shown in Figure 3-2) are described in this list:

» **Reports:** These are the meat of the Power BI stew; reports are the source of visualizations (sometimes called *visuals*), which is a fancy term for charts, graphs, maps and other kinds of graphical representations of a report. Each report can pull data from only one dataset.

» **Dashboards:** These contain tiles, each of which contains a visual from a report. You can pin multiple tiles onto one dashboard. When you click on a tile, it expands to the full report.

» **Workbooks:** These are special datasets geared entirely toward Excel files.

» **Datasets:** These are collections of data that you connect to (or sometimes import). A dataset can contain data from multiple database tables.

» **Workspaces:** These are areas on the Power BI Service that give you a space to organize and work with all the components listed in the bullets above; this is where you can create your own dashboards.

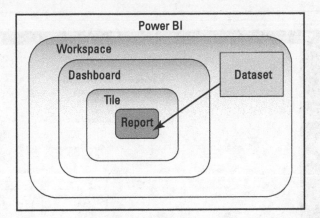

FIGURE 3-2:
How the various Power BI components fit together.

WARNING

Power BI is geared toward end users rather than IT professionals; nonetheless, because it's a powerful application with tons of features, it can be a bit overwhelming. Don't get discouraged. Take the tutorials and get some training, online or in person. Power BI, once you gain some level of mastery (even at a novice level), will open up a whole world of information for you. Knowledge is power. You will become more powerful (and have more job security) within your organization by learning to use Power BI.

REMEMBER

You can create your reports in Power BI Desktop (locally) and then share them with others on the Power BI service (the cloud website).

When using the Power BI service, you browse to the Power BI website at `https://powerbi.microsoft.com/en-us/landing/signin` and sign on. (See Figure 3-3 for a view of a successful sign-on using Chrome.) A variety of web browsers are supported for Power BI, including:

>> Microsoft Edge (Microsoft's newer and preferred web browser)

>> Microsoft Internet Explorer 11 (supported for backward compatibility)

>> Google Chrome desktop (latest version is recommended)

>> Safari Mac (latest version is recommended)

>> Firefox desktop (latest version is recommended)

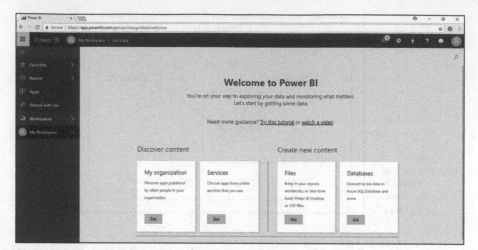

FIGURE 3-3:
Signed in to
the Power BI
services website
using Chrome.

Installing Power BI Desktop

To install Power BI Desktop for use with Dynamics 365, follow these steps:

1. **To start your download of Power BI Desktop to your laptop or PC desktop computer, visit the Microsoft Download Center.**

    The URL is https://www.microsoft.com/en-us/download.

2. **In the center's search box, type** Power BI desktop download.

    The search box is where it says *Search Microsoft.com* to the left of the Magnifying Glass icon, near the upper right corner of the window.

    Do not be confused by the Power BI desktop app (which is for mobile devices). Select *download,* not *app,* unless you're on a mobile device.

3. **From the search results, click on the blue link for Microsoft Power BI Desktop.**

4. **Select your language preference from the drop-down list that appears.**

5. **Click the red Download button.**

    A dialog box appears, asking you to choose the download you want.

6. **Select the check box for PBIDesktop.msi for the 32-bit application, or select the check box for PBIDesktop_x64.msi for the 64-bit application.**

    The 64-bit version is preferred because the processing power is significantly better and the stability of the application itself is superior.

7. **Click the blue Next button.**

The file begins downloading to your computer.

You can see the progress on the status bar in most web browsers — typically, in the lower left corner.

8. **To start the installation, click the** `.msi` **file (the Windows installation setup program) that you just downloaded.**

A wizard appears, ready to guide you through the installation.

You will need to reboot your computer.

Lastly, when you first run Power BI Desktop, you're prompted to sign in to Power BI. You can sign in using the same email address credentials you use to sign in to Dynamics 365.

Connecting to Dynamics 365 with Power BI Desktop

Power BI can be used to connect to almost any data source under the sun, so you can combine data from external sources with data from Dynamics 365. In this chapter, I focus on how Power BI connects to Dynamics 365. But first, let me help you understand how Power BI connects to data from a general point of view.

Power BI is a monster when it comes to being able to connect to data sources of all shapes and sizes. The general methods of Power BI connectivity are described in this list:

>> Connect to a file, such as an Excel file, XML file, or CSV (comma-separated values) text file.

>> Connect to a database such as SQL Server, Oracle, or IBM DB2 (and many more by means of other database connectors).

>> Connect to Azure (Microsoft's cloud services), including SQL databases stored in Azure.

>> Connect to Online Services, including the Power BI Service, SharePoint Online List, and — most importantly for our purposes — Dynamics 365 (online) services.

Power BI comes with database connectors to non-Microsoft databases such as Oracle, IBM DB2, MySQL, PostgreSQL, Sybase, Teradata, SAP HANA, Snowflake, Amazon Redshift, and more, but some connectors are not enabled by default, so in Power BI you may need to enable them. Go to File ⇨ Options and Settings ⇨ Options ⇨ Preview Features to enable the database connector. You can then see the database connector you enabled in the list of available databases.

Connecting to a file

Sometimes you may want to connect to a file, especially if you're just adding a bit of external information to a report, but generally speaking, files are rather limited. A file is usually the output of a report, not the source of a report. Excel files are sometimes sources of data rather than outputs of reports, but data stores are better housed in a relational management database system (RDBMS). Databases are where the action is. Databases contain tons of tables, each full of data. The real magic shows up when you can join related tables together using SQL queries and can summarize data using SQL GROUP BY clauses.

Connecting to a SQL View

A SQL *view* is a SQL query that has been stored in the database as a sort of virtual table. A great way for end users to work with data is for an IT professional to create SQL views that do the hard work of joining together related database tables, and aliasing cryptic table column names to human-readable field names — data element names that an end user can easily understand, in other words. The column in the database might be called EXPDELDT, but the SQL view will alias that field to something like Expected_Delivery_Date. The SQL view may also exclude fields that are not being used by your organization. For example, on sales orders, your billing clerks may not be entering any data in the Expected Delivery Data field because it's always assumed that the delivery date is the same as the invoice date, so in that case, that particular date field would be excluded from a SQL view of your sales order history.

The SQL view is an easier-to-understand view of the data in a database — easier than peering into the raw physical database tables and trying to make sense of all the many strange columns of data. (It also helps you understand how to join tables together without inadvertently duplicating rows.) It's a more user-friendly view that end users can then access as part of a dataset using Power BI to create their own reports, graphs, and dashboards. Some of these SQL views come built-in with the application you want to pull data from, and some can be written by your IT department or by IT consultants. Of course, because Power BI is able to connect to databases, you can easily connect to SQL views contained in those databases.

Connecting to Dynamics 365

Connecting Power BI to Dynamics 365 is quite doable. Let's face it: Microsoft built Power BI for end users to connect to the mission-critical data in their organizations, and Dynamics 365 is a vital source of information for Microsoft customers who are using Dynamics 365 for Customer Engagement (CRM), Finance and Operations (ERP), Talent (Human Resources), and more. It's also vital to Microsoft to migrate as many of its customers as possible onto Dynamics 365 (if they haven't already started using it), so Microsoft cannot neglect the connectivity to Dynamics 365; it's a top priority. Because connecting to Dynamics 365 from Power BI is such a high priority, Microsoft has tried to make it easy, and has provided several different means to do so.

REMEMBER

Like many Microsoft technologies, these connectivity methods make for somewhat of a moving target; some new bit of technology is always on the horizon, and some other bit is always on its way out. Always inquire to see whether a new connector is available for your target data source.

Where connecting Power BI to Dynamics 365 gets somewhat complicated is when you start thinking about the fact that Dynamics 365 is more of an umbrella of cloud-based applications rather than a single app. Each of these Dynamics 365 applications can have a slightly different preferred method of connecting. To further complicate matters, a single application can have more than one way to connect to Power BI. Recall that Power BI can connect directly to a database, can connect to Azure, and can connect to other services, such as Dynamics 365 online services. Let's take a look at some of the easiest and preferred ways to connect Power BI to Dynamics 365.

Connecting Power BI to Business Central

One of the quickest and easiest ways to connect Power BI Desktop to Dynamics 365 is to use the Online Services options found in the software's Get Data window. For example, setting up a connection to Business Central using Online Services is a breeze.

To connect Power BI Desktop to Dynamics 365 Business Central, follow these steps:

1. **From the Power BI Desktop menu, click Get Data on the Home tab.**

   The Get Data window appears, as shown in Figure 3-4.

   If, on your system, a pull-down menu appears, click the More button to open the Get Data window.

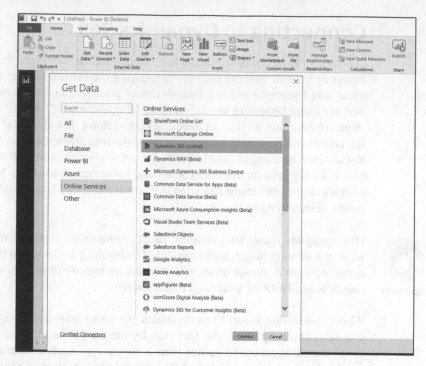

FIGURE 3-4:
The Power BI
Desktop Get Data
window.

2. **Click Online Services in the navigation menu on the left side of the window.**

   The list of Online Services appears on the right side of the window.

3. **Choose Microsoft Dynamics 365 Business Central from the list and then click the yellow Connect button.**

   A dialog box appears, prompting you to sign in to Microsoft Dynamics 365 Business Central.

4. **Click the Sign In button.**

5. **Use the same account credential that you use to sign in when running Dynamics 365 Business Central.**

   This is typically your work email address.

   Enter your password, if prompted (your password may already be stored as part of being signed in to Office 365, Dynamics 365, or Windows).

6. **Click the yellow Connect button.**

   The Navigator window appears.

   You're now connected to Business Central.

7. **Click Display Options.**

   A drop-down menu appears. As you select data, select the check box for Enable Data Previews if you want to see some of the rows of data retrieved on the right side of the window.

8. **Click the Microsoft Dynamics 365 Business Central Folder.**

   A list of companies (organizations) that you have access to in Business Central displays.

9. **Click the name of the company (organization) that you want to explore.**

   A list of queries appears, such as Chart_of_Accounts.

10. **Click the check box to the left of the query name.**

    If you have enabled data previews, the data retrieved by that query is displayed in a grid on the right side of the window.

11. **Click the yellow Load button.**

    The data is loaded into Power BI Desktop.

12. **From the Power BI Desktop menu, click Edit Queries on the Home tab.**

    A pull-down menu appears.

13. **Again, select Edit Queries.**

    The Power Query Editor window appears.

14. **In the gray navigation pane on the left side of the Power Query Editor window, click the right arrow (>), if it's not already expanded.**

15. **Click on the name of the query you loaded in the navigation pane.**

    The loaded data is visible and ready to work with.

REMEMBER

How you should connect Power BI Desktop to your organization's instances of Dynamics 365 is typically determined by your IT department, who will provide, and perhaps insist on, a standard approach. Please contact your IT department, Help desk, or system administrator to ensure that you're adhering to the recommended connection method.

Connecting Power BI to Finance and Operations

Connecting Power BI with Dynamics 365 for Finance and Operations (formerly Dynamics AX) is similar to connecting to Business Central (formerly Dynamics NAV). As explained in the previous section, you can use Online Services. The name of the service differs from the service used for Business Central because, after all, it's a completely separate application. The way you sign in is also slightly different.

To connect Power BI Desktop to Dynamics 365 for Finance and Operations, follow these steps:

1. **From the Power BI Desktop menu, click Get Data on the Home tab.**

If a pull-down menu appears on your system, you may need to click the More button.

The Get Data window appears. (Refer to Figure 3-4.)

2. **Click Online Services, on the left side of the window.**

The list of online services appears on the right side of the window.

3. **Choose Microsoft Dynamics 365 (online) from the list and then click the yellow Connect button.**

A dialog box appears, prompting you to specify the Web API URL of your Dynamics 365 for Finance and Operations instance. (See Figure 3-5).

In other words, it wants the website address you browse to when signed in to Finance and Operations.

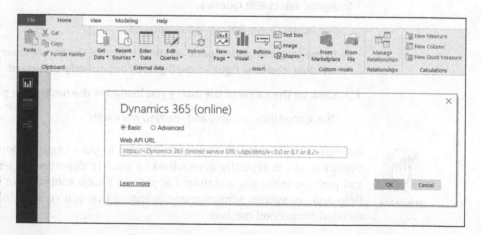

FIGURE 3-5:
The Dynamics
365 (online)
connection
prompt.

4. **Enter the required Web API URL.**

You can cut-and-paste the website address from your browser; just be sure to remove any text after dynamics.com and add the following text to the address:

```
/api/data/v8 or /api/data/v8.1 or/api/data/v8.2 (depending
    on your version number)
```

5. **Click the yellow OK button.**

You're now connected to Dynamics 365 for Finance and Operations.

Dynamics 365 for Finance and Operations is a cloud application, a Software as a Service (SaaS) solution. This means your data is stored on Microsoft's servers, not on your own servers, and you access it over the Internet. However, Microsoft gave in to customer demands and agreed to offer it as an on-premise solution (at least for now). Some organizations are still averse to putting their ERP data in the cloud, for various reasons. An alternative method to connect Power BI Desktop to Finance and Operations is to connect directly to the SQL database that stores the Finance and Operations data. This is a valid approach to take, especially for an on-premise installation of Dynamics 365 for Finance and Operations.

To connect Power BI Desktop directly to a SQL database, follow these steps:

1. **From the Power BI Desktop menu, click Get Data on the Home tab.**

   If a pull-down menu appears, click the More button.

   The Get Data window appears. (Refer to Figure 3-4.)

2. **Click Database in the navigation menu on the left side of the window.**

   The list of database connectors appears on the right side of the window.

3. **Select SQL Server Database from the list and then click the Connect button.**

   A dialog box appears, prompting you to specify the SQL Server database connection parameters.

4. **Click Advanced Options to expand the window.**

5. **Enter the server name (and, optionally, the database name) of the SQL Server for your Dynamics 365 for Finance and Operations on-premise installation. (See Figure 3-6.)**

   Ask your system administrator for the name of the server and the database. The database name is typically AxDB.

   You can look up the name of the SQL Server yourself within Finance and Operations; to do so, choose System Administration ➪ ➪ Setup ➪ Server Configuration from the main menu. After all that, you should see the SQL Server name in the AOS instance name field in the new window that appears.

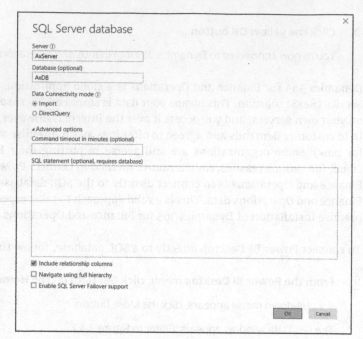

FIGURE 3-6:
The Power BI
Desktop SQL
Server Database
Connection
window.

SQL Server database

Server ⓘ
AxServer

Database (optional)
AxDB

Data Connectivity mode ⓘ
⦿ Import
◯ DirectQuery

◢ Advanced options

Command timeout in minutes (optional)

SQL statement (optional, requires database)

☑ Include relationship columns
☐ Navigate using full hierarchy
☐ Enable SQL Server Failover support

OK   Cancel

6. **Click the yellow OK button.**

   You're now connected to the SQL Server.

   You can now browse the tables and views in Navigator and then load the data you want into a memory table within Power BI Desktop.

REMEMBER

If you load data into Power BI Desktop, the load may take a while, but having the data loaded locally means that running your report is quicker.

Notable options (refer to Figure 3-6) that you can adjust when connecting Power BI Desktop to SQL Server databases include:

» **Data Connectivity Mode:** Set this to DirectQuery if you don't want to load the data into Power BI Desktop itself, but instead prefer to query the data each time you refresh the report. DirectQuery is recommended if you're connecting to a very large dataset with hundreds of thousands of rows of data. Another advantage to DirectQuery is that your data is always fresh, whereas if you set this to Import, you'll need to import again every time you want the most current information on your report, assuming that the underlying data has changed.

» **Command Timeout:** Normally, leave this one blank, but if you're getting a timeout error, specify a value that gives the server more time to retrieve the data before it quits (times out, in other words). Timeout is specified in number of minutes.

- **>> SQL statement:** Normally, leave this one blank, unless you're being precise about exactly which data you want from this connection (rather than seeing the full list of tables and views in the database). You must enter a valid SQL `select` statement if you decide to put something here.

- **>> Include relationship columns:** Normally, you should select this check box because, if you do, you will have an option in Navigator to let the system select related tables after you have selected a table. This is a handy way to determine which tables you will require for a report.

TIP

To find out the name of the table that has the data you're looking for, to act as a dataset for your report, you can right-click on data in a window within a form within Dynamics 365 for Finance and Operations. A pull-down menu appears. Choose Form Information ⇨ Administration ⇨ DataSource from the menu to see the name of the table where that data is stored.

REMEMBER

Connecting Power BI with Dynamics 365 Customer Engagement (CRM), which includes, among other things, the Sales application (for sales force automation), the Service application (for customer service), and the Marketing application (for marketing automation) can be done in more than one way. You can choose from the following two preferred methods to connect Power BI to Dynamics 365 Customer Engagement:

- **>>** Connect directly to your online instance.
- **>>** Connect using content packs (collections of predefined reports and dashboards).

Harnessing the Power of Apps and Content Packs

Power BI *content packs*, now referred to also as Power BI *apps*, are collections of dashboards and reports that have been preconfigured by someone else but that you can work with, and even modify to your own specifications.

Many content packs have been created and published by Microsoft and by third-party developers, and you can get these content packs when you sign in to the Power BI services website (`https://app.powerbi.com`). Microsoft is encouraging an ecosystem of developers to create content packs and apps related to Dynamics 365 (among other things) and to load them to the Power BI website, where they can be shared with end users, developers, and IT professionals.

To browse the content packs that are available for Dynamics 365, follow these steps:

1. Point your web browser to the Power BI website and sign in.

The URL is https://app.powerbi.com.

Normally, you're directed to the Welcome page.

2. Click on Apps in the navigation pane located on the left side of the window.

If you have already downloaded some apps, they appear in the window. If not, you see a message saying that you don't have any apps yet.

3. Click the yellow Get Apps button.

The AppSource window appears.

4. Click the blue Apps button.

Apps for Power BI appear in the window. (See Figure 3-7.)

FIGURE 3-7:
The Power BI
AppSource
window.

5. Click Get It Now next to an app you're interested in to initiate a download, or click on the top part of the tile to learn more about the app.

For example, Sales Analytics for Dynamics 365 is a content pack designed to report on data from the Dynamics 365 Customer Engagement Sales application.

Embedding Dashboards in Dynamics 365

To embed a Power BI Dashboard in Dynamics 365 Customer Engagement (CRM), you need to do some preliminary work. Before embedding any dashboard, for example, you need to first update a system setting. To do so, follow these steps:

1. **On the navigation bar (the black band at the top of the screen), click the down arrow to the right of Dynamics 365 to switch to another app.**

   A pull-down menu of apps appears.

2. **Select Sales from the list of apps, then click the down arrow to the its right.**

   Another pull-down menu appears, with the Sales tile already selected.

3. **Click the magenta Settings tile.**

4. **Under the System Group, click Administration.**

5. **Click System Settings.**

   The System Settings window appears.

6. **Click the window's Reporting tab.**

7. **To allow Power BI visualization embedding, click the Yes radio button to the right of this option, near the bottom of the window.**

8. **Click OK to save these settings.**

Now that the setting is enabled, to embed a dashboard, follow these steps:

1. **Click the down arrow to the right of Settings.**

   The pull-down menu appears.

2. **Click the blue Sales tile.**

3. **Under the My Work Group heading, select Dashboards.**

4. **Click the down arrow to the right of New.**

   A drop-down menu appears.

5. **Select Power BI Dashboard.**

   The Add Power BI Dashboard dialog box appears.

6. Select the dashboard you want to embed from the drop-down list of available dashboards.

You must have previously downloaded the dashboard to your Power BI workspace on the Power BI service (website).

7. Click the Save button.

The dashboard is embedded and is displayed in your Customer Engagement application. See Figure 3-8 for an example of a dashboard displayed within Dynamics 365 for Sales.

FIGURE 3-8:
Sales activity dashboard in Dynamics 365 Customer Engagement.

Chapter **4**

Extending Dynamics 365 with PowerApps

L et's face it: No matter how well designed a software program is, and no matter how flexible the developers try to make it by adding more and more settings for you to control its behavior, there always comes a point when the software just doesn't work the way you want it to. In the real world, software customization is inevitable and unavoidable. Nonetheless, customizing your business software involves a cost. Customization is notoriously time consuming (and therefore expensive) to build, test, deploy, and maintain. Customization is often a barrier to upgrading software. Worse yet, customization can bog down or even derail an implementation of a new system.

Many organizations have adopted an IT policy that discourages customization to off-the-shelf, best-of-breed software applications, as well as the inclusion of add-on products. The idea is to buy the software that has the features that provide the closest fit to your organization's business requirements and configure it appropriately, without straying into the perilous world of customization, even if you have to adapt your current business practices to conform to the way the software was designed to work. That being said, having an adverse and derogatory regard for business software customizations and add-ons is a conservative stance that made more sense in the past than it does today. Over the decades, business software has become more easily customizable, and Dynamics 365 is no exception to this general trend.

Ideally, your software should adapt to how you do business, not the other way around. This is not to say that you should stick with an inefficient, outdated business procedure just because that's the way you've always done it. You should embrace process reengineering and come up with an efficient and logical workflow. After you have determined how that business process should work, tailoring your business software to do precisely what you want it to do is quite beneficial, as long as you can avoid the pitfalls typically associated with developing and deploying customization to the base package or implementing add-on extensions.

Providing Power to Your People with PowerApps

Microsoft PowerApps, formerly known as Project Siena, was originally released in 2015. PowerApps is a Software as a Service (SaaS) offering hosted by Microsoft in the cloud on the Azure platform. Most license plans for Office 365 and for Dynamics 365 include licenses for PowerApps. If you're running Dynamics 365, in all likelihood you're already licensed for PowerApps as well and are thereby free to use it to extend what you can do with Dynamics 365.

PowerApps is a way to create mobile apps or web-based applications that have nothing to do with Dynamics 365 per se or that extend and enhance Dynamics 365 by connecting with data and processes inside of Dynamics 365 and providing additional functionality, akin to a software add-on or bolt-on product. PowerApps isn't the way you directly modify the screens within the Dynamics 365 core applications, such as Customer Engagement (CRM) or Finance and Operations (ERP). Each application that falls under the Dynamics 365 umbrella has its own modification features and proper way of customizing it. The focus of this chapter, however, is PowerApps.

WARNING

Most folks know that you can use PowerApps to create apps that run within the context of Office 365 and Dynamics 365, but PowerApps can also be used to create apps outside of Office 365 and Dynamics 365. If you have a license plan for Dynamics 365 that includes PowerApps and you want to create apps that run outside the context of Dynamics 365, be aware that you may need to purchase additional per-user licenses (or an enterprise license that covers multiple users) in order to use PowerApps in your organization.

PowerApps was conceived as a tool to allow nonprogrammers (nontechnical end users) to be able to create their own computer programs, without having to know computer programming languages or the nuances of operating systems, database technology, or software design principles. PowerApps is a point-and-click software development tool that includes an option to use prebuilt templates to speed up the development process and simplify the creation of applications. PowerApps is touted as a way for anybody — regardless of experience or software knowledge — to create useful business applications with a few clicks of the mouse.

Okay, now let's get more realistic: Point-and-click software development means that while you're pointing and clicking, behind the scenes the tool is writing computer code automatically. Obviously, some of the code it is automatically generating may not do precisely what you want or need it to do. To make point-and-click app development a reality, the designers of PowerApps needed to make some assumptions and also needed to limit and constrain what you can actually do with it. Furthermore, end users who are typically clerical workers and are often bogged down with tons of data entry work — and who rarely have time to code apps — feel more at home keying in data than they do designing computer programs. As you can see from Figure 4-1, the Design screen in PowerApps doesn't appear to be all that simple; it has a lot of menu items, tabs, navigation panes, and so forth. Many users may easily become overwhelmed by what is supposedly a "simple" app creation tool but is more akin to a programming development platform that requires extensive training even for an experienced IT professional.

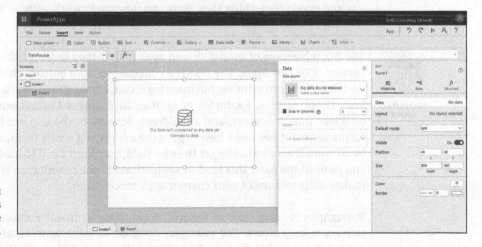

Finding out whether PowerApps is right for you

The good news is that if you choose the right type of app to build and don't get overly ambitious, an end user who is somewhat of a superuser in Dynamics 365 can achieve some amazing efficiency gains, all without having to be at the mercy of the IT department. This is truly awesome news, and I encourage you to try PowerApps if you're the type of person who is undaunted by learning new, advanced software features.

Furthermore, PowerApps isn't merely an end-user tool limited to prebuilt templates and simplistic scenarios. In PowerApps, you can build apps from scratch, starting with a blank template. In the hands of an IT professional, a programmer, or even a functional ERP or CRM Dynamics 365 consultant who doesn't necessarily know how to code any computer programming languages, PowerApps can be a rapid application development environment used to create robust apps, without requiring low-level coding.

When creating PowerApps, you can start with a data connection or you can start with the user experience. Microsoft classifies these two types of PowerApps this way:

>> **Canvas apps:** Start with the user experience

>> **Model-driven apps:** Start with your data connections

Canvas apps are the original PowerApps: You drop controls onto a free-form canvas and create something that users can intuitively work with — with little or no training. Model-driven apps are a newer addition to PowerApps.

TECHNICAL STUFF

The big advantage of model-driven apps is that they leverage the Common Data Service (CDS) for Apps. The CDS is a collection of data entities that includes relationships between entities, business logic concerning those entities, and forms to view those entities. Examples of entities in Business Central are an account, a business unit, a contact, and an address. Screens in the app are based on entity forms so that if you add a new field to the underlying entity form, all the apps you build from it automatically get the new field; you don't need to modify all the apps you built in the past; this kind of sophisticated code inheritance is automatic and makes maintenance of your custom apps much easier.

PowerApps is being used in the real world today by major corporations and top-tier consulting firms. For example, Avanade (a joint venture of Microsoft and Accenture), a global IT consulting firm with many thousands of employees, has created smartphone apps using PowerApps that employees (including every salesperson out on the road) use daily. These apps are used to tie together related information that is stored and managed in separate applications such as appointments in Outlook calendars and marketing literature in SharePoint.

Listed here are some examples of the kinds of capabilities that can be included in apps built by your organization or your authorized Dynamics 365 solution provider using Microsoft PowerApps:

>> Search through a document knowledge base stored on SharePoint for Office 365 from your smartphone and comment on articles.

>> Schedule technicians for appointments and automatically update their availability in the Dynamics 365 Resource Scheduling application.

>> Onboard employees by providing information about where to go, whom to see, what their login credentials are, and so forth, by securely transmitting the information to the new hire's smartphone.

>> Provide detailed, step-by-step instructions and easy-to-understand pictures and diagrams to manufacturing workers in a factory-floor shop via Android tablets to help improve quality control and adherence to state and federal regulations.

>> Capture customer sign-off when jobs are complete, and update that information back to Dynamics 365 for Finance and Operations to serve as backup for subsequent billing.

These are just a few examples. Use your imagination. There is truly no limit to the efficiency gains you can achieve by linking applications, workforces, customers and vendors, employees and administrators, email and databases, and on and on — and doing so in the cloud and using mobile applications. The advantages of creating and deploying solutions built on PowerApps include:

>> **Anytime/anywhere access:** Everybody has a mobile device (their smartphone) with them at all times.

>> **Global Microsoft cloud capabilities:** You can take advantage of them because everything is cloud based, so you don't need to design, purchase, install, and maintain your own computer network infrastructure.

>> **Available data connectors:** You can quickly integrate with disparate services from different SaaS providers.

Making external PowerApps connections

PowerApps is quite powerful, quite useful, and really cool. You can do some amazing things with it. But PowerApps isn't the only way that significant customizations are developed in each of the major applications that make up Dynamics 365.

REMEMBER

Dynamics 365 is an umbrella of applications that includes Customer Engagement (based on Microsoft CRM Online), Finance and Operations (based on Dynamics AX), Business Central (based on Dynamics NAV), Talent (HR), Retail, and much more. How you go about customizing each one of these applications at its core differs significantly. Each has its own customization features built into it and has techniques for controlling the versions and layers of customization.

PowerApps is more about extending processes within any of the Dynamics 365 applications and/or in Office 365 by creating apps that help to bridge the gap between different applications and organizations that coexist within a continuous business process. For example, you can create an app for use by subcontracted workers who are not logged on to your main network because they aren't full-time employees of your company; this app allows them to have a limited amount of access and update capability that is automatically integrated to your main Dynamics 365 ERP and/or CRM.

Although PowerApps can obviously connect to data and application services by means of connections, you can use one of five other methods or sources to incorporate data into your PowerApps creations. All these methods or sources are displayed in the black navigation pane to the left of the PowerApps Design Studio main window. From the navigation pane, when you select Data, the menu expands downward to display the data methods:

>> **Entities:** A set of records that is similar to a database table but is actually part of Microsoft's Common Data Service (CDS) for Apps.

   You can use the base set of standard entities that covers many common scenarios, but you're not limited to only these. In addition, you can create your own custom entities to meet your unique requirements.

REMEMBER

   Business rules such as data validation can be stored at the entity level instead of at the individual app level; in this way, you can create multiple apps that use the same entity and avoid having to recode and maintain the same data validation routines repeatedly. Other code-reuse features are also included.

>> **Option sets (picklists):** A drop-down list of fixed values that you can include in one or more apps.

   Option sets are also called picklists, and in general parlance are commonly referred to as value sets or (in old-school Windows terminology) a combo-box.

As with entities, they can be standard (factory-loaded) or custom lists that you create to suit your unique purposes.

>> **Data integration:** Data feeds from external or related systems.

These more complex data interfaces can be configured using either the Data Integrator feature or a newer capability called Microsoft Data Integration for Common Data Service.

Confer with your IT department and/or authorized solution provider for more details on how to design and configure complex data integrations, or, better yet, request that someone there create integrations for your use.

Integrating data from external applications into Dynamics 365, especially into the Finance and Operations (AX) application, is an important consideration because it can help you avoid time-consuming rekeying of data, increase data accuracy, and enhance automation of repetitive tasks and functions.

>> **Connections:** PowerApps comes with dozens of factory-loaded connections, which allow you to connect to other cloud services via the Internet.

A partial list of available connections appears later in this chapter in the "Adding a data connection" section.

Microsoft is continually expanding this list as new services become popular and widely used across the Internet.

>> **Custom connectors:** Work in a similar fashion to connections, as described earlier in this list.

If the connection you seek isn't available in the list of connections provided by Microsoft in PowerApps, consider asking your IT department to create a custom connector for you.

To do so requires knowledge of the REST API, short for *Representational State Transfer application programming interface*, to whatever it is that you want to connect to. That API must support at least one (of ten) authentication mechanisms and must use JavaScript Object Notation (JSON).

>> **Gateways:** Known as on-premise data gateways and run as a Windows service.

The on-premise data gateway is a method to get data from an on-premise system and integrate it into your cloud environment, where it can then be available as part of the apps you build with PowerApps.

Confer with your IT department for installation and configuration of on-premise data gateways.

Adding an Option set

Generalized descriptions of all available options in the PowerApps universe are all well and good, but it wouldn't hurt to walk through one particular PowerApps variant. For example, if you're building apps for your organization's marketing department to use to control the marketing materials they deliver to prospects — and these materials can be either case studies, brochures, or white papers — you might want to create a picklist that you can use throughout your application to categorize marketing materials. When users are prompted to tag the marketing material that they have uploaded to SharePoint using the app, they're presented with a drop-down list box giving them these choices:

>> Brochure

>> Case Study

>> White Paper

To create a new Option set (picklist) in PowerApps for the example just described, follow these steps:

1. **In your web browser, go to the PowerApps website.**

   The URL is https://powerapps.microsoft.com.

2. **In the upper right corner of the web page, click the Sign In link.**

3. **Provide your user ID and password credentials that you use to sign in to Dynamics 365 and/or Office 365, and then click Next.**

   Your browser is directed to an introductory web page.

4. **In the navigation pane on the left side of the web page, click the Data button.**

   The list of data sources/methods expands.

5. **Click Option Sets.**

   The Picklists (in other words, Option Sets) window is displayed to the right of the navigation menu.

   If you have previously created picklists, they appear in a list on this page.

6. **Click New Picklist, found in the upper right corner of the web page.**

   The New Picklist dialog box appears, as shown in Figure 4-2.

7. **Fill out the Name and Display Name fields.**

The name is one that you give to the object you're creating for your own purpose of managing that option set, whereas the display name is what the user of your app sees as a label for this field when running your app.

Typically, the display name is a more user-friendly descriptive name, but both names can be the same.

REMEMBER

The name cannot contain spaces.

Note that the Description field is optional.

A red asterisk following a field name label indicates that the field is required.

8. **Click the Next button.**

A new screen appears, displaying a blank list of items to be included in the picklist you just created.

The name of your picklist appears above the list of items.

The first item in the list says NewItem because the system doesn't yet know what you want to call it.

9. **Click NewItem, under the Items Name heading, to edit the name of the item.**

A rectangular text box appears.

10. **Mouse over NewItem and then type** CaseStudy **in the Name column,** Case Study **in the Display Name column, and** A write-up of a successful customer experience **in the Description column.**

Alternatively, you can leave the Description field blank. (The Description column is optional.)

FIGURE 4-2:
The New Picklist dialog box in PowerApps.

11. Click the Add Item button in the upper right corner of the web page.

A new line appears above the CaseStudy item you just entered.

12. Create two more lines — one for brochure and one for white paper — to complete the example.

13. Click the Save button in the lower right corner of the web page.

The picklist becomes available to you when creating apps in PowerApps.

Adding a data connection

Connections to an ever-expanding selection of services are available and easy to add within PowerApps. Here's a list of some of the well-known and widely used websites that you can find connections available for in PowerApps:

>> LinkedIn

>> Salesforce.com

>> OneDrive for Business

>> Trello

>> Twitter

>> Vimeo

>> Gmail

>> GoToMeeting

>> WordPress

>> YouTube

>> Workday HCM

To create a new app and add a connection to Google Gmail (for example) in Power-Apps, follow these steps:

1. Point your web browser to the PowerApps website.

The URL is https://powerapps.microsoft.com.

2. In upper right corner of the web page, click the Sign In link.

3. On the new screen that appears, enter the user ID and password credentials you use to sign in to Dynamics 365 and/or Office 365, and then click Next.

Your browser is directed to an introductory web page.

4. **In the navigation pane on the left side of the web page, click the Apps button.**

The apps you have created previously are displayed.

If you have not already created any apps, you see a No Apps Found message.

5. **Click the Create an App button, located on the left side of the menu bar.**

You may see a purple Create an App button located under the No Apps Found message in the middle of the page.

Whichever button you click, a new web page or web page tab (depending on how your browser settings are configured) launches, displaying shortcuts for creating a new app. Here are your options:

Start with Data

Start with a Blank Canvas

Start with a Template

6. **Choose the Start with a Blank Canvas option.**

Use Phone Layout if you're programming your app for a smartphone.

A new web page tab launches, and a Welcome dialog box appears that says "Welcome to PowerApps Studio," prompting you to either create a form, create a gallery, or take an interactive tour.

7. **Click the gray Skip button.**

You're now in PowerApps Studio in a blank app, ready to start creating the app.

8. **Choose File from the File menu in the upper left corner of the screen.**

The black navigation pane appears on the left side of the screen.

9. **Click Connections in the black navigation pane.**

10. **On the menu bar above the list of connections, click New Connection.**

A list of available connections displays.

You can sort this list by clicking the Name column heading — the first column of the list.

11. **Type the word** Gmail **in the Search text box, located above the column headings, toward the right side of the web page.**

The list of available connections is automatically filtered based on your search criteria.

The connector for Gmail should now be visible in the list of connections.

12. **Click the + sign or click anywhere on the Gmail Connector row.**

A dialog box appears that provides a brief description of what you can do with the connector (in this case, send or receive an email message to a Gmail account).

The dialog box prompts you to create the connection.

13. **Click the Create button.**

A dialog box appears, prompting you to sign in to a Google Gmail account.

14. **Select an existing account that is recognized by your browser (and thus will be listed), or select Use Another Account.**

15. **If you have chosen Use Another Account, enter the email address you want to use and then click Next.**

Another dialog box prompts you for a password.

16. **Again, if you have chosen Use Another Account, enter your password and then click Next.**

A dialog box appears, warning you that this action will allow Microsoft PowerApps and Flows to read, send, delete, and manage your email.

17. **Click the blue Allow button.**

You have now added Gmail as a connection that can be used in any apps you build in PowerApps or in any workflow you create in Microsoft Flow.

Making your app your own with App Settings

PowerApps provides easy point-and-click configuration to design your app to your liking. For example, many aspects of your app can be easily configured from the App Settings screen with a simple click of the mouse. (See Figure 4-3.)

These settings are among the ones you can configure from the App Settings screen:

>> **App Name:** Enter a short and distinctive name for the app you're creating; make sure the name isn't already used for another app.

>> **Background Color:** Click the colored square to change the color.

>> **Icons:** Use the slider bar on the right to see more preloaded icon choices, or load your own icon by clicking the Browse button; PNG, JPG, and JPEG file formats are accepted; the recommended image size for icons for PowerApps is 245 x 245 pixels.

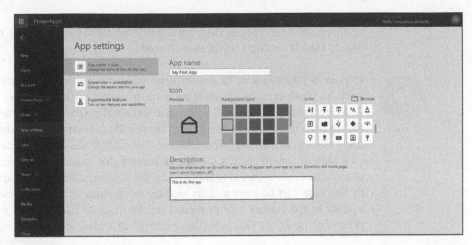

FIGURE 4-3:
App settings in
PowerApps.

>> **Description:** Be sure to enter a description that lets users know what your app can do.

>> **Screen Orientation:** Your choice is Landscape or Portrait.

>> **Screen Size:** Your choices are 16:9 (Default), 3:2 (Surface Pro 3), 16:10 (Widescreen), 4:3 (iPad), or Custom; if you choose Custom, you must enter a width and height.

TIP

On the App Settings screen, the options for Lock Aspect Ratio (which maintains the height and width in the same proportion) and Lock Orientation (which maintains the same screen orientation even if the tablet or smartphone is rotated) are defaulted to On. You might think it would be nice to let users rotate your app or resize it any which way they prefer, but both options can easily distort your app's display and render it useless. So, unless you truly know what you're doing and can successfully test your app in different aspect ratios and portrait and landscape positions, it's safer to leave these setting turned on, to simply lock both the aspect ratio and the orientation to ensure that your app displays correctly.

Connecting PowerApps to Dynamics 365

The real fun (and efficiency) comes in when you can create an app that can interact with data in your ERP (accounting software) system. For example, if you're running Dynamics 365 Business Central for ERP at your organization, you can create a self-service app that allows vendors to update their remittance email or mailing address; this app would save time because the Accounts Payable department would be free from having to field a phone call from a vendor every time one of them needs to update their remittance address (the email or mailing address where they want their invoices delivered).

TIP

If your organization or IT department has a policy that forbids external parties, such as vendors, from directly altering or inserting information in your ERP or CRM system, you can still allow the external parties to interact electronically rather than make time-consuming phone calls (or wait for a return call after leaving a voice mail). The app you create in PowerApps can create a data change request as a task in Dynamics 365 Customer Service, for example. The task would appear in a queue or view that is monitored by the Accounts Payable department. The data in the task can be reviewed by authorized agents in your organization, and the update to the vendor master record can be made at the touch of a button without rekeying the data. (This is just an example of a nifty idea for a PowerApps app.)

To create a connection to Dynamics 365 Business Central, follow these steps:

1. **Back on the PowerApps site, click Data in the black navigation pane to expand the data selections underneath.**

   When the data selections are expanded, you see Connections listed under Data Integration.

2. **Click Connections in the black navigation pane.**

3. **Click New Connection on the menu bar, above the list of connections.**

   A list of available connections displays.

   You can sort this list by clicking the Name column heading — the first column of the list.

4. **Type the word** Dynamics **in the Search text box, located above the column headings toward the right side of the web page.**

   Doing so filters the list of available connections based on your search criteria.

   Several connectors for Dynamics should now be visible in the list of connections.

   Among these are Dynamics 365, Dynamics 365 for Operations, and Microsoft Dynamics 365 Business Central.

5. **Click the + sign or anywhere on the Microsoft Dynamics 365 Business Central Connector row.**

   A dialog box appears that provides a brief description of what you can do with the connector.

   The dialog box prompts you to create the connection.

6. **Click the Create button.**

A dialog box appears, prompting you to sign in to Business Central with your Microsoft account credentials.

7. **Select an existing account that is recognized by your browser (and thus will be listed), or select Use Another Account.**

8. **If you have chosen Use Another Account, enter the email address you want to use and then click Next.**

Another dialog box prompts you for a password.

9. **Again, if you have chosen Use Another Account, enter your password and then click Next.**

A dialog box appears that asks whether you want to stay signed in.

10. **Click the blue Yes button.**

You have now added Business Central as a connection that can be used in any apps you build in PowerApps or in any workflows you create in Microsoft Flow.

I encourage you to explore what PowerApps can do to extend and expand the capabilities of Microsoft Dynamics 365.

Chapter **5**

Going with the Microsoft Flow to Enhance Dynamics 365

We've all suffered through the frustrating experience of having something go wrong with an order or a delivery, calling in to complain about it, and not getting the issue resolved because we keep getting shuffled around from one person to the next. None of the new folks knows what the previous person has done or what to do next, so we end up having to explain the problem over and over again to each new clueless person in the chain of ineptitude. Our initial reaction to this painful pinball-machine-style of customer service is to blame the people who are trying to help us — we may even gripe about how lazy and stupid we think they are. But if we examine the true cause of the inefficiency, it's not the fault of the workers, who are most often conscientious and reasonably intelligent; rather, it's the computer system they're working with that is at the root of the problem. The software application they're using isn't well integrated with related applications inside and outside their organization, and, furthermore, the system they're using lacks automated workflow capability. Without integration and workflow, you end up with isolated silos that can deal with only one small piece of a rather large and complicated puzzle. If the workers can't see the big picture — if they can't rise above the forest canopy, so to speak — they can't guide you out of the woods.

More than ever, Microsoft's business software development efforts, as well as its marketing strategy concerning those efforts, is placing the emphasis on connecting applications together. The idea is to have a fluid, interconnected ecosystem of loosely coupled special-purpose apps rather than one giant, monolithic application that can't talk to anything other than itself. To make this dream a reality, you need standard technologies for rapid customization, robust workflow, and seamless integration. Customization capability is needed so that you can create apps that act as a bridge between previously disconnected systems. Workflow is needed so that you can route cases, incidents, or documents to multiple parties within your organization as well as outside your organization and through multiple applications so that the process doesn't get bogged down with any single person or in any single application. Integration is needed so that your custom apps (many of which will contain custom workflows) can communicate with a wide variety of other applications, web services, Windows services, databases, and other elements across the Internet.

Setting Up Basic Workflows Using Microsoft Flow

Customization, workflow, and integration are already seen to be crucial for the future of business development software. Microsoft has devised the following new cloud technologies that address these three essential ingredients of an interconnected world of loosely coupled applications:

>> **Microsoft PowerApps:** For customization

>> **Microsoft Flow:** For workflow

>> **Connectors:** Available for Microsoft PowerApps and Microsoft Flow for integration

PowerApps is used to create apps that can run in either a web browser or on devices such as tablets and smartphones. Those apps can contain one or more workflows created using Microsoft Flow. Also, workflows created in Microsoft

Flow can run independently without being embedded in a PowerApps app. (For more on PowerApps, see Chapter 4.)

At the PowerApps and Microsoft Flow development sites, you find what Microsoft calls *connectors* (sometimes referred to as *connections*). These prebuilt connectors can be tapped within both PowerApps and Microsoft Flow to connect you to all kinds of data and services over the Internet. You can also connect to on-premise data within your organization using an on-premise data gateway. Furthermore, you aren't limited to the available off-the-shelf connectors (connections) that come with PowerApps and Microsoft Flow; you can instead build custom connectors and data integrations in situations where a prebuilt connector isn't available for whatever you're looking to connect to.

REMEMBER

Like PowerApps, Microsoft Flow is a cloud service, designed and built from the ground up, for the Internet and Internet-enabled mobile devices.

The following Microsoft connectors are among the most popular connectors available for Microsoft Flow:

>> SharePoint

>> Office 365 Outlook

>> OneDrive for Business

>> Dynamics 365

The following connectors to non-Microsoft websites are among the most widely used connectors available for Microsoft Flow:

>> Dropbox

>> Adobe Sign

>> Gmail

>> Twitter

>> Facebook

Microsoft has created hundreds of templates for Microsoft Flow that make it easy to create a workflow. The templates are available on the Flow website, as shown in Figure 5-1.

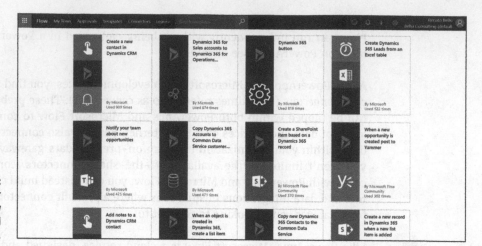

FIGURE 5-1:
Templates for
Microsoft Flow
workflows related
to Dynamics 365.

To see the Microsoft Flow templates available for Dynamics 365, follow these steps:

1. **Point your web browser to the Microsoft Flow website.**

   In the United States, the correct URL is https://us.flow.microsoft.com/en-us.

2. **In the upper right corner of the screen that appears, click Sign In.**

3. **Provide the user ID you use to sign in to Dynamics 365 and/or Office 365 and then click Next.**

4. **On the next screen, enter your password and then click the Sign In button.**

   An introductory web page appears.

5. **On the black navigation bar at the top of the web page, click Templates.**

   The templates for all flows appears.

6. **In the search box above the templates, type** Dynamics 365 **and then click the Magnifying Glass icon to run the search.**

   The Flow templates for Dynamics 365 appear in the window. (Refer to Figure 5-1.

7. **Click the template of your choice to call up the wizard that will guide you step-by-step in creating the workflow.**

   The system prompts you to enter information such as credentials and company name, as you're guided through the workflow creation. You'll be able to edit the workflow on the Microsoft Flow Designer screen after the wizard completes creation of the workflow, as shown in Figure 5-2.

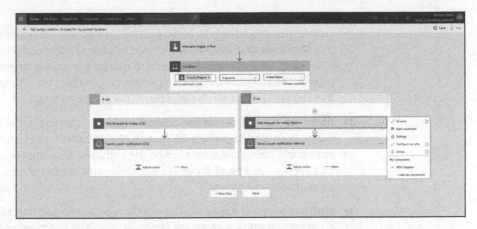

FIGURE 5-2:
The Microsoft
Flow Designer
screen.

Grasping the Relationship Between Document Management and Workflow

Traditionally, workflow capabilities have been most prominent in document imaging systems. Document imaging systems evolved into document management systems and are now more formally referred to as enterprise content management (ECM) systems. The reason that ECM systems tend to be workflow intensive is that their primary goal is a paperless routing of electronic documents for data entry, approval, electronic signatures, archival storage, and sometimes for funds disbursement.

Typical functions handled by ECM systems include:

>> Processing insurance claims

>> Reviewing mortgage applications

>> Managing contracts and other legal documents

ECM system designers were among some of the first proponents of workflow software. However, most of these workflow engines were proprietary technologies that were part of the ECM document storage software itself, rather than all-purpose tools or a standard technology that could be used to create workflows for a variety of different applications from different vendors. That being said, ECM systems tend to have powerful and robust workflow engines. A powerful ECM workflow engine should include these components:

>> **Graphical workflow designer:** You should be able to drag and drop the workflow steps onto a blank canvas (screen) and connect the steps with

arrows. You should be able to right-click on a step and set properties for what that step does, and so forth. You should be able to insert conditional logic processing blocks between the steps to change the routing based on selected criteria. The workflow designer application should be a user-friendly interface that requires little or no low-level computer programming.

>> **Ability to apply complex conditional logic:** You should be able to base the if-then logic used to redirect the routing of a document on as many attributes as possible, such as who sent it, who the author is, what the status is, whether it's signed, what type of document it is, dollar amount thresholds, day of the week, and product lines.

>> **Multiple levels of approval:** The workflow engine should handle multiple approval scenarios, such as one approver, any valid approver, approver in a group or team, all approvers, a chain of approvers, or approvers based on who the manager is, rather than on only a single approver per document.

>> **Approval delegates:** If the approver is on vacation or is too busy to approve the document, the document should be approvable by a delegate; this strategy avoids having the document get stuck in the workflow.

>> **Automatic actions:** The power of a workflow engine is largely contingent on having as many system and application actions available to be triggered by some other event in the workflow or by a command button. In other words, you should have an extensive menu of possible actions that you can auto-mate using the workflow, such as deleting or copying a document, deleting a master record, posting a transaction, or sending an email; you shouldn't be constrained to only being able to either approve or reject the document.

Seeing How Microsoft Does ECM

Microsoft's enterprise content management (ECM) system is called SharePoint. SharePoint, although very widely adopted, isn't a typical ECM system, partly because it was originally envisioned to be more of a development platform than a document imaging or document management system. Unlike many other ECM systems, SharePoint didn't start out as a document imaging system and then, over the years, add capabilities to evolve into an ECM. Rather, SharePoint started out as an ambitious next–generation development environment from Microsoft that was supposed to take over the world, so to speak — an ambition thwarted by the fact that SharePoint lacked a powerful workflow engine. Originally, the answer to Sharepoint's workflow engine problem was supposed to be Microsoft InfoPath *forms*, which were objects that you could create in the SharePoint environment. InfoPath forms acted as a graphical user interface (GUI) screen for users to key in data — a form to provide data capture, in other words). The InfoPath forms could then be routed around the organization, much like a workflow. InfoPath never caught on, and is now considered obsolete.

REMEMBER

As InfoPath is being phased out, Microsoft PowerApps and Microsoft Flow are being touted as its replacement. Just keep in mind that PowerApps and Flow aren't constrained to working within SharePoint. They can work with SharePoint, just like any other application, by means of connectors. PowerApps and Flow run in the cloud and can connect to a wide variety of applications, including Microsoft Power BI (the business intelligence reporting tool). PowerApps and Flow are also inherently mobile enabled; the idea of running them anytime and anywhere using a smartphone was the original conception, not a later development.

Understanding Workflow in the ERP and CRM Realms

Enterprise resource planning (ERP) systems are financial and operations software, sometimes referred to as *back-office* accounting systems. ERP lagged behind ECM in providing workflow capabilities. When ERP developers finally started to add workflow capability into their applications, rather than create generic workflow tools to create any kind of workflow, they tended to provide prebuilt (canned) workflows for the following ERP functions:

>> General ledger journal-entry approval

>> Requisitions (creation and approval)

>> Purchase orders (requisition promotion to P/O and budget approval)

>> Accounts payable (vendor invoice approval)

>> Budgeting collaboration

Many ERP systems included some document imaging capabilities, using their own proprietary document storage capabilities. However, many ERP workflow modules were created by third-party add-on developers rather than by the ERP vendor, and these add-on products sometimes made use of more widely used or standard document imaging systems. The add-on product's workflow engine, however, was most often purely proprietary.

Generally speaking, workflow has been an afterthought in ERP, but less so in customer relationship management (CRM) systems. CRM systems became popular and widely adopted after ERP systems had been around for many years, so they tended to include more workflow capabilities. Also, a CRM system isn't burdened with having to include the complexity of accounting, so it's more free to focus on the routing of cases, incidents, emails, and documents instead of on having to get each transaction correct with regard to accounting impact (and all the other issues, such as tax implications) that an ERP system must address.

Considering your workflow options in Dynamics 365

Dynamics 365 has one CRM application and two ERP applications. The CRM application (formerly called Microsoft CRM Online) is now referred to as Customer Engagement for Dynamics 365. It contains Sales, Service, and Marketing, among other applications. With ERP, you have a choice between Business Central (formerly Dynamics NAV) for smaller organizations and Finance and Operations Enterprise Edition (formerly Dynamics AX) for larger organizations. Each of these three applications — CRM, NAV, and AX — have their own workflow engines. These internal (native) workflow engines aren't part of Microsoft Flow; they in fact predate Microsoft Flow. However, these internal engines are in many respects more robust than Microsoft Flow, which is a newer, cloud-based workflow tool geared especially toward user-friendly simple workflow scenarios. If you're writing a workflow for which the actions, approvals, and processes are internal to the application, then in many such circumstances it makes more sense to use the internal workflow engine rather than Microsoft Flow. Microsoft Flow is newer and lacks all the bells and whistles that the internal workflow engines have, yet it's powerful especially because of how many connections you can make to external applications and services.

TIP

When considering developing a workflow for Dynamics 365, carefully consider which workflow engine to use — internal or Microsoft Flow. As a rule of thumb, if the workflow steps take place mostly within a single application or require advanced actions to occur within the application, then the internal workflow tool is probably preferred. Consult with your authorized Dynamics 365 solution provider for advice on which tool is right for your particular purposes.

TECHNICAL STUFF

Workflow notifications are more extensive in Microsoft Flow than in CRM business process flows. Dynamics 365 workflows native to Dynamics 365 for Customer Engagement (CRM) send email-based notifications to alert users to attend to a step in the workflow, such as approving a transaction or document. Though email is convenient and handy in most cases, sometimes you don't want to notify users by email because doing so tends to clog up their inboxes. Sometimes you need to send a text message, possibly to a customer who isn't a licensed user of your Dynamics 365 instance. With the Twilio connector for Microsoft Flow, you can send and receive SMS text notifications for events that occur within Dynamics 365. Also, with the Microsoft Flow app installed on your mobile device, you can receive notifications on your smartphone that have been triggered by an event that was initiated within Dynamics 365.

The native workflow capabilities are implemented in a variety of ways within these three Dynamics 365 applications: Customer Engagement (CRM), Business Central (NAV), and Finance and Operations (AX). As a general guide, you can establish workflows in these three applications in the following manner:

>> **Customer Engagement (CRM):** Use Dynamics 365 workflows.

   The native workflow engine of CRM is still available in Customer Engagement, the Dynamics 365 version of CRM.

   The native workflows in CRM are a type of process that you configure in the Settings area. (These are also referred to as *business process* flows.)

   To create a Dynamics 365 workflow in Customer Engagement, choose Settings ➪ Process ➪ New from the main menu to access the Create Process screen. (See Figure 5-3.)

>> **Business Central (NAV):** The direction that Microsoft is leaning toward is to encourage you to create workflows for Business Central using Microsoft Flow, which is why there are many templates available to do so. (Available templates include vendor approval, sales quote approval, low stock warning, and more.)

   See Figure 5-4 for more templates available for Business Central on the Microsoft Flow website.

>> **Finance and Operations (AX):** Workflows are available for a variety of transactions and functions within a module, such as the Procurement and Sourcing module.

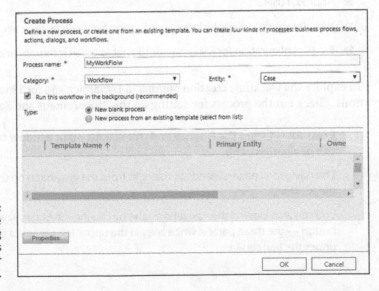

FIGURE 5-3:
The Create Process dialog box in Dynamics 365 for Customer Engagement.

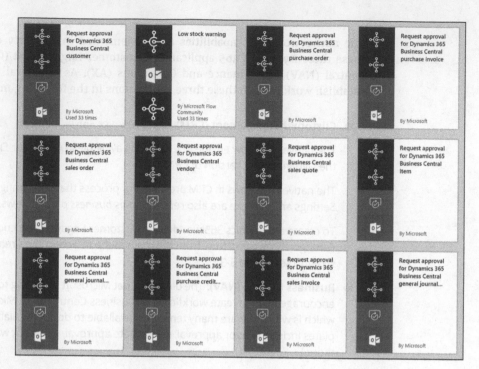

FIGURE 5-4:
Microsoft Flow
templates for
Business Central.

Workflow creation in Business Central's native workflow engine involves more setup and configuration than using the template in Microsoft Flow. The steps for the Business Central workflow creation include setting up these components:

>> Workflow users and user groups

>> Approval users

>> Workflow notifications including notification batching by time allotments

>> Email configuration for SMTP server to enable email internally and externally

To explore the workflow creation options in Dynamics 365 for Finance and Operations, check out the process for setting up the Procurement and Sourcing module:

1. **Press Alt+F1 from the Finance and Operations main window to display the navigation pane.**

   The navigation pane expands to the right from the gray band on the left side of the window.

   You can also expand the navigation pane by clicking the Show Navigation Pane button — the three parallel white lines in the upper left corner of the window under the teal square.

REMEMBER

In Finance and Operations for Dynamics 365, the navigation pane displays a large menu that can be used to navigate anywhere in the system.

Alternatively, you can navigate by entering search criteria in the search box, which becomes visible when you click the Magnifying Glass icon located near the upper right of the window on the black navigation bar.

2. **Select Modules from the navigation pane.**

   The list of modules in the Finance and Operations application expands underneath.

3. **Select Procurement and Sourcing from the modules list.**

   The Procurement and Sourcing menu items appear to the right of the list of modules in the navigation pane.

4. **Choose Setup from the menu.**

   The menu items for procurement and sourcing appear underneath.

5. **Click Procurement and Sourcing Workflows.**

   A list of existing Procurement and Sourcing workflows appears.

6. **Click New.**

   The Create Workflow window appears, showing the types of workflows that are predefined in the system for the Procurement and Sourcing module. (See Figure 5-5.)

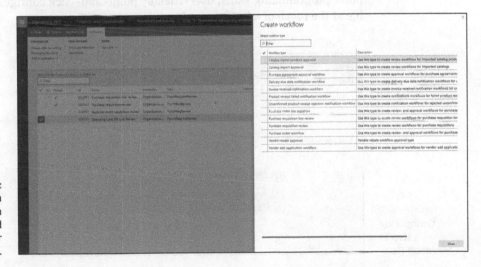

FIGURE 5-5:
Creating a workflow in Finance and Operations for Dynamics 365.

7. **Click the Close button when you're finished reviewing.**

Confer with your Dynamics 365 Finance and Operations solution provider for the details on how to create workflows in Dynamics 365 for Finance and Operations (AX).

Comprehending the Microsoft Flow advantage

A proprietary workflow engine can be a powerful capability within a single application. Workflow technology is most powerful, however, when a more standard or all-purpose workflow engine stands outside of any particular application and can act as the conduit for a seamless flow of incidents, documents, issues, and cases across multiple organizations, applications, and user groups. Microsoft Flow is designed to integrate disparate applications and services.

Microsoft Flow has a life outside the world of Dynamics 365 because it's not simply a workflow capability within some other application that can reach outside of the main application; rather, Microsoft Flow is a pure workflow engine itself. Because it doesn't have a native application — a home, as it were — it can be used to automate processes within any application or applications that it can connect to. Essentially, Microsoft Flow is a SaaS (Software as a Service) offering that can be used to create workflows inside and outside of Microsoft. Configuring steps, actions, and conditional business logic in Microsoft Flow doesn't require computer programming skills; user-friendly point-and-click configuration is available at the touch of a button, as shown in Figure 5-6.

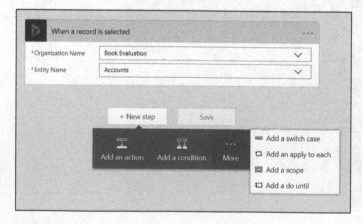

FIGURE 5-6:
Configuring
a step in
Microsoft Flow.

Though Microsoft Flow is designed for power users to set up their own quick workflows by means of prebuilt templates, the native workflow engines of the Dynamics 365 CRM and ERP applications are more often regarded as tools used by CRM and ERP consultants (as well as other IT professionals) to automate business processes on behalf of users. These business processes have to first be studied carefully, and requirements have to be gathered by internal business analysts or external consultants acting in a business analyst role.

To get the most out of Microsoft Flow and its ability to enhance Dynamics 365, you should go beyond the templates that let users quickly create simple workflows. Though these simple workflows are certainly worthwhile (and even neat-o), they won't necessarily make a major impact on your organization's productivity. Consider engaging your Dynamics 365 solution provider to fully explore how many of your existing business processes can be significantly enhanced and automated by means of a more complex design and configuration of a workflow created with Microsoft Flow.

TIP

If you want the ability to schedule a workflow rather than have it kick off as a result of an event, you may want to use Microsoft Flow rather than the native workflow engines in Dynamics 365, which lack a scheduling feature. In Microsoft Flow, use the Recurrence option when you create the flow, and set a frequency and a time interval so as to initiate the workflow when and how often you desire.

2

Customer Engagement (formerly Dynamics CRM Online)

Chapter 6

Turning Relationships into Revenue with Sales

The purpose of customer relationship management software is to foster efficient and effective communication with both prospective and existing customers, thereby improving customer satisfaction and increasing sales revenue. Customer relationship management systems began as simple lists of leads and prospects and have evolved into complex applications which handle a wide range of business functions. This chapter sets out to help you gain a better understanding of customer relationship management systems and to see how this type of software could be of use to your organization.

Understanding CRM-Related Terms

To help you gain a better understanding of Dynamics 365 for Customer Engagement (formerly Dynamics CRM Online), a quick history of CRM-related terms is in order. In this brief history lesson, I clear up any confusion you may have about the acronyms CRM, SFA, and ERP and the terms *front office* and *back office*.

The following are CRM-related acronyms and terms:

>> **CRM:** Customer relationship management

>> **SFA:** Sales force automation

>> **ERP:** Enterprise resource planning

>> **Front Office:** Operations

>> **Back Office:** Accounting

The first CRM software that became widely adopted was developed by Siebel Systems in the early 1990s. Another popular CRM software was ACT!, first developed in Dallas, Texas, and later acquired by the Sage Group. ACT! (a sort of computerized Rolodex for managing sales contact information) was geared toward smaller companies, whereas Siebel was focused on larger enterprise clients. Both CRM offerings were on-premise software products that initially focused on sales force automation; in other words, giving salespeople a way to track their leads and opportunities. As Siebel grew, it added more features, and eventually many of its large clients used its software as a development platform to create complex applications that became entangled in more aspects of their daily operations. CRM became a hot button issue for many organizations, and competitors sprung up to compete with Siebel and ACT! and get in on the action. Originally, Microsoft Dynamics touted Siebel as its go-to partner for CRM, but eventually Microsoft decided to create its own CRM system, Microsoft CRM.

REMEMBER

The subject of this chapter, Dynamics 365 for Sales (which is only one part of Microsoft's CRM software application, now called Dynamics 365 for Customer Engagement) encompasses sales, service, marketing, field service, project service, and resource scheduling. Microsoft is now using the term *customer engagement* rather than *customer relationship management* because the new term seems more descriptive of the broader range of functionality that the company has added to the Microsoft CRM offering over the years.

Although the *c* in CRM stands for customer, as opposed to prospect, one of the main functions of a CRM system is automating the sales force. Of course, your sales force deals mainly with prospects as well as with customers. The term *sales force automation*, or SFA, was coined as a marketing term to help popularize CRM software. The reasoning of the CRM software marketers was that they could sell more CRM software by claiming that using it will increase sales revenue, and thus increase profits, with the happy result that the software pays for itself. This strategy worked, and CRM became wildly popular. These days, most sales managers cannot even imagine what life would be like without a proper CRM system to organize and automate their sales efforts.

Microsoft got into the CRM game by developing its own CRM software from scratch — Microsoft CRM, first released in 2003. The original Microsoft CRM, built by Microsoft on the .NET platform, has evolved into today's version, Microsoft Dynamics 365 for Customer Engagement, now offered in the cloud as a Software as a Service (SaaS).

The goal of a sales force is to turn prospects into steady customers by sending out quotes to prospects and getting back signed purchase orders. This process of onboarding customers is commonly referred to as *front office*. After you get your first order, that prospect is now a real customer, and the *back office*, the place where the accounting happens, comes into play. You'll need to create the customer master record, process their billing, accounts receivable, and all the rest in your company's back-office accounting software system. The back-office is usually referred to as ERP. ERP stands for *Enterprise Relationship Management*, another term devised by software marketers, but what it really means is accounting and supply chain software: financial reporting, general ledger, payables, receivables, billing, inventory control, and so forth.

As shown in Figure 6-1, customer and order data starts out in front-office applications and eventually makes its way to back-office applications. That being said, for the sake of efficiency, data integrations between front-office and back-office applications most often should be bidirectional. (For example, if you update the customer address in either the ERP or the CRM, the address change should be reflected in both systems.)

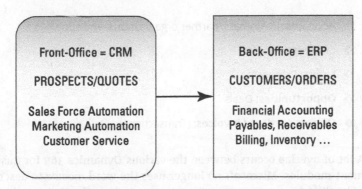

FIGURE 6-1: Traditional front/back office terminology.

Historically, ERP systems have tended to be more complex than CRM systems, for the simple reason that almost all transactions recorded in an ERP system require debits and credits to the financial ledger and thus have tax and financial reporting implications, whereas in CRM systems, much of the activity that is recorded doesn't require the same kind of rigorous financial mappings and audit trails. However, as CRM systems have become more widely adopted and have added more features and functions, ERP systems no longer seem so much more complex by contrast.

Originally, CRM was focused on sales force automation, but over time CRM software expanded, offering capabilities to track the activities of your marketing department (such as campaign management) as well as the activities of your customer service department (such as support cases and complaint handling).

In Dynamics 365, Microsoft provides CRM capabilities in these major areas:

The traditional (core) CRM modules:

>> **Sales:** Sales force automation

>> **Service:** Customer service

>> **Marketing:** Marketing automation

CRM expansion:

>> **Field Service:** Delivery, inventory, purchases, and returns

>> **Project Service:** Time and billing

>> **Resource Scheduling:** Worker scheduling

This chapter focuses on showing what you can do — and which benefits you can gain — by using Dynamics 365 for Sales, which includes features to help you track all of the following areas and more:

>> **Accounts:** Customers, partner organizations, and suppliers

>> **Contacts:** People

>> **Leads:** Prospects

>> **Opportunities:** Deals

>> **Quotes / orders / invoices:** (Transactions)

REMEMBER

A lot of overlap occurs between the various Dynamics 365 for Customer Engagement modules. Microsoft no longer uses the word *module* to describe these areas of its CRM for the most part. Sometimes you hear the term *application*, and sometimes *module*, but you can think of it as one big, happy system. For example, both your sales and marketing teams are interested in leads, so it's hard to say whether leads fall into the Sales module or the Marketing module. The areas are not truly separate, because the navigation bar at the top of the screen allows you to easily jump to any area.

Navigating the Navigation Bar

The *navigation bar* in Dynamics 365 for Customer Engagement is the black bar at the top of the screen. In a lot of places, you can click, so it can be a bit confusing until you get the hang of it. (Figure 6-2 shows buttons on the left side of the navigation bar, and Figure 6-3 shows more buttons on the right.)

FIGURE 6-2:
The left side of the navigation bar in Dynamics 365 Customer Engagement.

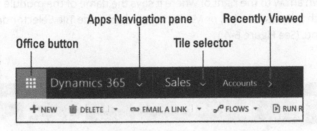

Apps Navigation pane   Recently Viewed

Office button   Tile selector

FIGURE 6-3:
The right side of the navigation bar in Dynamics 365 Customer Engagement.

Categorized Global Search

Advanced Find   Settings

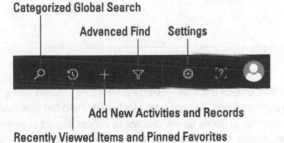

Add New Activities and Records

Recently Viewed Items and Pinned Favorites

To get you up to speed on the navigation bar, I have created this quick guide for you:

REMEMBER

>> **Office 365 button:** This is the button to click if you want to navigate somewhere in the greater world of Microsoft cloud applications — outside of Dynamics, in other words — but still in the Microsoft Azure cloud.

You can still get to Dynamics-related web pages such as the Dynamics home page from here as well.

Click the Office 365 button to display on the left side of the screen a navigation pane that has icons for Office 365 applications such as Word, Excel, PowerPoint, and SharePoint.

When you click an Office 365 application icon from this navigation pane, a separate web page displays, with the online version of the application rather than a desktop version.

>> **Apps Navigation pane:** Click the down arrow to the right of where it says *Dynamics 365* to display the Apps Navigation pane.

From the Apps Navigation pane, you can navigate to any of the Customer Engagement applications *(modules)*, including those applications that are part of the expanded CRM offerings, such as Field Service and Project Service.

>> **Tile selector:** The Tile selector lets you switch to another module. Click the down arrow to the right of where it says the name of the module you're in (such as Sales, Service, or Marketing) to display the Tile Selector drop-down menu. (See Figure 6-4.)

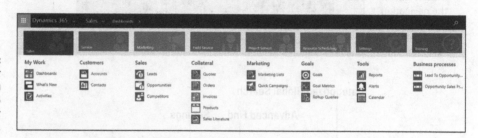

FIGURE 6-4:
The Tile Selector drop-down menu in Dynamics 365 for Customer Engagement.

When you click one of the tiles — those colored rectangles along the top of the menu such as Sales, Service, and Marketing, Field Service, and Project Service — the menu items below change to reflect the most relevant menu items for that module. For example, if you click the Field Service tile, a choice for Inventory & Purchasing displays, whereas if you click the Marketing tile, a choice for Marketing Lists and Campaigns displays.

>> **Recently Viewed:** When you click the arrow for the next drop-down menu — the menu to the immediate right of the Tile selector (refer to Figure 6-2) — you get a clickable list of all recently viewed objects. Simply click an item in the list to go back to that screen.

>> **Categorized Global Search:** Click the Magnifying Glass icon to display a Search text box. Then you can enter search criteria to search Dynamics 365 data.

The global search allows users to enter a search string on the navigation bar and conduct a global search of up to ten *entities* (or types of records, such as customers, vendors, or cases) at a time. You can use the asterisk character (*) as a wildcard to specify Begins With, Ends With, or Contains.

>> **Recently Viewed Items and Pinned Favorites:** Click the Clock icon to display a pull-down menu showing your recent views and recent records as well as all pinned views and pinned records. (To pin an item in the list, hover the mouse

over the item until the Pin icon appears to its right, and then click the icon. Pinning the item keeps that item visible on this menu, even if you haven't viewed it recently.)

Simply click the item itself to navigate to that item. Doing so doesn't launch a new web page or web page tab, but rather the web page you're on switches to the recently viewed or pinned item.

» **Add New Activities and Records:** Click the Plus Sign (+) icon to display a pull-down menu showing you the activities (tasks, phone calls, emails, and appointments) as well as the records (accounts, cases, contacts, and leads) that you can add.

Simply click the icon for the activity or record type you want to add, and the screen changes to a blank data-entry window for that type of activity or record.

For example, when you click the Opportunity icon, the Quick Create Opportunity window displays. Fill out the required information and click the Save button to add the opportunity.

» **Advanced Find:** Click the Filter icon to open the Advanced Find window. This window opens in its own separate web page.

The Advanced Find feature is a query tool that allows you to create views that you can save and use over and over again, as well as share with colleagues. You can search for just about any kind of entity that exists within Dynamics 365, select whichever columns you want to see, arrange them in the order you want to view them, and apply conditional logic and filters to limit the data to the relevant records.

» **Settings:** Click the Gear icon to display a pull-down menu for your Settings preferences. You can then click, say, Options to open the Set Personal Options window. This window has many tabs, and these settings affect many options that can control the behavior of Dynamics 365 for your personal use.

TIP

On the Set Personal Options window's General tab, be sure to set your time zone and default currency to reflect where you're geographically located.

Working with Leads, Accounts, and Contacts

In Dynamics 365 for Customer Engagement, leads, accounts, and contacts are common entities shared across most modules, including Sales, Marketing, and Service. Figure 6-5 presents the relationship between these three important entities.

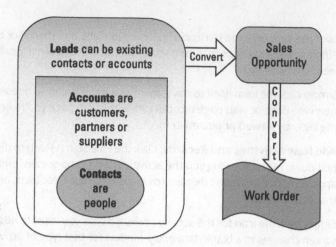

FIGURE 6-5:
Converting leads to work orders.

A *contact* is a person. The person can be tagged with an account. What this means is that an account can have an unlimited number of contacts who belong to that account. The typical scenario is that the account is a company that is your customer. Several contacts may be working at that customer, such as the person in the Accounts Payable department and the main buyer who issues purchase orders to buy goods and services from your organization.

A *lead* is a person — a person whom you're evaluating and pursuing to determine whether he qualifies as a legitimate sales opportunity. A lead can be tagged with an existing account and/or an existing contact at that account, but doing so is optional; you can enter from scratch a lead who is not associated with an existing contact or account.

Leads can be qualified (worthy of follow-up), disqualified (not worth a follow-up), or abandoned (not enough info to make a decision, but not digging any deeper). Leads can also be added to marketing lists. Leads can be converted to sales opportunities. Opportunities can in turn be converted to work orders.

When working with a lead, an account, or a contact, you and your colleagues keep a record that acts as an audit trail of your activity related to them. You can record what you did as well as what you need to do in the future, such as make a phone call at a predetermined future date and time. The Lead Summary, Account Summary, and Contact Summary forms (windows where you edit these entities) all have a place in the center of the form to add:

>> **Posts:** Quick comments that can be posted by a user or automatically by the system. Posts are similar to the brief remarks you see on Twitter.

>> **Activities:** Phone calls, emails, appointments, approvals, and booking alerts. An activity has a status so that you can track its progress, and it can act as a

sort of tickler file. You mark activities as complete after they're done, to get them off your to-do list, so to speak.

» **Notes:** Longer, more descriptive explanations that are used to document what has transpired or other notable information related to that lead, account, or contact.

Leads, accounts, and contacts have many data elements, including phone numbers, email addresses, and so much more. In addition, you can connect these entities to other entities — connecting a contact with an account, for example. You can assign them to users in your organization so that those users will know that they are responsible to follow up with them.

REMEMBER

The exact configuration of your leads, accounts, and contact forms — including which fields and functions are available — depends on how Dynamics 365 for Customer Engagement was configured at your organization. Remember that Dynamics 365 is a highly customizable system that is meant to be tailored to your unique requirements by using the built-in customization tools.

WARNING

You don't have to code custom computer programs in order to customize Dynamics 365; rather, you can use the tools found on the Settings menu. (Choose Settings ➪ Customizations ➪ Customize the System.) For the best results, though, be sure to confer with an authorized Dynamics 365 solutions provider before customizing your system, because even though customization in Dynamics 365 for Customer Engagement doesn't require low-level computer programming, it does require a deep knowledge of the Customer Engagement entities and customization features to do it properly and successfully.

Leading the way with leads

In Dynamics 365 for Sales, working with leads is where it all begins. Leads are the lifeblood of any sales force automation system. For example, a typical sales force automation process might work this way:

» Leads are loaded into the CRM system from an external marketing list.

» Leads are assigned to sales reps by the sales manager based on geographical regions or other relevant criteria.

» Sales reps begin to call, email, or otherwise reach out to the leads, perhaps via social media such as LinkedIn.

» Sales reps keep track of their phone calls, appointments, emails, and other tasks using the CRM software.

» Sales reps convert leads to opportunities and eventually send out quotes and, ideally, promote the lead (prospect) to an account (customer).

TECHNICAL
STUFF

You can use the Data Import Wizard to import leads, accounts, contacts, or other data into Dynamics 365, but you probably should set up duplicate detection rules to avoid importing duplicate records. (These rules are specified under Settings ⇨ Data Management ⇨ Duplicate Detection Rules.) Also, you must first prepare any file you want to import in the proper layout. Files with .csv, .txt, .zip, .xml, and .xlsx extensions are acceptable. Under the Settings tile, under the System Column heading, select Data Management and then Imports, and then click the Import Data button to launch the wizard.

Whatever your organization's process is for working with leads, Dynamics 365 for Sales can accommodate it, streamline it, and automate it. By default, the Dynamics 365 for Sales module has a built-in business process flow called the Lead to Opportunity sales process. The stages of this process are listed here:

>> **Qualify the lead.**

>> **Develop the lead.**

>> **Present a proposal.**

>> **Close the deal.**

The stages of business process flow in Dynamics 365 for Customer Engagement can be tailored to your precise requirements. You define stages and the steps that fall within each stage. You can specify the information that is required to be entered before the user can proceed to the next stage. The point of these business process flows is to guide the user through using the system so that the data that eventually gets collected in the system is more consistent and complete. Using or modifying the built-in business process flows as part of your organization's way of working with Dynamics 365 is optional. The business process flow feature was devised by Microsoft as a means to help you control and optimize the entering of data in Dynamics 365.

TIP

Creating, modifying, and specifying business process flows in Dynamics 365 for Customer Engagement is not a task that each user should do for herself, but rather it's an important design consideration in configuring and implementing Dynamics 365 that should be handled by the consultants or system administrators. Please consult with your Dynamics 365 authorized solution provider for more information on modifying the default built-in business process flows.

Typically, the main thing you will want to do in Dynamics 365 for Sales is work through your list of leads. To view your assigned leads, follow these steps:

1. **Click the down arrow to the right of the module name you're in (such as Sales, Service, or Marketing) to display the Tile Selector drop-down menu. (Refer to Figure 6-2 for which arrow to click.)**

   A pull-down menu appears. (Refer to Figure 6-4.)

2. **Click the Sales tile.**

3. **Under the Sales column heading, click Leads to go to your list of leads.**

   A view of leads displays.

   The view you see depends on the view you were working with the last time you were in the View Leads window.

You can easily change the view — how the list of leads is filtered, in other words. For example, you can switch to the view called My Open Leads, to see leads assigned to you that still require your attention. Here's how:

1. **Click the down arrow immediately to the right of the view name (such as All Leads) in the upper left corner directly above the list of leads.**

   A pull-down menu displays, showing all the views you can use to filter the list of leads.

2. **Select My Open Leads.**

   The list of leads is filtered to show your open leads.

   You can sort the list by any column by clicking on that column's column heading.

   You can filter the list further by clicking the Filter icon, which is to the far right of the column headings. (The Filter icon looks like a funnel.)

To open any Sales Lead form, simply click the name of the lead in the list. With the form open, you can add, delete, or update information related to the lead. (See Figure 6-6.)

A command bar (directly underneath the black navigation bar) is decked out with command buttons such as New, Delete, Disqualify, Assign, and Share. (Refer to Figure 6-6.) The command buttons available to you will depend on how your system has been configured by your system administrator.

TIP

If you want someone else in your organization to work on a sales lead but you also want to continue working on that lead, use the Share command button on the command bar rather than the Assign command button to assign to your colleague access to that lead. In this way, your colleague is assigned the lead, but at the same time, you don't lose access to the lead.

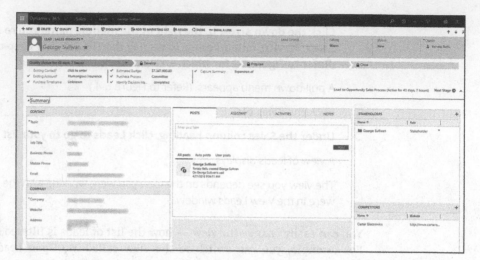

FIGURE 6-6:
The Dynamics 365 for Sales Lead form.

Working with accounts

In Dynamics 365 for Sales, customers are called *accounts*. Referring to customers or clients as accounts is typical sales terminology. However, the term *account* can be confusing because in many business software systems, such as ERP systems, one normally refers to general-ledger financial account numbers as accounts. In any case, in Dynamics 365 for Customer Engagement (CRM), the term *account* is used instead of *customer*, mainly because the term *account* is a more generic term than *customer*. Accounts can refer to not only companies that you sell to (customers) but also companies that you partner with or buy from, such as suppliers (vendors).

To create a new account, follow these steps:

1. Click the down arrow to the right of the module name you're in (such as Sales, Service, or Marketing) to display the Tile Selector drop-down menu. (Refer to Figure 6-2 for which arrow to click.)

A pull-down menu appears. (Refer to Figure 6-4.)

2. Click the Sales tile.

3. Under the Customer column heading, click Accounts to go to your list of accounts.

A view of accounts displays.

The view you see depends on the last time you were in the View Accounts window.

4. **Click the New button.**

   The New Account form displays. (See Figure 6-7.)

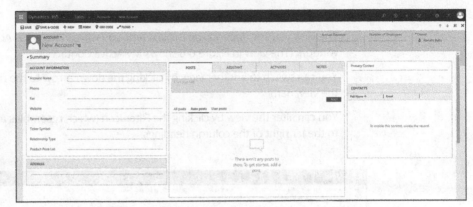

5. **Enter a name in the Account Name field.**

   Account Name is a required field.

   A red asterisk to the left of the field label indicates that the field is required. The other fields are optional.

REMEMBER

6. **Fill out more information where appropriate and based on the needs of your organization.**

7. **Click the Save & Close button.**

   The account is saved. The New Account form closes, and you're taken back to the view of accounts.

Connecting with contacts

Dynamics 365 for Sales is jam-packed with useful features to connect with your contacts. Besides adding posts, notes, and activities, you can take many other actions directly from the View window (a list of contacts that can be filtered).

To view contacts in Dynamics 365 for Sales, follow these steps:

1. **Click the down arrow to the right of the module name you're in (such as Sales, Service, or Marketing) to display the Tile Selector drop-down menu. (Refer to Figure 6-2 for which arrow to click.)**

   A pull-down menu appears. (Refer to Figure 6-4.)

2. **Click the Sales tile.**

3. **Under the Customer column heading, click Accounts to go to your list of accounts.**

   A view of your accounts displays.

   The view you see depends on the last time you were in the View Accounts window. (The view in Figure 6-8 shows My Active Contacts.)

   You can switch to another view by clicking the down arrow to the right of the view name.

   You can filter the view by clicking the Filter icon (which resembles a funnel) to the far right of the column headings.

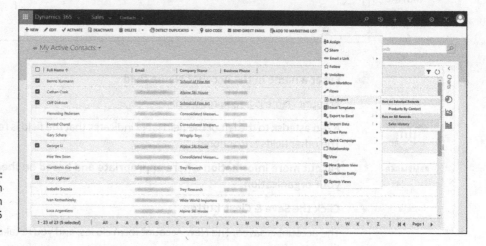

FIGURE 6-8:
Working with Contacts view in Dynamics 365 for Sales.

TIP

On the command bar, the last button to the far right is the Ellipse button — three periods (. . .) — and when you click it, a pull-down menu appears, displaying more commands that will take actions related to the contacts in your view of contacts. (Again, see Figure 6-8.) Using this pull-down menu, you can run reports, export data to Excel, and set up quick campaigns, among other tasks.

On the command bar — the white bar underneath the black navigation bar — you can find several command buttons, including the ones described in this list:

>> **New:** Add a new contact record.

>> **Edit:** Open the Contact form and make changes or add information to an existing contact.

>> **Deactivate:** Make a contact inactive, knowing that you can reactivate this person in the future if necessary.

>> **Delete:** Remove a contact from the system that you're sure is not needed now or in the future.

>> **Detect Duplicates:** Weed out duplicate records from your contacts. You can run a duplicate detection algorithm against all contacts in the view or only those you have selected by selecting the check box to the left of those records.

>> **Send Direct Email:** Send an email based on an email template. To save time, you can send the email to more than one contact by selecting multiple contacts or by filtering the view list to only those contacts you want to send the email to.

TIP

One of the handiest features of Dynamics 365 for Sales is the ability to select multiple contacts in the view by selecting the check box located in the first column of the view list. With multiple contacts selected, you can perform an action that will apply to all the contacts simultaneously. For example, you can send out an email based on an email template. Separate emails will be sent to all the contacts at the same time. The email template swaps in the contact's name and other pertinent information to personalize the message. You can send out these mass emails using the Send Direct Email button on the command bar, which opens the Send Direct Email window, shown in Figure 6-9.

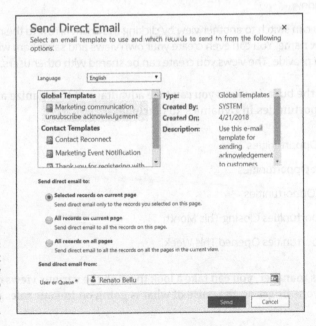

FIGURE 6-9:
The Send Direct
Email window
allows you to
send emails to
multiple contacts.

Tracking Opportunities

In Dynamics 365 for Sales, opportunities are, in a sense, the most important entity of the module. Opportunities act as your sales pipeline. If sales force automation is your goal, having the ability to track your sales pipeline in an automated fashion is paramount. One way to study your opportunities to assess the healthiness of your sales pipeline is to use the built-in views.

To view opportunities in Dynamics 365 for Sales, follow these steps:

1. **Click the down arrow to the right of the module name you're in (such as Sales, Service, or Marketing) to display the Tile Selector drop-down menu. (Refer to Figure 6-2 for which arrow to click.)**

   A pull-down menu appears. (Refer to Figure 6-4.)

2. **Click the Sales tile.**

3. **Under the Sales column heading, click Opportunities to go to your list of opportunities.**

   A view of opportunities displays.

   The view you see depends on the last time you were in the View Opportunities window.

   You can switch to another view by clicking the down arrow to the right of the view name. You can even create your own views and save them with a name you provide. The views you create can be shared with other users.

Some of the built-in views you can take advantage of to organize and analyze your sales opportunities in Dynamics 365 include:

>> All Opportunities

>> Lost Opportunities

>> My Opportunities

>> Opportunities Closing This Month

>> Opportunities Opened This Week

As a sales manager, you can take a look through the various views of opportunities to keep your finger on the pulse of what is going on in your sales pipeline.

As with leads, there's a built-in business process flow in Dynamics 365 for opportunities that can be used as is or tailored to your organization's requirements. You define stages and define the steps that are part of each stage. You can also specify the fields that are required to be filled out before the user can proceed to the next stage.

REMEMBER

An opportunity is normally assigned a contact. The contact is displayed on the Opportunity Summary form under the Opportunity Contact heading, as shown in Figure 6-10.

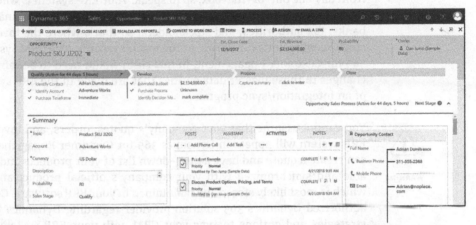

FIGURE 6-10:
Quick links for the opportunity contact in Dynamics 365 for Sales.

Quick links for contact

TIP

Generally speaking, the data that is shown in blue on the Opportunity form not only is informational but also provides a link to open another form or take action on that information. You should take advantage of these quick links to navigate the system more efficiently. For example, in the Opportunity Contact section of the Opportunity form (refer to Figure 6-10), the full name, business phone, and email are all displayed in blue, and clicking them has the following results:

>> **The name of the contact:** Displays the contact form and automatically navigates you to the associated contact (the person whose name you clicked).

>> **A phone number:** Automatically calls that phone number using Skype for Business.

>> **The email address:** Launches Outlook for Office 365 and creates a new email with the recipient already filled out with the proper email address.

Creating Quotes, Orders and Invoices

To create quotes, orders, and invoices in Dynamics 365 for Sales, your organization will most likely need to have some fairly extensive data integrations and synchronizations set up between your CRM system (Dynamics 365 for Customer Engagement) and your ERP system — which may or may not be a Dynamics 365 ERP such as Dynamics 365 for Finance and Operations (formerly Dynamics AX) or Business Central (formerly Dynamics NAV). Even if you're using Finance and Operations or Business Central, the synchronization isn't automatically there from day one out-of-the-box, so to speak. Your ERP system is where you actually control inventory, actually bill customers, and actually provide financial reports to banks, tax authorities, and stockholders, so that's where the inventory items or stock keeping units (SKUs) are as the master records. The CRM system (Dynamics 365 for Customer Engagement, in this case) would need to be refreshed with any changes to those master data entities that are made in the ERP system by means of an integration/sync program.

WARNING

You cannot assume that your company's quotes, orders, and invoices from your ERP system will appear in Dynamics 365 for Customer Engagement, or that you can create a quote and have a drop-down list of your products and services available and synchronized with your company's official product and services list, which is most likely stored and maintained in your ERP software. Confer with your authorized Dynamics 365 solution provider regarding Dynamics 365 integration strategies and options to sync your CRM with your ERP system's billing- and inventory-related master data.

If you're using Dynamics 365 for Field Service or Project Service Automation, you will have more extensive built-in integration between your quotes, orders, and invoices if you bill out of those applications directly rather than use a separate ERP system; this is because Field Service and Project Service automation are Dynamics 365 CRM-related applications (modules), which share many entities with the Sales module, including accounts and contacts.

IN THIS CHAPTER

» **Understanding customer relationship management (CRM) terminology**

» **Getting to know the key components of Dynamics 365 for Customer Service**

» **Working with service cases**

» **Publishing knowledge articles**

» **Viewing service queues and dashboards**

Chapter **7**

Connecting with Customers Anytime, Anywhere with Customer Service

Nowadays, customer service is more important than ever. In a service-based economy, it's not enough to simply offer lower prices and better products. Customer service is the main point of contact between your business and your customers. A customer who has a frustrating experience during a customer service call is likely to move to a competitor.

Dynamics 365 for Customer Service has a wide range of capabilities that allow your agents to assist customers efficiently, by providing information that is easily searchable, automated, integrated, and widely visible throughout your entire organization. At the heart of Dynamics 365 for Customer for Service is the case, which is sort of an incident or a support ticket. The case is assigned to customer service agents (users or teams of users) who can assign the case to other agents or route the case to work queues. Learning how to search for, add, annotate, and relate other information to cases is essential to working with Dynamics 365 for Customer Service.

REMEMBER

You see the case, which is a built-in (out of the box) entity, through a customizable form — in other words, a window or screen layout. Cases can be tailored to fit the exact needs of your organization, and you can configure multiple types of cases for different types of customer service issues that track different pieces of information. Talk to your system administrator for more information on modifying case forms.

WARNING

Dynamics 365 is a highly customizable application. If you're already using Dynamics 365 for Customer Service at your organization, the screens you see may look different from the screen shots in this book — they're out-of-the-box screens as found in the trial version of the software.

Knowing Your Way Around Dynamics 365 for Customer Service

Dynamics 365 for Customer Service is designed along the lines of the Customer Service module of a traditional CRM system, with most of the typical components one would expect, but with some additional unique capabilities. Understanding the key components of Dynamics 365 for Customer Service — Microsoft refers to such components as *entities*, by the way — is essential to becoming adept with the software.

These are the key components (entities) of Dynamics 365 for Customer Service:

>> **Users:** People in your organization

>> **Accounts:** Your customers

>> **Contacts:** People who work for your customer

>> **Cases:** Customer incidents or issues to resolve

>> **Activities:** Things to do to get the case resolved, such as Phone calls, emails, and appointments related to the case

>> **Posts and notes:** Comments and attachments on the case

>> **Tasks:** A type of activity that requires action and completion

>> **Queues:** Lists of activities and cases used to manage the workload among users and teams of users

>> **Views:** Lists of accounts, contacts, cases, or other things that can be sorted, filtered, and adjusted to show useful columns of information and then saved as personal views, similar to an ad hoc query

Some of the relationships between these key components are illustrated in Figure 7-1.

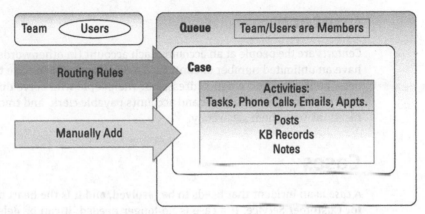

FIGURE 7-1:
Key components
(entities) of
Dynamics 365 For
Customer Service.

Users

Users are, of course, the application users. Your network administrator will have already created you as a user of the overall Microsoft network, and will then have assigned appropriate permissions for you in your organization's instance of Dynamics 365.

One key benefit of using Dynamics 365 is that it's tightly integrated with other Microsoft applications, especially Microsoft Active Directory (the network) and Microsoft Outlook (the email). For example, Dynamics 365 recognizes your Windows Active Directory (AD) network login and Outlook email account. Because of that, your system administrator doesn't have to set up a separate user ID for you in Dynamics 365, and you won't need a separate password.

Users can become members of teams and members of queues. Teams and queues are important for sharing workload. For example, if you go on vacation, because your work has been assigned to a team rather than to just you, your team members will handle the work while you're away. Likewise, if you're overloaded with work, other members of the work queue can pick up the slack. Having teams and queues in place means you can avoid having to reassign all your work to someone else before you go away. The same benefit occurs if somebody quits or retires from your company — team members and queue members are already assigned to the work.

Accounts

Accounts are your customers. The same account record is shared among all the CRM-related capabilities of Dynamics 365: Sales, Service, Marketing, Field Service, Project Service, and Resource Scheduling.

Contacts

Contacts are the people at an account. Each account (in other words, customer) can have an unlimited number of contacts. In this way, you can have the phone numbers, addresses, and email addresses of the people who serve different roles for your customer, such as buyer and accounts payable clerk, and track your communications with them separately.

Cases

A *case* is an incident that needs to be resolved, and it is the heart of Dynamics 365 for Customer Service. If a case is no longer needed, it can be deleted or canceled rather than resolved.

Each case is assigned to an owner of the case. The case is owned by a user or a team of users. The owner of the case has the primary responsibility to resolve the case.

A case can be added to a queue. Users or teams of users who are members of the queue will see the case appear in their queues and then have the responsibility to work the case.

A case can be routed. Routing rules can be configured by your administrator that will apply *business logic* (the rules and policies your organization has established for workflow) to direct the case to the appropriate queue, depending on information that has been filled out on the case and other factors specified into the routing logic.

The following list shows some of the many ways a case can come into being. A case can be

>> **Imported from an external system** such as a warehouse management or order fulfillment system

- » **Created at the click of a button** by a user from an email (email converted to case)
- » **Generated automatically by the system** from an incoming email
- » **Created manually, while on a phone call with a customer, by a user** who is a customer service representative

Posts and notes

Posts and notes are "sticky notes" that you can attach to a case to provide or log information related to the case that you're in the course of trying to resolve. A post is more like a simple quick note, whereas a note allows you to attach documents such as PDF files to the case and to write a lengthier comment.

Activities

Activities include phone calls, tasks, emails, appointments, approvals, and booking alerts. Phone calls that you have made or received related to the case can be logged against the case. Doing so provides an audit trail of the communication that has occurred in your attempt to resolve the case.

Emails and appointments are tightly integrated into your Outlook email. For example, you can create a quick email within Dynamics 365 for Customer Service and click the Send button from within Dynamics 365 without having to toggle out to Outlook. Your email will be associated and visible on the case, without your having to download or copy the email and then upload and attach it as a note in your case. In other words, when you set up emails and appointments on the case, they get incorporated into Outlook automatically.

Tasks

A *task* is one of several types of activities that you perform in the course of resolving a case; it has a due date and a priority. In this sense, a task can act as a *tickler* file — a to-do list, in other words. You can even create a task to take some action in the future on behalf of a customer to help resolve a case.

Because a task can be assigned a different owner than the owner of the case, you can assign a task to another user or team of users. In this way, a task acts as a sort of mini-case within the case. You can convert a task to a case, at the click of a button, if it turns out that the task becomes more complicated than you originally had envisioned. In a similar vein, tasks can be converted to sales opportunities (part of Dynamics 365 Sales).

When you finish the task, you mark it as Complete. You cannot resolve the case until all open tasks are marked as either Complete or Canceled. Deleting a task requires several steps, because the software is designed to maintain an audit trail of activities surrounding the case. So, in that sense, it's better to cancel a task and keep a record of it than to delete it entirely. However, sometimes you may add a task by mistake and need to get rid of it.

To delete a task, follow these steps:

1. **Open the activity window by clicking the rightward-pointing arrow — referred to as a *pop-out* button — in the far-right corner of the activity listed on the Activities tab, normally found in the center of the Case window. (See Figure 7-2.)**

Pop-out button

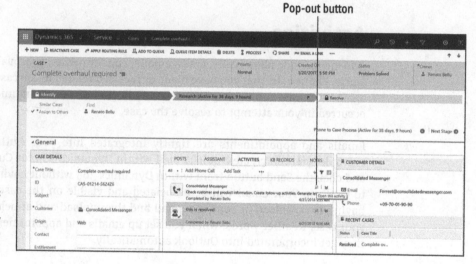

FIGURE 7-2:
How to open the activity window using the pop-out button.

2. **Click the Close Task button.**

   The Close Task window appears.

3. **Change the state from Completed to Canceled.**

4. **Click the Close button.**

   The Delete button now appears on the command bar.

5. **Click the Delete buttons.**

   The Confirm Deletion window appears.

6. **Click the window's Delete button.**

   The task is deleted from the system.

Queues

The purpose of a queue is to organize your work in a centralized manner. A queue provides a command center of pending activities and open cases. When tasks are assigned, prioritized, routed, redirected, and sorted, customers can be serviced efficiently, as their cases are resolved by a team of customer service agents working collaboratively with other members of your organization. Queues provide maximum visibility into what needs to get done — and who is responsible for getting it done.

Queues contain cases or activities in a communal fashion. If you're a member of a queue, you can see all items in the Queue list. A case is either routed automatically or added manually to a queue. Later, the case or activity is taken out of the queue (accepted, in other words) by a user who assumes responsibility for working it. As a user, you can choose the case or activity in a self-service fashion, or, alternatively, a user who has manager permissions (in other words, a customer service manager) may divvy up the workload among users and teams of users by directly assigning items or routing items using routing rules.

TIP

Using a shared Office 365 Outlook mailbox will make the queue even more communal, increase visibility, and enhance collaboration. The customer can email the shared mailbox associated with the queue, and then all those emails will be visible to users who are members of the queue. Talk to your administrator about configuring CRM queues to work with an Office 365 shared mailbox.

Views

A *view* is a list of items that can be filtered and sorted so that you can find them quickly. You can also add columns to views so that the list of items shows more fields, giving you more columns to sort and filter on and more information at your fingertips.

After you have filtered the view and included all the columns you want, you can save that configuration (called a *view definition*) as a personal view by giving it a name. Doing so saves you from having to set up all that filtering and choosing the column layout each time. In addition, Dynamics 365 for Customer Service comes with dozens of built-in (system) views, such as My Active Cases and Cases Opened in the Last 7 Days. All these system views have a descriptive name that makes it easy to understand what you're looking at. You can see the views in the View list.

To create a personal view of cases based on an existing view, follow these steps:

1. **Click the down arrow immediately to the right of the View name.**

A pull-down menu of views, which starts with System Views, appears; is followed by My Views (personal views); and, lastly, has a few command buttons at the end.

2. Click the Create Personal View button at the bottom of the pull-down menu.

Doing so launches the Advanced Find window. (Note that the Advanced Find window has a Save As button.)

The Look For field is already defaulted to Cases, so you won't need to change that.

3. Click the downward-pointing arrow to open the drop-down list to the right of Used Saved View.

4. Select the name of the view to base your personal view on.

The query and criteria used to retrieve the cases are populated automatically. You won't need to change that unless you want to tweak it by adding, deleting, or modifying criteria.

5. Click the Edit Columns button.

The Edit Columns window appears.

6. Select a column by clicking in the Column Heading area.

A green border appears around the column to indicate that the column is selected.

7. In the Common Tasks controls located to the right of the column headings, click the left or right arrow to move the column to the left or right.

You can add columns, remove columns, or change the properties of columns using the appropriate button in the Common Tasks controls.

8. After you have the column layout set up the way you like it, simply click OK in the Edit Columns window.

The Edit Columns window closes, taking you back to the Advanced Find window.

9. Click the Save As Button.

The Save as New View window appears.

10. Give your personal view a name by entering a name in the Name field.

The name field is required. (Note the red asterisk.)

Optionally, you may enter a description of the personal view.

11. Click Save.

Your personal view appears in the View list, under the My Views heading, which is bolded. Personal views are shown lower in the list, after the System views.

TIP

Dynamics 365 for Customer Service has lots of views to find all kinds of items, such as accounts (customers), contacts, activities, and, yes, the all-important cases. You can navigate to a case by finding it in a view. Because views can be filtered and sorted, it's easy to find the case you're looking for using a view. Because they're so easy to find, views themselves can be used as a sort of queue. In other words, you can monitor a view, in the same way you can monitor a queue.

Working with Cases

Each case has its own, unique case number. A saved set of filters that you apply to filter a Queue list is called a *view*. The drop-down list of all your saved views is called the *View list*. The particular cases that appear in the Queue list are determined by the filtering applied by the view you have selected.

The case should also have Customer, Status, Create Date, Priority, and Owner fields. A list of cases is called a *Queue list*. You can search, sort, and filter on all these fields, and many more, in the Queue list. The Queue list is where you can see a list of cases, and you can even create your own, personal views that are filtered exactly the way you want them.

Finding a case

To navigate to a queue of cases, follow these steps:

1. **On the navigation bar (the black band at the top of the screen), click the down arrow to the right of Dynamics 365 to switch to another app.**

   A pull-down menu of apps appears.

2. **Select Customer Service from the list of apps.**

3. **Click the down arrow to the right of Service to navigate to the Service tab.**

   Another pull-down menu appears, with the Service tab already selected.

4. **Click on Cases, found under the Service heading, to navigate to the System Views of cases.**

You can change your default view by clicking the Pin icon to the left of the View name in the View list.

TIP

You can sort by any column in the Queue list by simply clicking the column heading, add filters to one or more columns by clicking the Filter icon located on the far right end of the column heading, or jump to any letter in the alphabet by clicking that letter at the bottom of the list.

To find a particular case and open the case form, follow these steps:

1. **If you know the case number, enter the case number into the Search Box, which is to the far right, above the column headings.**

2. **Click the Search icon (magnifying glass), or press the Enter key to start the search.**

The name of the view switches to Search Results, and you can see your case in the list of search results, or Queue list.

TIP

You don't need to enter the entire case number, because the search finds all cases that begin with the characters you entered in the search box. You can use the asterisk character (*) before and/or after your search term as a wildcard to increase your matching results.

If you don't know the case number, search by another field or combination of fields, such as the customer and the status. For example, if you're looking for an active case for a customer called Humungous Insurance Company, follow these steps:

1. **Select the view called All Cases to ensure that all cases are in the queue before you start filtering that queue.**

Optionally, you can select any view that you know includes the case you're looking for, such as My Active Cases.

2. **Click the Filter icon on the far right end of the column headings.**

A small down arrow appears to the right of all the column headings.

REMEMBER

Generally speaking, Dynamics 365 conforms to standard Microsoft Office icons, so the Filter icon, which looks like a funnel, is the same Filter icon you may be familiar with from Microsoft Excel.

3. **Click the down arrow to the right of the Customer Column heading.**

A pull-down menu appears, offering various methods to filter that column.

4. **Select Custom Filter.**

The Custom Filters window appears, as shown in Figure 7-3.

5. **Select Contains from the first Select Operator drop-down menu.**

6. **In the text box immediately to the right of the menu, type part of the customer name, such as Insurance or Humungous, and then click OK.**

The view is automatically filtered to show only cases where the customer name contains the text you entered.

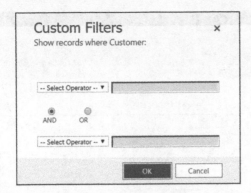

FIGURE 7-3:
The Custom
Filters dialog box.

7. **Click the down arrow to the right of the Status column heading.**

   A pull-down menu appears, offering various methods to filter that column, including check boxes for Active, Resolved, and Canceled cases.

8. **Check the Active check box and then click OK.**

   The already filtered view is further filtered to limit the list to only active cases.

TIP

You can clear all column filters with one click by simply clicking the Filter icon to the far right of the column headings. The Filter icon, which is white when the filters are on, toggles to black when the filters are off. If you turn off the filters, the filters are cleared and the filter criteria you just added is lost.

REMEMBER

You can always create a personal view that filters the list any way you want.

Toward the bottom of the View list is a feature named Save Filters as New View, whereby you can save the criteria you just entered into your column filters.

TIP

Adding a new case

To add a case, follow these steps:

1. **On the navigation bar, go to Service ⇨ Cases.**

2. **On the command bar, click New Case.**

   The Case Summary window appears. (See Figure 7-4.)

3. **Click the Click to Enter link to the right of Find Customer.**

   You can enter the first letter of the customer name before you click the Magnifying Glass button to speed your search.

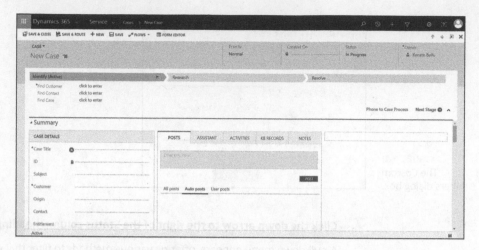

FIGURE 7-4:
The Case
Summary
window.

4. **Enter the case title, which is a description of your case.**

   The case title is a required field. You must enter a case title before you can save the case.

   The Owner field, which is also a required field, automatically defaults to the user who created the case. If you want, you can make another user the owner of the case by editing that field.

5. **Fill out any other fields appropriate for your organization.**

TIP

Notice the red asterisk to the left of the field label near all the required fields.

Which fields are required may vary depending on how your administrator has configured the case entity for your organization.

REMEMBER

When you select the customer, the customer details are filled out automatically. You can also see other recent cases for this customer, if they have any.

After you have the case set up with the minimum amount of information required, you can save the case. Three command buttons are available that can save the case:

>> **Save:** Save the case and allow you to continue editing it.

>> **Save & Close:** Save and close the case window.

>> **Save & Route:** Save and route the case using routing rules.

When you save and route the case, the Route Case window appears. You can click the Route button to automatically route the case to a user, team, or queue, based on the routing rule that has been configured for your organization by your administrator. If no routing rule has been set up, this option isn't available.

Annotating an existing case

Front and center in the case summary window, you'll find four handy ways to annotate your case:

>> **Posts:** Similar to an audit trail

>> **Activities:** Phone calls, emails, appointments, and other tasks you need to follow up on

>> **KB Records:** Knowledge Base articles

>> **Notes:** Can contain file attachments

There are two types of posts: *auto posts*, which are system generated, and *user posts*, which you need to create yourself.

To create a user post, follow these steps:

1. **In the General section of the Case Summary window, click the Posts tab.**

2. **Enter a comment in the large text box labeled Enter Post Here.**

3. **Click the Post button.**

   Your post is automatically tagged with your username and the date and time that you posted it. The post is also visible to other agents who are working the case and may also be visible on one or more dashboards. The post will become part of an audit trail of comments and actions made by agents who are working on resolving the case.

TIP

A post is a helpful way to quickly communicate a comment that you have concerning a customer's case to other workers in your organization.

REMEMBER

Cases, including user posts that convey useful information, may be made visible to many members of your organization, not just those who work in the customer service department. Posting comments as the case is routed through various departments is an effective way to share information, and thereby collaborate effectively to resolve customer incidents more quickly.

Activities are similar to posts, but they have the added benefit of allowing you to specify a due date, as well as a status, so that you can see which activities have been completed and which are still open and need to be followed up on. This list describes a few types of activities:

>> **Phone call:** Use the Add Phone Call button.

You log the phone calls that have been made to the customer, specify the direction as incoming or outgoing, and indicate whether you left a voicemail, using the Voice Mail check box.

>> **Task:** Use the Add Task button.

A task is an activity that you need to follow up on. You specify a due date and a priority. You track the status of the task and ensure that you cancel or complete it, before resolving the case.

>> **Email:** Use the More Commands button, which looks like an ellipsis — three dots, in other words.

Selecting Appointments from the More Commands drop-down list opens the New Email window. After writing your email, clicking the Send button immediately sends the email to the recipients you specified. Because of tight integration with Microsoft Outlook, the email automatically appears in your Outlook Sent folder.

>> **Appointment:** Again, use the More Commands button,

Selecting Appointments from the More Commands drop-down list opens the New Appointment window. After you fill out the required information, clicking the Save & Close button returns you to the Case Summary window. Appointments, like emails, are integrated with Outlook, so they appear in the Outlook calendar of the attendees.

Taking action on an existing case

You can take several actions on a case to speed it toward resolution. There are command buttons on the command bar for most actions — most notably:

>> **Resolve Case:** When you resolve a case, you're completing it or, in other words, closing it out. You need to be certain that all activities related to the case get done first.

TIP

Always ensure that there are no open activities on a case before you resolve the case; otherwise, you'll receive a warning message and you won't be able to resolve the case.

>> **Cancel Case:** When you cancel a case, you're prompted to confirm the cancellation. By default, the case status is set to Canceled. You can change the case status to Merged by clicking in the Status field and selecting Merged.

As soon as you cancel a case, the Cancel Case button on the command bar disappears and a Reactivate Case button appears instead. If it's needed, you can reactivate the case and then cancel or resolve it later.

>> **Add to Queue:** When you add a case to a queue, you're establishing in which queue the case will appear. You can assign the case to an individual user, to a team of users, or simply to a queue. Your organization can establish rules to ensure that each queue is monitored by one or more users. Those users are assigned as members of the queue.

>> **Assign:** When you assign a case, you are, in effect, handing the baton to the next employee or employees in your organization who will continue working the case. Doing so changes the owner of the case to the user or team to whom you assigned the case.

By clicking the three dots (the More Commands button), you can see even more actions you can take. (See Figure 7-5.)

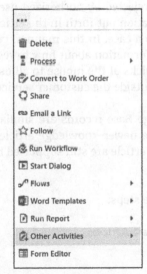

FIGURE 7-5:
The More
Commands
button
on the Case
command bar.

To see how this works in practice, check out how to resolve a case:

1. **Click the command bar's Resolve Case button.**

   This step opens the Resolve Case window.

2. **Select a resolution type from the drop-down list that appears.**

   The resolution type is required.

3. Enter a resolution description.

This free-form text field is also required.

4. Enter the billable time in minutes, if any billable time is associated with resolving the case.

Optionally, you may enter a comment in the Remarks text box.

The Total Time option is automatically filled in by the system.

5. Click the Resolve button to set the case as resolved.

Adding knowledge articles (KB records)

A *knowledge article* is a way to share information among members of your organization. This information can be used to help resolve cases.

Users can create knowledge articles and publish these to the interactive Service Hub. The articles can be approved or rejected by authorized users, as a way of verifying that you can trust the information put forth in the article. A link to the knowledge article can then be added to a case. In this manner, customer service agents begin to build up a wealth of information about how to resolve cases, and that information is available in a few clicks of the mouse to all users of the software in your organization, inside and outside the customer service department.

Knowledge Base articles and Knowledge Base records are similar to knowledge articles, but were made obsolete by the newer knowledge articles. Nonetheless, these earlier versions of the knowledge article are still supported by Microsoft for reasons of backward compatibility.

To add a knowledge article, follow these steps:

1. On the navigation bar, go to Service ⇨ Articles.

2. On the command bar, click New.

The Article Template window appears.

3. Choose an appropriate template.

For example, if your article is about how you resolved a case, select Solution to a Problem.

4. Click the window's OK button.

The New Article window appears. (See Figure 7-6.)

5. Enter a title in the Title field.

This is a required field.

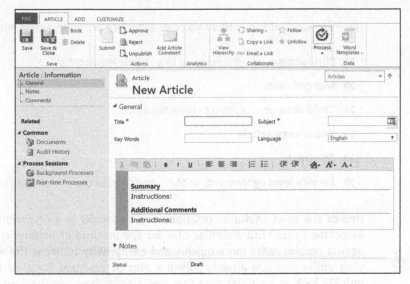

FIGURE 7-6:
The New Article window.

6. **Choose a subject from the drop-down list of subjects.**

   The subject is important because it allows users to find your article when looking for solutions related to the subject at hand.

7. **Optionally, you may enter keywords in the Keyword text box.**

   A keyword, like the subject, helps users retrieve your article during a search of the knowledge articles.

8. **Enter a problem in the Problem text box.**

   This is free-form text.

9. **Describe the solution in the Solution text box.**

   Be thorough in your description of the solution.

10. **Optionally, add a comment or attach other documents that contain pertinent information about the solution.**

11. **Click Save & Close.**

    Your knowledge article is saved, and can now be added to a case.

Relating a case to other information

Dynamics 365 for Customer Service gives you a whole host of ways to associate a case with other cases and other information. Information is power. If you have instant access to related pertinent information, you have the power to resolve the case quickly and efficiently.

Here are some of the entities you can associate or relate a case with:

» **Similar case,** which is referred to as a *case relationship*

» **Merged case**

» **Child case**, or *subcase,* a case within a case

» **Knowledge article**

» **Contract**

» *Service level agreement,* **or SLA,** used to track the time it takes to resolve a case

One of the most useful associations you can make is a *case relationship*, used to associate a case with a similar case for the purpose of helping customer service agents resolve cases more quickly and easily. Why reinvent the wheel? If one of your colleagues has already solved a similar problem for a customer, you can quickly look at a similar case that has already been resolved and then read the posts and notes and other information on that similar case to glean a solution.

To establish a case relationship, follow these steps:

1. **Click the plus sign (+) to the right of where it says Similar Cases under the Case Relationships heading. (See Figure 7-7.)**

   The Find Similar Cases window appears. (See Figure 7-8).

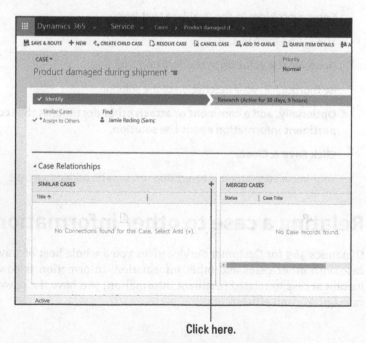

<figure>
FIGURE 7-7:
Establishing a
case relationship.

Click here.
</figure>

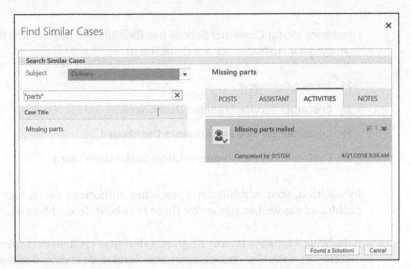

FIGURE 7-8:
The Find Similar
Cases window.

2. **Select a subject in the Subject drop-down box.**

   Cases with that subject appear in the grid under the Case Title heading, and the Search text box appears below the Subject text box.

   You can add search terms there that will search on the case title for related cases. Use the asterisk (*) as a wildcard character before and/or after the search term to increase your chances of getting a match.

3. **Click a case title that you believe to be relevant to your case.**

4. **Toggle between the Posts, Activities, and Notes tabs to the right of the window to see more information about the related case.**

   If you find a similar case that you want to relate to your case, you can add a link to the similar case on your case by following Step 5.

5. **Click the Found a Solution button to add the link.**

   The link is added to the Similar Cases grid in the Case window.

Gaining Control with Dynamics 365 for Customer Service Dashboards

The dashboard is an important part of Dynamics 365 in general, and the customer service dashboards are great examples of how dashboards can provide a bird's-eye view into the goings-on in your organization.

Dynamics 365 for Customer Service has four built-in dashboards that can help you manage your customer service department:

>> **Service Overview**

>> **Customer Service Manager Dashboard**

>> **Customer Service Performance Dashboard**

>> **Customer Service Representative Social Dashboard**

In addition, your administrator, or other authorized users, can configure more dashboards as well as customize these four built-in dashboards.

A *dashboard* consists mainly of graphs that provide a visual representation of the underlying data. For example, in the Service Overview dashboard, one graph shows Active Cases by Agent. (See Figure 7-9.)

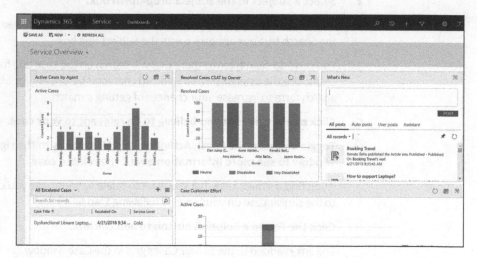

FIGURE 7-9: Service Overview dashboard.

You can always see the data that is behind the graph by clicking the View Records button, located between the Refresh button (the Circular Arrow icon) and the Enlarge the Chart button (the arrow icon pointing toward the upper right corner). Doing so opens another window where you can see the view that is the basis of the data in the graph.

TECHNICAL STUFF

You can create a custom personal dashboard completely from scratch in Dynamics 365. You need to choose a layout and then add charts, lists, web resources, or iFrames. Be sure to select the Enable for Mobile check box on the Dashboard Properties form to view your dashboard on your smartphone or another mobile device.

Chapter **8**

Profiting from Project Service Automation

Dynamics 365 offers several options for accounting for *project-based* operations — operations that are primarily focused on people delivering services rather than wholesale or retail distribution of hard goods. Two of these options are modules of Dynamics 365 for Customer Engagement (formerly called Microsoft CRM Online):

» Dynamics 365 for Project Service Automation

» Dynamics 365 for Field Service

Dynamics 365 for Project Service Automation is the main topic of this chapter. This module, sometimes referred to simply as Project Service, was developed in-house by Microsoft to address the high demand for professional services automation (PSA) software in the United States (which is largely a service-based economy) as well as in other regions of the globe where start-ups focused on delivering services are starting to outpace manufacturing ventures.

If your projects are more like service calls — quick projects performed by technicians in the field, usually within one day — then most likely a more appropriate choice for your organization is the Dynamics 365 for Field Service module (formerly called FieldOne, an application that was acquired by Microsoft in 2015 and is now fully incorporated within today's Dynamics 365 Customer Engagement cloud offering). The Dynamics 365 for Field Service module is the main topic of Chapter 10.

Project functionality also exists in both Dynamics 365 ERP applications: Business Central (formerly Dynamics NAV) and Finance and Operations (formerly Dynamics AX). Most organizations that are running Dynamics 365 choose either Business Central (geared toward smaller companies) or Finance and Operations (geared toward larger enterprises). Few organizations run both Dynamics 365 ERP offerings at the same time. Some may opt to run an ERP application that isn't even part of Dynamics 365 for their project software needs. The choice of project software in Dynamics 365 usually comes down to a choice between the two aforementioned CRM modules (Project Service and Field Service) and the project management module of either Business Central or Finance and Operations.

REMEMBER

The decision whether to use Business Central or Finance and Operations is usually based on the overall size and complexity of an organization rather than on just the project accounting requirements.

Though both Dynamics 365 ERP offerings provide some level of project functionality, neither Dynamics AX nor Dynamics NAV was especially known for its project accounting prowess. AX and NAV were known more for manufacturing and supply chain, not for professional services automation; in other words, these ERP packages had more robust features for moving inventory around than for tracking the billable time of consultants assigned to projects. In fact, over the years Microsoft has touted Dynamics SL (formerly Solomon) as its premier project-based ERP solution; however, SL was not ported to the cloud, so it isn't available in Dynamics 365; also, it's more of a job costing system than a professional services automation application. Dynamics GP (formerly Great Plains) also has a widely used project accounting module, but several add-on products for projects are favored over the core GP project accounting module. The module, though powerful, isn't so highly regarded due to the complexity of configuring it as well as the difficulty of writing reports for it. As with Dynamics SL, Dynamics GP isn't part of Dynamics 365, so neither SL or GP is an option in the cloud.

Disregarding any third-party add-on software, your choices for project software in Dynamics 365 come down to these four:

>> **Customer Engagement (CRM) – Project Service Automation module:** This module is geared toward professional consultants charging fees for billable consulting hours performed for client work.

» **Customer Engagement (CRM) – Field Service module:** This module is geared toward technicians performing service calls to maintain and repair equipment in the field. It includes robust features for resource dispatch, assignment, and scheduling.

» **Finance and Operations (AX ERP) – Project Management and Accounting module:** This module's feature set includes project phases, utilization analysis, project budgeting and forecasting, project costing and invoicing with fixed-price or time-and-material project types. This module can handle the more complicated project accounting requirements of larger enterprise organizations.

» **Dynamics 365 Business Central (NAV ERP) – Project Management module:** This module's feature set includes resources, jobs, estimates, and timesheets as well as other capabilities found in a typical job costing application.

TIP

A careful and thorough software selection engagement should be conducted in which the project accounting and project tracking requirements of your organization are matched against the features available in the four Dynamics 365 project modules. Third-party add-on software that enhances, extends, or replaces the native project modules of Dynamics 365 should also be considered, as well as industry-specific applications created by independent software vendors (ISVs). Confer with your authorized Dynamics 365 solution provider before implementing project software within Dynamics 365.

Categorizing Project Software

Project software comes in a few basic types, which are referred to using common terminology. When selecting project software to fit your organization's needs, you must understand the differences between these few basic types and know which term is used for each one so that you know which category to focus on when making a software-selection short list of possible solutions. The three basic types are PSA, job costing, and field services. (See Figure 8-1.) Also keep in mind that many industry-specific applications focus on one particular type of business, such as architectural, legal, civil engineering, or what-have-you.

Professional services automation is commonly abbreviated as PSA, which is a fairly recent software term. In the old days, a PSA system was called a *time-and-billing system* — an accounting system used by a professional services organization such as a law firm, a management consulting firm, or a certified public accounting (CPA) firm. In fact, any organization whose revenue is generated mainly by the hourly services performed by its workers, will need some kind of PSA application or module. Because software marketing folks love to create new names for old concepts, to make them sound more sophisticated and snazzy, we now have the term *PSA*. But to be fair, time-and-billing systems have evolved as developers have added more features and functionality, so in that sense, the name change makes sense.

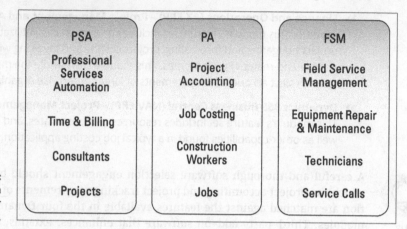

PSA	PA	FSM
Professional Services Automation	Project Accounting	Field Service Management
Time & Billing	Job Costing	Equipment Repair & Maintenance
Consultants	Construction Workers	Technicians
Projects	Jobs	Service Calls

FIGURE 8-1: Common terminology for project software.

Originally, a time-and-billing system had only two main components: timesheet capture and billing — hence the term *time-and-billing*. Now PSA systems have the capabilities to not only capture the timesheet information and bill customers for the time entered but also tackle the project management and resource scheduling requirements of even large-scale, service-oriented organizations. The Dynamics 365 for Project Service Automation module can be classified as a PSA application.

Most professional services consulting firms perform work for clients not so much on an hour-by-hour basis, but rather on a project-by-project basis; for example, a client may engage its CPA firm to conduct an annual audit. When it estimates a job and creates an engagement letter or statement of work (SOW), it tends to propose the work as a project to be performed by multiple consultants, and an overall estimate of fees is included for the consulting hours that will be incurred to accomplish the scope of work detailed in the proposal (as well as a budget for the cost) so that it can assess profitability on a project-by-project basis. Because these firms organize their efforts in a project-oriented fashion, they can be said to require project accounting software.

PSA software is geared toward professional services organizations. Typical hot button issues for these organizations are the need for user-friendly mobile timesheet capture and employee expense reporting, along with the ability to quickly and easily bill the timesheets entered by the consultants. Measuring utilization rates of consultants (how billable they are), as well as profitability on a project-by-project basis is also highly desired.

Job costing software is geared toward construction companies, which handle materials. The physical materials they use (such as building materials) may make up a large percentage of the cost of their projects. Typical hot button issues for these organizations are the integration of the project software with requisitions, purchase orders, and inventory. Because the jobs involve physical inventory, the accounting (especially the costing) tends to be more complex than for a service-only business where the only cost is for labor. Often an industry-specific add-on or separate application is the most viable solution for job costing.

Field service software is clearly in its own category, but because each service call can be considered a project, that generic project software is sometimes used to handle this requirement — hence the overlap. Field service is project accounting at its core, because you're billing for the time of a consultant (who is a technician) who provides service at an hourly or fixed-price rate, and that person tends to use some materials to get the job done. The difference is that, in field service, projects are typically completed in one or two days rather than stretched out into long, drawn-out affairs that take several months or years to complete. A key capability desired in the field service space is contract management, as in keeping track of service contracts on equipment that is dispersed in the field at customer sites. There's an emphasis on equipment, serial numbers, warranties, and returns, and on the dispatching of technicians to geographical locations to perform the repair and maintenance work.

Avoiding complicated project accounting

Project accounting can get complicated because of the various ways in which deals can be structured. Often the projects are quoted at a fixed price, revenue is recognized based on a percentage of completion of the work, and a separate billing-and-payment schedule is based on yet another set of factors. In a *fixed-price* contract, the price of the project is based on a predetermined agreed-on amount, not on how many hours it takes to complete the project. Other projects may be accounted for on a *time-and-materials* basis, which means that the client must pay for whatever hours are incurred regardless of when the project is finished; it's a sort of pay-as-you-go arrangement. The materials part of "time and materials" refers to the fact that the customer is also billed for expenses such as travel or material used in the job, such as parts (as in parts and labor). Generally speaking, clients prefer a fixed-price arrangement so that they know up front the cost of getting the work done.

REMEMBER

Though it's true that you have only two basic project types — fixed-price and time and materials — each of these two types can be accounted for using several different methods. The accounting methods address the timing of when you're allowed to recognize revenue — when you have truly earned the money, in other words — as opposed to when you have billed the customer or collected the cash.

Generally speaking, the time-and-materials method is easier to account for. When you get into fixed-price projects, the accounting can get hairy.

Fixed-price projects can be accounted for using several accounting methods, including, but not limited to, these:

» **Completed contract:** You recognize all the revenue when the entire project is complete. Sadly, this simple and straightforward method isn't the method most companies use, because they don't want to wait several months or years to record revenue on their financial statements while waiting for long-term projects to be completed. If business is steady, then theoretically it shouldn't matter, because each month a number of projects will be completed, so some revenue will be recognized; if it's just a rolling amount, it should make no material difference. In actual practice, however, it rarely works out that way, and most auditors will insist that if the projects are fixed-price and are completed over a course of several accounting reporting periods, then the completed contract method will not be accurate, and you will have to calculate the revenue recognition amount rather than simply recognize the entire price of the project.

» **Percentage of completion:** You recognize revenue every month based on how much of the project is complete. On a project priced at $100,000, for example, if the work is deemed to be 40 percent complete in the first month, you would recognize $40,000 that month. How you deem the project to be a certain percentage complete can vary. One method is to look at your budgeted costs and then see how much cost you have incurred; for example, if that same $100,000 project were going to cost you $70,000 to complete, it would earn you a gross profit of $30,000; if you incurred $35,000 in cost in the first month, then you would be 50 percent complete, and therefore recognize half the $100,000 ($50,000). Keep in mind that the cost amount you have budgeted might not be all that accurate, so this is a guessing game as far as how complete the project truly is. Exceeding the budget is a common occurrence. Another method is to base the calculation of completeness on the percentage of consulting hours incurred, regardless of cost. Yet another is to look at certain milestones to see where you are; for example, if the roof is on the building, the project must be 60 percent complete.

There are many other subtle nuances to the various contract arrangements for consulting projects, and many generally accepted accounting principles (GAAP rules) that apply to these various arrangements. Revenue recognition is a complicated calculation that considers various factors and spits out an amount to record as earned revenue for management reporting and tax filing purposes. Many organizations require project accounting software to perform these complex revenue-recognition calculations, and to map the amounts to the appropriate general ledger accounts for posting to the ledger. The number of general ledger accounts you need in order to track all this stuff — and how they clear out and offset one another — can get overwhelming.

A further complication of revenue recognition is that it's generally separate from billing-and-payment arrangements, and therefore separate from when the cash is collected from the client. You can have a billing arrangement for the client to pay you, which isn't at all connected to how you recognize revenue. Most people think that the money is earned when the customer pays up, but that is *cash basis* accounting, which is rarely used. Others believe that revenue is earned when the customer is billed and an accounts receivable is established. This is indeed a revenue recognition method (called the *when billed* method), but it's seldom used for project accounting. More often, the billing-and-payment arrangement doesn't fall in lock step with the revenue recognition accounting, so you have to track the differences in work-in-process or work-in-progress (WIP) accounts and several other general ledger accounts. Then you can keep track of the differences between what is billed and what is earned. (Project accounting isn't for the faint of heart.)

Fortunately, Dynamics 365 for Finance and Operations (AX) has the robust accounting features to handle very complex project accounting rules. If your organization has complex accounting requirements related to accounting for projects, then Finance and Operations should be considered as the most likely Dynamics 365 solution for projects.

Rules of thumb for selecting project software in Dynamics 365

You don't have to follow any hard-and-fast rules for selecting project software in Dynamics 365, and, as noted at the beginning of this chapter, you should confer with your authorized Dynamics 365 solution provider in evaluating project software. That being said, here are some general guidelines:

>> **Finance and Operations (AX) Project Management and Accounting:** This module gives you the benefit of being directly within the ERP application along with the General Ledger module; therefore, no interface development is required in order to post the transactions to the ledger. AX also has the more robust features for handling complex accounting requirements as well as other requirements of large enterprise global operations.

>> **Business Central (NAV) Project Management:** NAV is generally for smaller organizations than AX, and is somewhat easier to set up, configure, and maintain. The NAV Project Management module is geared toward job costing, but can also be a PSA solution. This module, as with the AX project module, provides the benefit of being a fully integrated module of the ERP system. (It requires no custom interface.)

>> **Customer Engagement (CRM) Field Service:** You should probably not consider using this module unless your business is clearly a field service operation, where technicians in the field service equipment while out on repair-and-maintenance service calls. This module could be used for time and billing professional services consulting work, but it has so many features specifically tailored for field service that it's unlikely to be the best-of-breed choice in any case other than pure field service.

>> **Customer Engagement (CRM) Project Service Automation:** This module is part of CRM, not a module in one of the ERP offerings. Some interfaces will be required with your ERP system — but on a positive note, being part of CRM means that it's already totally tied into the common CRM entities, such as the CRM accounts, contacts, and leads, which is a huge advantage if you're using, or planning on using, CRM. This is Microsoft's newest, snazziest project accounting system, and it's geared toward professional services consulting firms. If you're running a people-centric operation, as opposed to an inventory-centric operation, where you need your employees to enter their time on projects using mobile timesheets — and where you want lots of features for collaboration, custom reporting, dashboards, and project budgeting and forecasting — this module may be your best choice.

Knowing Your Way around Dynamics 365 for Project Service Automation

Navigating in Dynamics 365 for Project Service is easy. By clicking the Project Service tile on the Tile Selector drop-down menu accessed from the main navigation bar (the black bar at the top of the web page), you can see many of the choices you have for navigating to project-related forms. To access this menu, follow these steps:

1. **Sign in to Dynamics 365 for Customer Engagement.**

   Doing so takes you to the home screen.

   Normally, the home screen is a dashboard.

2. **Click the down arrow to the right of the module name you're in (such as Sales, Service, Marketing, or Project Service) to display the Tile Selector drop-down menu.**

   See Figure 8-2 for which down arrow to click.

   A pull-down menu appears.

3. **Click the Project Service tile.**

The menu headings and menu item selections change to reflect those items most closely related to the Project Service module. (Again, see Figure 8-2.)

Click the down arrow.
This pull-down Tile Selector menu displays.

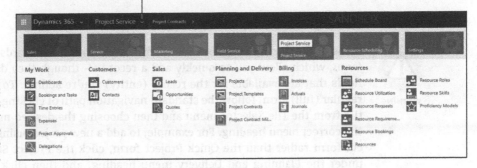

FIGURE 8-2:
The Dynamics 365 Tile Selector menu, with the Project Service tile selected.

Another handy way of navigating is to click the New button — the one with the plus sign (+) on the black navigation bar, found at the top of the screen. When adding new records in the Dynamics 365 for Project Service Automation module, you can find many of the master records that you need to add to the system on the New Activities and Records pull-down menu. (See Figure 8-3.)

Click the plus sign (+) to pull down the New Activities and Records menu.

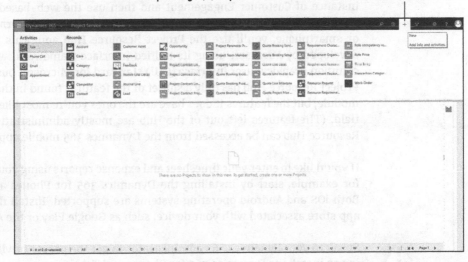

FIGURE 8-3:
Click the New button / plus sign (+) to access the New Activities and Records menu.

From the New Activities and Records pull-down menu, you can add a number of project service automation master records, including these:

>> Projects

>> Project contract-line details

>> Project contract-line milestones

>> Time entry

WARNING

Some of the forms that open from the New Activities and Records menu are *quick forms*, which allow you to quickly add a record — though they don't contain all fields that are available for the record (entity) you're adding. To navigate to the regular (full) form, follow the standard navigation path of clicking the appropriate tile from the Tile Selector menu and then choosing the desired menu item under the correct menu heading. For example, to add a new project using the New Project form rather than the Quick Project form, click the Project Service tile, look under the Planning and Delivery menu heading, and then click Projects. From there, click the New Project button.

Connecting remotely with the Project Service Hub

A great benefit of using Dynamics 365 for Project Service is that it's available anywhere and on any device. On the desktop, you sign in to your organization's instance of Customer Engagement and then use the web-based Project Service module. But if you're out of the office and connected to the Internet using a tablet or smartphone, you'll use the Project Resource Hub app. This mobile app was developed by Microsoft using its unified interface framework, which is the new common graphical user interface (GUI) standard for Microsoft business apps. The Project Resource Hub has only a subset of the features found in the Project Service module, but the features it does have are the ones you're most likely to need in the field. (The features left out of the Hub are mostly administrative.) The Project Resource Hub can be accessed from the Dynamics 365 mobile app.

If you'd like to enter your timesheet and expense reports using your mobile device, for example, start by installing the Dynamics 365 for Phones and Tablets app. Both iOS and Android operating systems are supported. Install the app from the app store associated with your device, such as Google Play or the Apple App Store.

WARNING

Speak to your Dynamics 365 administrator to get the proper privileges *before* trying to install the Dynamics 365 for Phones and Tablets app.

Getting familiar with the components of Project Service Automation

The main components of Dynamics 365 for Project Service are organized into the following menu headings:

- **My Work:** Fill out your timesheet and other project-related expenses, approve projects, and delegate others to fill out your timesheet on your behalf.

- **Planning and Delivery:** Set up projects and contracts.

- **Billing:** Bill your clients.

- **Resources:** Manage the people who do the work on your projects.

Grouped under these menu headings you'll find the following main components of Dynamics 365 for Project Service:

- **Projects:** Create a new project here, and enter the header level information about that project. Creating projects is normally done by a project manager or, sometimes, an administrative person. The consultants or other workers don't typically create their own projects. To record time and expenses, the project needs to be created and set up properly beforehand, including setting up a *breakdown structure,* which specifies the tasks, timing, and roles that will be used for the project. In other words, the breakdown structure is a sort of to-do list or project plan for the project.

- **Project Templates:** Using project templates is advisable because the template provides default values and helps you to adhere to your organization's standards when setting up each new project.

- **Time Entries:** Enter your timesheet information here. Microsoft doesn't use the term *timesheet,* but rather calls them *time entries;* however, *timesheet* is a common and well understood term. Its user interface is based on a calendar, and the time you enter here can be billed to clients.

- **Expenses:** Enter your employee expenses. The expenses you enter can be reimbursed to you. Expenses can be billable, in which case your clients are invoiced for the expenses incurred on their behalf.

- **Delegations:** You can allow somebody else to fill out your timesheet and enter your expenses on your behalf here. Often, an administrator who is in the office and responsible for ensuring that all timesheets and expenses get posted each week will be a delegate for others who are out in the field. In this way, the administrative person can assist consultants, sales reps, or others in the field in entering their timesheet and expense information into the system.

>> **Project Contracts:** A contract should be created after a customer or prospective customer has accepted a quote. You create one or more contracts for each quote that is accepted. Contracts can consist of both project-based lines and product-based lines.

>> **Resources:** A resource is usually a user of Dynamics 365 — in other words, an employee of your organization who will be entering a timesheet. However, other resource types are available to make the system flexible, including crews, equipment, contacts and accounts.

>> **Schedule Board:** The schedule board is the master control center, where you can see where everyone needs to be and when they need to be there. This schedule board is quite flexible, having the ability to instantly switch the view between hours, days, weeks, or months, or viewing a person's schedule horizontally in rows or vertically in columns. You can create a booking (schedule a resource) directly from the schedule by clicking the Book button located at the top of the schedule.

>> **Invoices:** You create invoices to bill customers for the services your organization has performed for them as well as products you have delivered. Invoices can be generated based on your invoice frequency settings.

Recognizing the importance of planning the setup of Project Service

Before you can use the Project Service Automation module, your authorized Dynamics 365 solution provider should work with you and your team to configure the module and thereby tailor it to your organization's precise requirements. Though Project Service Automation (sometimes referred to simply as Project Service) is an easy-to-use module that can be quickly configured for use without requiring custom programming, some essential setup needs to be performed up front. A thorough and careful requirements discovery should be undertaken by competent business analysts who are familiar with project accounting in general and Dynamics 365 specifically, and they should create a detailed design document that can act as a blueprint for the configuration of the module. Don't simply start filling out setup screens before having thought through the entire design of how your organization will use the module and how that module will interact with the rest of the Customer Engagement applications — as well as other Dynamics 365 components and your back-office ERP system (which may or may not be a Dynamics 365 ERP system).

Have someone in the IT department or your system administrator install the Dynamics 365 for Project Service demo data. The demo data can be loaded up in a sandbox (test) instance. You can use the demo data to run what-if scenarios. Seeing the actual screens with some data loaded into them makes it easier to visualize and discuss the various options you have for configuring the module during the design phase of your implementation.

To see the Configuration Settings menu items for Dynamics 365 for Project Service Automation, follow these steps:

1. **Sign in to Dynamics 365 for Customer Engagement.**

   Doing so takes you to the home screen.

   Normally, the home screen is a dashboard.

2. **Click the down arrow to the right of the module name you're in (such as Sales, Service, Marketing, or Project Service) to display the Tile Selector drop-down menu.**

   Refer to Figure 8-2 for which down arrow to click.

   A pull-down menu appears.

3. **Click the Project Service tile.**

   The menu headings and menu item selections change to reflect those items most closely related to the Project Service module. (Again, refer to Figure 8-2.)

   You'll find on the Settings menu many of the settings that should be configured before using the Project Service module, as shown in Figure 8-4.

FIGURE 8-4:
The Settings menu for Dynamics 365 for Project Service Automation.

To ready your Project Service module for use, your administrator or solution provider will need to define and configure some of these master data elements and settings:

» **Time units:** If you're like most organizations and you keep track of time in units of hours and days, this setup is straightforward. Other types of time units can be specified as well.

» **Currency and exchange rates:** The currency setup conforms to the International Organization for Standardization (ISO) codes. Simply choose your currency from the drop-down list. Exchange rates are needed only if you require multicurrency accounting.

» **Organizational Units:** Project Service organizational units are a way of categorizing the various types of work you perform (lines of business) or geographic areas you work in or how your teams are managed or another differentiator that you need to keep track of to provide meaningful reporting on your Project Service transactions. These organizational units don't need to mirror your Dynamics 365 business units. In Dynamics 365, business units are related to application security and financial reporting, and can be structured in a different manner than Project Service organizational units.

» **Invoice Frequencies:** The invoice frequency is basically a billing cycle. Besides monthly, weekly, and biweekly, you can specify a certain day of the week or a certain number of times per month to run the billing.

» **Transaction Categories:** These are the things your workers do for your customers against which their timesheets are recorded. There are no hard-and-fast rules about what these categories should be. A general rule of thumb is that you should have more than one category, maybe a dozen or so, but not hundreds of them. Don't get too granular in your categorization and analysis, because your setup will become cumbersome to maintain and administer, and just confuse everyone anyway. These categories help you distinguish on reports and dashboards what kinds of work you're doing and how profitable each type is.

» **Expense Categories:** The expense categories are similar to the transaction categories except that they relate only to employee expenses incurred for the business. Typical expense categories are items like airfare, parking, hotel, and business meals. As with transaction categories, you can define these to suit your needs.

» **Product Catalog Items:** The Dynamics 365 for Project Service module can access the same products as the Dynamics 365 for Sales module. In other words, the products you define in the Customer Engagement application (CRM) are universal to CRM. But keep in mind that they may not be synchronized automatically with the products (inventory items) that you have in your back-office ERP system, even if your ERP is Finance and Operations (AX) or Business Central (NAV). Project Service is generally concerned with service — or billing the transaction categories, not selling goods. Nonetheless, most businesses have a mix of products and services, so it's good to know that you can tap into the products lists from the Project Service module to invoice customers for a mix of products and services.

>> **Price Lists:** You can set up price lists for your transaction categories (typically, tasks you perform) and for roles (typically, consulting roles priced on an hourly basis). For example, you can create a role called senior consultant that is priced at some currency amount per hour, and that role, regardless of which employee is being billed out to your clients, will be priced at that standard price. Of course, the price can be adjusted on an individual project or invoice basis. You can also set up price lists for products. The prices can be based on a markup or a flat price, called a currency amount. The pricing method determines how the price will be calculated.

To add a new project to Dynamics 365 for Project Service Automation, follow these steps:

1. **Click the down arrow to the right of the module name you're in (such as Sales, Service, Marketing, or Project Service) to display the Tile Selector drop-down menu.**

Refer to Figure 8-2 for which down arrow to click.

A pull down menu appears.

2. **Click the Project Service tile.**

The menu headings and menu item selections change to reflect those items most closely related to the Project Service module. (Again, refer to Figure 8-2.)

3. **Click the Project menu item.**

The Project menu item is found under the Planning and Delivery menu heading, to the right of the menu headings for My Work, Customers, and Sales.

A list of projects (in Project view) displays. The particular view you see depends on the last view you navigated to when you were last using that window.

4. **Click the New Project button.**

The New Project button is located to the far left of the screen, just under the Dynamics 365 navigation bar.

The New Project form displays, as shown in Figure 8-5.

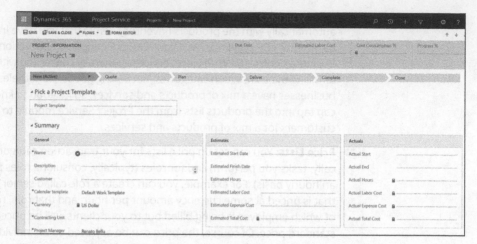

FIGURE 8-5:
The New Project
form in Dynamics
365 for Project
Service
Automation.

5. **Enter a name for your project in the Name field.**

The Name field is required.

Contracting Unit and Project Manager are also required fields. Exactly which fields are required will depend on how your instance has been configured by your Dynamics 365 administrator.

TIP

To help you identify required fields, a red asterisk to the left of the field label indicates that the field must be entered before you can save the record.

6. **Fill out other pertinent information for this project.**

The fields you need to fill out are based on how the Project Service module has been configured for your organization.

There's a built-in business process flow to help control, standardize, and speed up the data entry for the project. This business process flow is visible at the top of the form; look at the green labels that look like arrows pointed to the right. The steps of the business process flow are Quote, Plan, Deliver, Complete, and Close.

7. **Click the Save button.**

The project is saved. Alternatively, you can click Save & Close, which saves the project and takes you back to the Project View window.

TIP

To get the most out of your Dynamics 365 for Project Service Automation module, it's essential to configure your instance of the software to match the unique requirements of your organization. Modifying the built-in business process flow steps to more closely follow your actual business process is just one of many ways to tailor the software to your needs. The more you take the time to fully understand and carefully describe your unique requirements, and seek the advice of experts to carefully analyze, design, and plan your Project Service configuration, the more you can benefit from this feature-rich, flexible, and powerful module.

IN THIS CHAPTER

» Bridging the gap between your marketing department and your sales force

» Understanding the new capabilities recently added to Dynamics 365 for Marketing

» Navigating within Dynamics 365 for Marketing, including advanced settings

» Exploring lead scoring models, customer journeys, and marketing segments

» Creating better emails using email templates

Chapter 9
Creating and Nurturing Leads with Marketing

In the spring of 2018, Microsoft added a whole slew of exciting new capabilities to Dynamics 365 for Marketing. A new marketing menu called a site map (See Figure 9-1) lets you navigate to previous features such as Accounts, Contacts, Leads, and Opportunities but also gives you access to lots of new selections, including:

- **Lead Scoring Models**
- **Customer Journeys**
- **Marketing Emails**
- **Marketing Pages, Forms, and Websites**
- **Segments**

Dynamics 365 for Customer Engagement (formerly known as Microsoft CRM Online) has always had accounts, contacts, marketing lists, opportunities, and campaigns as the core entities of the marketing module. These core entities still exist in the newer releases of the marketing module, and they're fully compatible with the newer features; nothing important was taken away, though a whole lot of cool stuff was added.

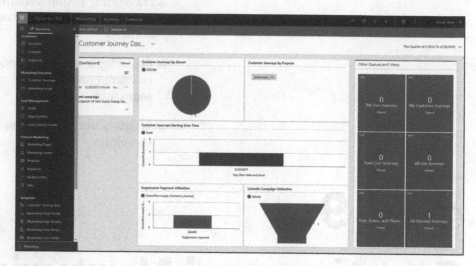

FIGURE 9-1:
Marketing Site Map menu in Dynamics 365.

Connecting Marketing to Sales

Many organizations suffer from a "disconnect" between their marketing and sales departments. How it's supposed to work is that the marketing department generates leads for the sales department to follow up on. All too often, the sales department ends up ignoring the leads they have been given by marketing, because the marketing department has no accurate way to qualify the leads. *Lead scoring* is a systematic method for qualifying leads in which numeric values are assigned to leads based on activities that the prospective customer has fulfilled, such as clicking a website link or responding to an email or filling out a survey. A lead that gets a qualifying high score is passed to the sales department. If leads are not properly qualified, the sales department may begin to feel that the leads they receive are a waste of their time, and may end up digging up their own leads, which takes time away from what they're supposed to be doing — selling. Or it may happen that the sales reps don't have enough leads to keep them busy, and nobody wants that. Sales reps want to sell, earn commissions, and contribute to the organization's success, and the only way they can do that is to have access to a consistent stream of qualified leads.

For marketing departments to properly qualify leads for the sales department, they must have a lead scoring methodology and — ideally — flexible and powerful software to help guide them through the lead scoring process, to log the scores, and to make the results visible to the sales team. Unfortunately, marketing departments all too often have neither the methodology nor the software for effective lead scoring. Microsoft has sought to address this problem by providing advanced features for lead scoring in the Dynamics 365 for Marketing module.

Marketing departments often fail to not only score leads but also, worse, to nurture leads — or, indeed, they may simply have no concept of lead nurturing whatsoever. Sadly, too many marketing departments do little more than bombard random recipients with spam emails containing a download link to a brochure thinly disguised as a white paper. These emails are promptly deleted by the annoyed victims. What a waste of everyone's time.

Lead nurturing means developing relationships by effectively communicating with prospective customers — listening to their input as well as answering questions and providing information — at every step of the buyer's journey. Rather than pester people with unwanted emails, you define a customer (or buyer) journey. The journey is a multipronged approach that consists of a variety of engaging activities, such as events, surveys, targeted and well-designed emails, or links to informative and well-crafted marketing pages on your website. The lead is then scored on how deeply they participate in the activities of the journey. In this way, potential customers are nurtured each step of the way, as they're funneled down the sales pipeline and the sales team becomes instantly aware of the most promising prospects in real-time. To help marketers nurture leads more effectively, Microsoft has added a feature called the Customer Journey to Dynamics 365 for Marketing. This feature includes a graphical drag-and-drop designer for defining the steps of the customer journey. (See Figure 9-2.)

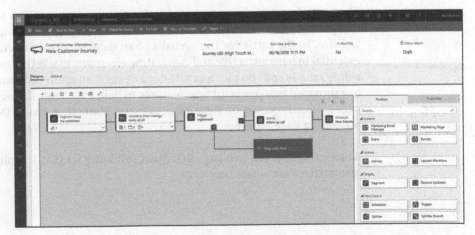

FIGURE 9-2: The Customer Journey Designer in Dynamics 365 for Marketing.

Escaping the Doldrums of Drab Emails and Boring Web Pages

In most industries — including business-to-business (B2B) sectors — much of the marketing effort involves encouraging prospects to read emails and view web pages as the initial way to find out about the products and services being promoted. The emphasis on electronic communication is partly because cold calling is becoming less and less effective, as most people nowadays let their cellphones ring through and some even turn the ringer off entirely. Many folks have a policy of never answering numbers that they don't recognize. Landline desk phones are mainly gathering dust these days, as the workforce has become more mobile, and working from home by telecommuting has become increasingly commonplace. However, because people are swamped every day by an onslaught of unsolicited and unwanted emails, typically many marketing emails are deleted by the recipient without being read. What a waste of effort and money.

The first part of the cure for this pointless and senseless spamming is for marketers to build meaningful marketing lists. Often, a good list comes from existing customers who may not be aware of the new products and services you can offer them, but because they have done business with you in the past, they may be receptive to whatever you want to present to them. Dynamics 365 for Marketing has always had a feature for working with marketing lists. There's a handy way to quickly import these lists into Dynamics 365, and lists can be built from your existing accounts already stored in Dynamics 365 for Customer Engagement. Of course, the list is just a starting point; guiding the prospective (or existing) customers through a meaningful customer journey is what will make your marketing lists bear fruit, and that's where the aforementioned Customer Journey and the Lead Scoring features come into play.

The second part of the remedy for ineffective email campaigns is to create more compelling emails as well as more persuasive web pages on your organization's website. In the battle for the eyeballs of an increasingly distracted populace, it's essential to have attractive and captivating electronic marketing materials. Boring, wordy emails with no pictures just doesn't cut it anymore. Fortunately, Microsoft has provided two powerful new features to help you create emails and marketing pages directly inside of Dynamics 365: the Marketing Email Designer and the Marketing Page Designer.

A *marketing page* is a web page that Microsoft hosts for you; it typically includes an interactive form where users can

» **Update contact information**

» **Unsubscribe or subscribe to mailing lists**

» **Register for special offers or events**

The Marketing Email Designer and the Marketing Page Designer are drag-and-drop graphical designer tools that allow you to quickly create professional emails and web pages without necessarily having to write any code. At the same time, they allow for someone with a more technical background to directly access the HTML code so that they can tailor the email or web page to your precise specifications without the limitations inherent in a drag-and-drop tool. Having the tools to create professional content within the same software used to launch campaigns, score leads, and guide the prospect through a customer journey is convenient and powerful because of the time you save by having a connected, integrated system for deploying your marketing strategy.

REMEMBER

The ease of posting your content to the web due to the tight integration between Dynamics 365 and the Microsoft Azure cloud hosting services is a key benefit. Dynamics 365 for Marketing provides you with a comprehensive end-to-end solution for deploying your marketing strategy and seamlessly connecting your sales pipeline generated by your marketing efforts to your sales force.

Using templates to get up to speed quickly

Microsoft didn't design all these snazzy new features just to see them wither on the vine. The designers of these powerful features really want to see them put to good use. To that end, they have taken the time (and invested the money) to provide templates for most of the features. The templates — professionally designed by ad agencies — provide all these benefits and more:

» **Responsive design formatting that renders a pleasing view on a variety of screen sizes, including smartphone, tablet, and desktop**

» **Color palettes that ensure a coordinated range of hues**

» **Professional designs that have been proven to get consistent results**

For example, when you create a customer journey, you can choose from a template of predefined journey types. The journey is already populated with targets, content, and actions. Likewise. the Marketing Email Designer comes with a wide choice of templates that include a column layout, a color scheme, and some sample content. There's also a blank email template, which gives you a sort of plain-vanilla starting point.

WARNING

Anytime you start with an email template in Dynamics 365 for Marketing and make your own changes to tweak the email template design to your organization's needs (such as branding the template with your logo), save the template under a new template name (any name that's different from the default name of the template or other any other default template). By giving the template a unique name, you ensure that it won't be overridden when the Dynamics 365 cloud software is periodically updated behind the scenes by Microsoft. If you don't save the template under a different name, you may lose your changes due to a system upgrade.

Segmenting your contacts for marketing and subscription lists

Microsoft has beefed up the marketing list functionality in Dynamics 365 by adding the concept of market segments. Segments are defined in Dynamics 365 for Marketing, but they go live (are published) in the Customer Insights service. Dynamics 365 for Microsoft Customer Insights is built on the Azure and Cortana intelligence service; it enables you to ingest data from any data source — including social media such as Facebook and Twitter, as well as your traditional back-office ERP system — and consolidate it all into one centralized 360-degree view of your customer and prospective customer contacts.

To help make the Customer Insights service more widely adopted and useful in a variety of settings, Microsoft, along with partners (most notably, Adobe) has created a standard data structure for the Customer Insight contact. Adobe, of course, is the creator of the PDF file format, which is a standard format for electronic documents. Having a contact layout that is compatible with Adobe and other important players such as Dun & Bradstreet is clearly beneficial. For example, Dun & Bradstreet supplies marketers with marketing lists (for a price, of course). It's great to know that the list will be formatted in a language that Dynamics 365 already understands without having to pay programmers to write custom integration programs.

These firms are among those participating in the new customer data standard:

>> **Microsoft**

>> **Adobe**

>> **Dun & Bradstreet**

>> **Zendesk** (a customer service and support-desk ticketing system)

>> **MasterCard**

>> **AppDynamics** (application performance and monitoring, now part of Cisco)

>> **Acxiom** (high-tech, savvy marketing database company)

Segments are similar to marketing lists because they are, in essence, lists of contacts that you plan to solicit with a targeted marketing campaign. However, segments are more sophisticated than plain old marketing lists because they can change in real-time to reflect changes in your contact data; they can employ complex query logic to automatically create themselves, and they can combine with other lists to create specific, surgically focused lists. When you first define a marketing segment in Dynamics 365, you save it in draft state; when you're ready to use it, you select the Go Live button on the command bar to set the segment to a live state.

In Dynamics 365 for Marketing, you can define these three basic types of marketing segments:

>> **Dynamic:** This term means "able to change as conditions change"; for example, if a contact changes her address, that may push her to a different geographically targeted segment. You can think of dynamic segments as queries that pull together a list of contacts based on criteria and conditional business logic that you define.

>> **Static:** This term means "unchanging"; nonetheless, these lists can be changed, but only manually, not automatically by the system. You can think of static segments as old-school marketing lists; you create these lists by adding contacts one by one based on factors that exist outside the system and your personal knowledge of who should be included in the segment.

>> **Compound:** Compound means "a mixture of two or more elements"; in this case, the elements can be either dynamic and/or static segments, but they must be in a live state (as opposed to a draft state) before combining them into a compound segment.

REMEMBER

Most of the features in Dynamics 365 can be accessed from the *site map*, a pull-out menu that extends from the left side of the screen. If you look at the top left corner of the screen, the Site Map button — the one with an image of a megaphone — is located directly under the Navigate to Other Applications button — the one with the three horizontal white lines. (You can see the Site Map menu itself in Figure 9-1; the button you click to open the Site Map menu is shown in Figure 9-3.)

Adding a static marketing segment.

To add a dynamic marketing segment in Dynamics 365 for Marketing, follow these steps:

1. **Click the Site Map button. (Refer to Figure 9-3.)**

   The Site Map pull-out menu appears.

Click here to open the site map.

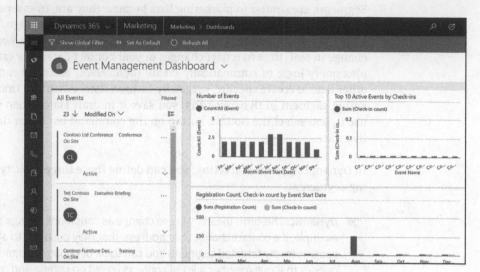

Click here to open the site map.

FIGURE 9-3:
The Site Map
button in
Dynamics 365 for
Marketing.

2. **Click Segments, found under the Customers menu heading on the site map.**

   The Active Segments view appears.

   This is a list of all segments you have created in your system that are in an active state.

3. **Click the New button.**

   A New Segment form appears. (Refer to Figure 9-4.)

   The General tab is selected by default.

   The Activation Status field defaults to Draft.

   The Owner field defaults to your username.

4. **Enter a name in the Name field.**

   The Name field is required; a red asterisk to the right of the field label indicates that you must fill out that field in order to save the record.

5. **If desired, enter a description in the Description field.**

   Adding a description is optional.

6. **Choose Static from the Segment Type drop-down menu.**

   Doing so indicates that this segment will be managed manually.

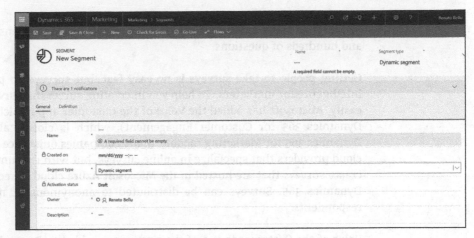

FIGURE 9-4:
The New
Segment form,
used for creating
marketing
segments in
Dynamics 365.

7. **Use the Definition tab to select contacts.**

   The Definition tab lists all contacts, with a check box next to each one. Select the check box for each contact you want to include in the static segment.

   Use the next-page control at the bottom of the page to see more contacts.

   Use the search filter at the top to the list to restrict the list of contacts in order to focus on the contacts you want to include.

8. **Click the Save & Close button to save the segment.**

   You're taken back to the Active Segments.

Listening to the Voice of the Customer

Soliciting feedback from your customers can provide valuable information that may lead you to make important changes in the products and services you offer them. Marketers want feedback in order to tailor their messages to fit the major concerns of their customers. Let's face it: The customer is king. If you don't care about what your customers think and you take them for granted, your company is likely to fail.

Unfortunately, people have been bombarded by survey requests so often that many have become averse to taking them. Just going out to buy a cheeseburger has become an opportunity for marketers to entice you to fill out their surveys. Often the marketers will bribe you to take surveys by offering a discount or a chance to win a vacation to Hawaii or some other kind of come-on. Sometimes, to be nice, you agree to take the survey, only to find out that it consists of 20 pages and hundreds of questions.

Getting people to take surveys is no easy feat, but surveys do provide valuable intelligence for marketers. To help you in creating successful surveys quickly and easily, Microsoft has added the Voice of the Customer app (which is a module of Dynamics 365 for Customer Engagement), which is closely aligned with the Dynamics 365 for Marketing module. Many companies outsource their surveys to cloud providers that specialize in online surveys, but with Dynamics 365, you can create surveys that are hosted in the Microsoft Azure cloud, directly from within Dynamics 365. Surveys can be distributed to anonymous or non-anonymous respondents.

Voice of the Customer is one of the newer apps added to Dynamics 365 for Customer Engagement that is directly related to marketing. You can see the features for surveys and collateral listed as menu choices on the Site Map menu for Voice of the Customer, as shown in Figure 9-5.

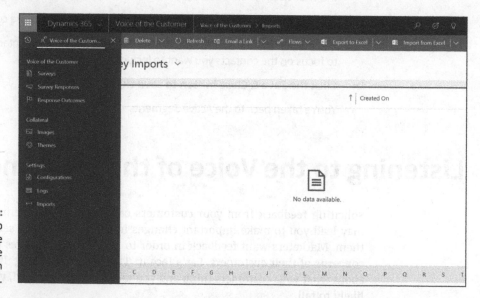

FIGURE 9-5:
The Site Map menu for the Voice of the Customer app in Dynamics 365.

REMEMBER

To display the Site Map menu for the Voice of the Customer app, you first need to make that app current (if it isn't already). To do so, click the down arrow to the right of where it says *Dynamics 365* on the navigation bar at the top left of the screen. (See Figure 9-6.)

Click the down arrow to switch to another app.

Current app name is displayed here.

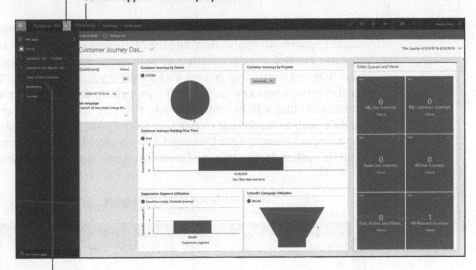

FIGURE 9-6:
Switching apps
(or modules)
from Marketing
to Voice of the
Customer.

Click the app name to switch.

When you design a survey in the Dynamics 365 for Voice of the Customer app, for each question you ask, you must decide on a question type. Voice of the Customer supports all these question types, and more:

>> **Short answer:** A 1-line answer

>> **Long answer:** Allows multiline answers

>> **Rating:** Typically, from one to five stars

>> **Single response:** Radio button controls where the respondent selects one mutually exclusive choice

>> **Multiple response:** Check box controls where the respondent makes one or more selections

>> **Date:** Calendar control

>> **Numerical:** Text box that accepts only numbers (for questions that ask the respondent how many times something has happened, for example)

>> **CSAT:** Slider control, from very dissatisfied to very satisfied

>> **Upload file:** Allows the respondent to upload a file of up to 5MB

>> **Smileys:** An emoticon, clicked by a respondent, that is a happy or sad face or something in between

Dashing Off to Marketing Dashboards

The dashboard is an important concept throughout the Dynamics 365 for Customer Engagement application, and the Marketing module is no exception. Microsoft has created a wide selection of built-in, preconfigured dashboards packed with lists and charts that convey useful information at a glance. (See Figure 9-7.) Furthermore, users can create their own private dashboards (referred to as *user dashboards*) that will be visible only to them in their work areas in a particular module such as Marketing, Service, or Sales. (Built-in dashboards are referred to as *system dashboards*.) Your Dynamics 365 system administrator can customize the built-in system dashboards, and even create new system dashboards from scratch.

Click here to see more dashboards.

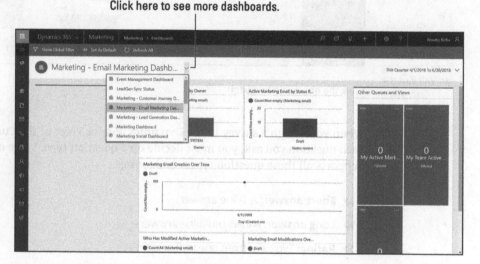

FIGURE 9-7:
Viewing Marketing dashboards in Dynamics 365.

Configuring Advanced Settings in Dynamics 365 for Marketing

Dynamics 365 for Marketing is a seriously robust marketing application, and in order to configure it to optimally, your Dynamics 365 administrator or authorized solution provider will need to adjust several Advanced settings. Even if you're not the one configuring the Advanced settings, it may be helpful to check out the Advanced Settings options. Often, someone is unsure about how flexible an application is because he's unaware of where the switches and levers that control the behavior of the software are located within the software's maze of menus. Navigating to the Advanced settings in Dynamics 365 for Marketing isn't all that intuitive for many users, but there's a handy way to get there from the Marketing Site Map menu. (Refer to Figure 9-3 to see how to display the site map.)

To navigate to the Advanced settings in Dynamics 365 for Marketing, follow these steps:

1. **Click the Site Map button. (Refer to Figure 9-3.)**

The Site Map pull-out menu appears.

2. **Click the ellipse (. . .) button — the one with three consecutive dots.**

A small pop-up menu appears immediately to the right.

3. **Choose Settings from the pop-up menu.**

A check mark appears next to the item after it has been selected.

When you click Settings, the Site Map menu to the left of the screen changes to show the Marketing Settings heading, as shown in Figure 9-8.

4. **Under the Marketing Settings heading, click Advanced Settings.**

The Advanced Settings menu page appears, as shown in Figure 9-9.

1. Click the **three dots** to display the pop-up menu.

2. Click Settings to navigate to the Advanced Settings menu.

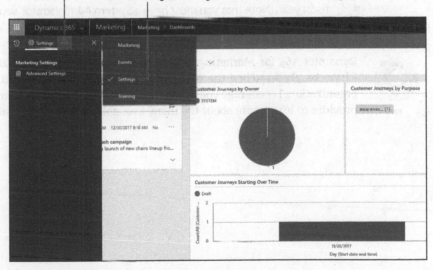

FIGURE 9-8:
Navigating to the
Advanced
Settings area In
Dynamics 365 for
Marketing.

Some of the highlights that I'd like to point out in the Advanced Settings for Marketing include the ones in this list that describe what you can do:

>> **LinkedIn Lead Gen:** Generate leads directly from LinkedIn.

>> **Import Data:** Import leads, accounts, contacts, opportunities, and more from an Excel or CSV file.

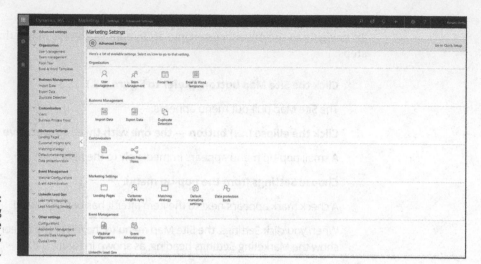

FIGURE 9-9:
Marketing
Settings available
in Dynamics 365
for Marketing.

>> **Default Marketing Settings:** Set the default contact on your marketing emails as well as the default time zone when you create a new customer journey, among other defaults.

>> **Fiscal Year:** Specify the starting and ending months of your organization's fiscal year. (Note that you must have a System Administrator security role or the equivalent in order to change the fiscal year settings.)

Dynamics 365 for Marketing is a super-robust, end-to-end marketing solution. I have barely scratched the surface in this chapter about what it can do for your organization. I encourage you to confer with your authorized Dynamics 365 solution provider to learn more about the many available options and capabilities.

TIP

Chapter **10**

Going Mobile with Field Service

ield service management (FSM) software is designed to fulfill the needs of organizations with a mobile workforce composed of technicians who provide installation, repair, and maintenance services for equipment located "in the field" at customer sites. The type of service performed isn't always equipment-related, as in fixing a broken water heater; it might be killing bugs or mowing the lawn. Here are some examples of types of businesses that have traditionally used FSM software:

» HVAC installers (*heating*, *ventilation*, and *air* conditioning)

» Janitors (housekeeping)

» Gardeners (landscaping and lawn care)

» Electricians (electrical, cabling, and networking)

» Plumbers (plumbing, sewers, water works)

» Exterminators (pest control)

The demand for FSM software is growing steadily. Service companies are no longer able to compete by relying on the old-school, paper-based system. Technicians in the field are expected to do more, and to do it right, from their vehicles or handheld devices in the field, whether it means connecting to the back-office ERP system to determine parts availability, interacting with the sales department to upsell services, or taking credit card payments and assessing the creditworthiness of customers on the fly. A vital goal of service companies is to get the job done on the first visit, because sending the technician back the next day makes the profit margin plummet. To that end, it's essential to match the skills of your technicians with the types of service that need to be performed. A good FSM application must have intelligent tools to efficiently assign work orders to technicians based on skill, geographic location, and parts availability, for example.

A tipping point has been reached where most companies in search of a new FSM system would rather pay monthly for a cloud service than purchase an on-premise software package, acquire additional hardware such as computer servers, install the software, install the database, and maintain it all themselves. Field service management has moved to the cloud, and that makes a lot of sense, especially when you consider the nature of field service requirements where mobility is king because the workers are out in the field all day long. In fact, most technicians park their vehicles at home and drive directly to customer sites in the morning. They may stop at various depot locations, but they don't necessarily visit headquarters often. Cloud services are mobile-ready by design; after all, they're built to run on the Internet, not on a server based at headquarters.

In July of 2015, Microsoft announced that it had acquired FieldOne Systems LLC, a provider of FSM software that's based in Mahwah, New Jersey. What made FieldOne especially attractive to Microsoft was that the application was developed on the Dynamics CRM Online (now called Dynamics 365 for Customer Engagement) platform; in other words, it was basically an add-on for Microsoft CRM. Because FieldOne was developed for CRM, it was already cloud based, and was built to connect to the standard CRM entities (master records) such as accounts, contacts, cases, and products. Incorporating FieldOne into the Dynamics 365 Customer Engagement suite of modules was therefore a natural fit, giving Microsoft a strong field service solution to supplement its existing CRM capabilities of sales force automation, customer service, and marketing automation.

TIP

Go to the App Store (Apple) or to Google Play (Android), depending on your mobile device's operating system, and search for *Field Service Dynamics 365* to install the Field Service mobile app from Microsoft Corporation. Your system administrator will have to provide additional instructions for the URL that needs to be specified in the Setup section of the app.

Assessing Microsoft's FSM Competitors

Microsoft has plenty of competition in the FSM arena. The sheer number and variety of cloud-based FSM developers is staggering. There's a Software as a Service (SaaS) solution for nearly every type of service business; some examples are PestRoutes for exterminators, ZenMaid for cleaning services, and Pronexis Lawn for lawn care. This market has literally hundreds of competitors, and most of them are like Microsoft Dynamics 365 for Field Service: They're generic Field Service applications, devoid of any industry-specific features. Furthermore, some on-premise solutions still have a large installed client base and haven't yet ported their applications to the cloud; many of these on-premise FSM packages have a loyal and entrenched following.

However, when compared to Microsoft Dynamics 365 for Field Service, what all these competitors lack is the comprehensiveness and depth of functionality that only Microsoft itself can offer: cloud hosting in Azure, fully integrated CRM, robust cloud ERP, and native Office 365 integration. Furthermore, most of these competitors are small companies that lack the financial wherewithal to invest in the research and development that will be needed to keep pace with Microsoft's cloud FSM capabilities — which are improving all the time, especially with regard to how these capabilities are becoming increasingly intertwined with other Microsoft services.

With Dynamics 365 for Field Service, Microsoft is poised to capture a significant chunk for the SaaS FSM software market. Because Dynamics 365 for Field Service is the only FSM SaaS solution offered directly by Microsoft, it has a unique advantage over all its competitors. Most of the competitors use or rely on Microsoft's programming languages — SQL Server database, cloud services, office automation suite (Word, Excel, Outlook, and so on) — whereas Microsoft isn't dependent on any other software developer in quite the same way. Also, Dynamics 365 for Field Service is a slick application that's hard to beat in many ways.

REMEMBER

When evaluating field service management software, you have a lot to choose from because lots of good applications are out there. Dynamics 365 for Field Service is a powerful application with tons of cool features, but it's still a generic field service offering that tries to be everything to everyone. Industry-specific offerings from competing vendors may have some important off-the-shelf capabilities that Dynamics 365 for Field Service lacks. Some may offer more advanced features such as sophisticated vehicle routing. At the other extreme, some may be cheaper, simpler, and easier to work with. Finding just the right fit all depends on matching the size, complexity, and industry specialization of the software to the size, complexity, and unique and industry-specific requirements of your organization.

Taking the Back-office ERP into Consideration

Dynamics 365 for Field Service is a part of Microsoft's CRM application; it's not part of either of Microsoft's ERP applications: Business Central (NAV) or Finance and Operations (AX). The ERP is typically referred to as the back office and the CRM as the front office. Because Dynamics 365 for Field Service isn't an ERP module, but rather a CRM module, it isn't seamlessly and fully integrated with the general ledger, accounts payables, accounts receivables, inventory control, and purchase order processing, as an ERP module would be. The parts (inventory items), warehouse locations, price lists, and other elements are typically part of the ERP system, and the ERP system is the master (the horse's mouth, so to speak) for those master data elements. What this means is that the CRM system has to keep refreshing a copy of information from the source information (maintained in the ERP by use of custom integrations, which may prove to be somewhat tricky to set up and potentially problematic to maintain). True, Microsoft is striving to make all of Dynamics 365 one big, happy and fully integrated system between front office and back office, but it isn't quite there yet. Here are some of the obstacles in its way:

» Because CRM has no general ledger, you can't produce financial statements out of a CRM system.

» You can't report to the tax authorities, banks, or stockholders using CRM reports alone.

» You can't avoid having a proper financial ledger.

The bottom line? You can't get away from having an ERP system.

You can take one of several approaches to deal with the disconnect between the front office (CRM) and back office (ERP). One approach is to duplicate many entities (master data records) in both systems, such as customers, inventory items, and work orders, but that approach calls for more integration programs. In an alternative approach, and one that involves fewer integration programs, you use the CRM system as your operational system and use the ERP as your financial ledger; in other words, you use CRM to do the work and use ERP to crunch the numbers.

The ERP can be used primarily for its three main ledgers: general (for financial statements, such as balance sheet and profit and loss statement), accounts receivable (what your customers owe you), and accounts payable (what you owe your vendors and suppliers). Some capabilities, such as the worker scheduling calendar (called the *schedule board* in Dynamics 365) obviously will exist independently in the CRM, so there's no integration issue for those bits of functionality.

Regardless of whether you will use a Dynamics 365 ERP or another ERP system, you should consider many integration interfaces between CRM and ERP, including but not limited to these:

» CRM Accounts = ERP Customers

» CRM Contacts = ERP Customer Contacts

» CRM Parts = ERP Inventory Items

» CRM Warehouses = ERP Inventory Site Locations

» CRM Transfers & Adjustments = ERP Inventory Transactions

» CRM Purchase Orders = ERP Purchase Orders

» CRM Invoices = ERP Sales Orders and Accounts Receivables

Avoiding the duplication of data is usually a good idea because, if your system is reliant on integrations and an integration program fails (yes, they do fail from time to time, for a variety of unavoidable reasons), your entire system may come to a standstill, operations may be disrupted, and customers may get angry and go to a competitor the next time they need service. That being said, the most realistic and feasible scenario still calls for some significant level of integrations; this is because the CRM system isn't really built to handle the financial general ledger mapping, posting, and audit trails of a true accounting system — the kinds of things an ERP system does so well.

REMEMBER

The Microsoft Common Data Model and Common Data Services help make the integration of CRM and ERP entities easier to accomplish and maintain. Microsoft is clearly moving in the direction of making Dynamics 365 a fully integrated system among all its many parts, at which point the distinction between CRM and ERP will become a thing of the past. Keep in mind, however, that until CRM and ERP are seamlessly connected in Dynamics 365, the integration issues need to be carefully thought out and their solutions intelligently planned in advance. There will be some design work and configuration effort and ongoing maintenance involved in hooking Dynamics 365 for Field Service into your ERP, even if you're using one of the two Dynamics 365 ERP offerings.

Getting Acquainted with the Key Components of Dynamics 365 for Field Service

The main menu items for Dynamics 365 for Field Service are shown on the Tile Selector pull-down menu when you click the Field Service tile.

To view the main Field Service–related menu items, follow these steps:

1. **On the black navigation bar at the top of the screen, click the down arrow to the right of the name of the module you're in.**

   The Tile Selector pull-down menu appears.

2. **Click the Field Service tile.**

   The Field Service tile is the blue tile to the right of the orange Marketing tile.

   The menu items and menu item headings change to reflect the choices most closely related to the Field Service module. (See Figure 10-1.)

FIGURE 10-1:
Dynamics 365
for Field Service
Tile Selector
menu items.

This list describes the key components of Dynamics 365 for Field Service:

>> **Work order:** The work order is the heart of the Field Service module. It's where you specify all the facets of a service call: where to go, what needs to be done, what parts are used, who is doing the work, and so forth.

>> **Schedule board:** The schedule board is your master control center — you can see at a glance where everyone is and where they need to go next. Color coding is used to show the status of each booking in real-time. This schedule board is flexible. You have the ability to instantly switch the view between hours, days, weeks, or months or to view a person's schedule horizontally in rows, or vertically in columns. You can assign a technician to a service call directly from the schedule. You can see the work orders on a map (like Google Maps or Bing Maps) that you can zoom in or out. The work orders appear as pushpin icons that are located on the map where the work is to be performed. Pushpins are color coded, with each technician having her own color. Unassigned work orders appear with a gray pushpin.

>> **Resource booking:** A resource booking is the assignment of a resource to a work order. A resource is usually a technician or another worker, but it can also be a piece of equipment that is needed for the job or even another resource type.

>> **Customer asset:** A customer asset is a piece of equipment that is located at a customer's site in the field. You can specify subcomponents, which is especially useful if the equipment has parts inside that have their own, separate serial numbers and warranties, such as a condenser coil or a compressor inside of an air conditioning unit.

>> **Agreement:** An agreement is a sort of template for generating work orders and invoices and is similar to a contract that you have in place with your customer. The agreement can specify the price of the service and can contain one or more schedules; this way, you can have one agreement that covers different types of work that are performed at different periodic intervals.

>> **Time-off request:** A time-off request is important because, after it has been approved, it shows up on the schedule board as a grayed-out area for the technician who is taking time off. In this way, the dispatcher avoids booking technicians who are on vacation or otherwise unavailable for work.

>> **Purchase order:** A purchase order can be used to acquire inventory (parts) that can be either stocked in a warehouse or sold directly to a customer on a work order.

>> **Inventory transfer and adjustment:** Inventory transfers record the movement of inventory items between warehouses so that the system knows the correct on-hand quantity at each warehouse location. Inventory adjustments are used to correct the on-hand quantity, usually after a physical count has revealed that the quantity in the system doesn't agree with what is actually on the shelf. You could use an inventory adjustment to add inventory to the warehouse, but normally you add purchases of inventory using a purchase order receipt; so adjustments are mainly for error correction.

>> **Warehouse:** A warehouse is a physical location where inventory is stocked. A warehouse doesn't necessarily have to be a warehouse building; it can be a van, a truck, a room in an office building or any place you want to isolate inventory for managing it more effectively.

>> **Return merchandise authorization (RMA):** The term *RMA* is commonly used in inventory management parlance related to inventory returns. You issue an RMA so that your customer can return a bad or unwanted piece of equipment to you. Usually, it's the technician who is returning it on the customer's behalf, because it's the technician in the field who has probably assessed that the equipment is faulty in some way. You have three options for returns: Return to the warehouse, return to the vendor (supplier), or change the equipment

ownership. When you return an item to the warehouse, it usually means that the part is still good and you can use it elsewhere later on for a different customer. If you return an item to the vendor, doing so involves a return-to-vendor (RTV) order. In the RMA approval process, more than one part can be added to a single RMA. You may also need to issue a credit memo to your customer for the return.

>> **Return to vendor (RTV) order:** RTVs are used to track inventory items that you have returned to a vendor. Use RTV substatuses to track the status of the individual parts of the RTV.

TIP

The schedule board is an exciting functionality that can be used in several areas within the Dynamics 365 for Customer Engagement application. In other words, the schedule board is a global feature of Customer Engagement. Even though scheduling is an essential feature of Field Service applications, you can also use it in the Sales module. For example, you can schedule opportunities as part of the Sales module, not just work orders as part of the Field Service module.

Living the Dream of Efficient Field Service: The Work Order Lifecycle

In Dynamics 365 for Field Service, the work order completes a lifecycle. (See Figure 10-2.) The work order lifecycle consists of several sequential steps (some of which are optional), including these:

>> **Work order creation:** Work orders can be created in several ways, including being keyed into the system manually (from scratch), generated automatically from an agreement, or converted from a case.

>> **Schedule (booking):** The work order then needs to be added to the schedule (in other words, *booked*). You can do this manually on the schedule board from the list of unscheduled work orders, directly on the work order using the Add Bookings button, or by using the schedule assistant (a tool that uses a complex query to match a technician to a work order based on a variety of factors, such as distance and skill set).

>> **Dispatch:** A technician is dispatched to the customer site.

>> **Approval:** Approval is a status change. A manager reviews and then approves the work order if she is satisfied that everything looks in order — changing its status from "unapproved" to "approved".

>> **Billing:** Customers are invoiced for completed work orders.

>> **Return:** Returns are optional, based on the discretion of the technician, who assesses whether any parts need to be returned. RMA and RTV functionality is available.

>> **Inventory adjustment:** Inventory adjustment transactions may sometimes be necessary to account for parts used on the service call.

>> **Credit memo:** You may need to issue a credit memo to a customer to give credit for a part, listed on an invoice, that was paid for but later returned because it was eventually determined that it wasn't needed.

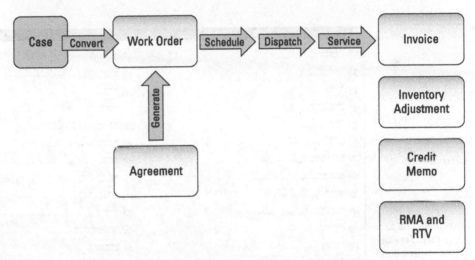

FIGURE 10-2:
The work order lifecycle in Dynamics 365 for Field Service.

Configuring Administrative Settings for Dynamics 365 for Field Service

To view the Field Service menu items related to the configuration (settings), follow these steps:

1. **On the black navigation bar at the top of the screen, click the down arrow to the right of the name of the module you're in.**

The Tile Selector pull-down menu appears.

2. **Click the Field Service tile.**

The Field Service tile is the blue tile to the right of the orange Marketing tile.

The menu items and menu item headings change to reflect the choices most closely related to the Field Service module. (Refer to Figure 10-1.)

3. **Under the Settings menu heading, click Administration.**

The Administration menu item is the blue box that has the Gear icon inside it.

Dozens of settings related to configuring the Field Service module appear, each with an icon, a title, and a short description of which features that setting controls. (See Figure 10-3.)

One setting has the Gear icon and the title Field Service Settings. Clicking this icon opens even more settings related to Field Service. Keep in mind that all these icons are related to the Field Service module, not just the one labeled Field Service Settings.

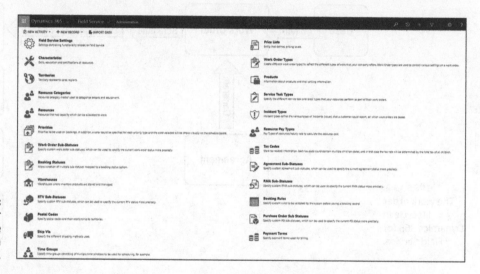

FIGURE 10-3:
Dynamics 365 for Field Service Administration menu items.

TIP

As you can see in Figure 10-3, the Field Service module has lots of different settings; some of these are optional, but many are required, and many optional settings are still likely to be appropriate for your organization. Setting up the Field Service module requires expertise and careful analysis. You'll be wise to set up a sandbox (test) instance to try out some of these settings during the design phase of your implementation. Consult with your authorized Dynamics 365 solution provider about configuring Dynamics 365 for Field Service to ensure that you're provided with a detailed project plan. Also, when the solution provider prepares a design document, be sure that you read it carefully and provide feedback about it, before the setup is performed in your production Dynamics 365 instance.

Working with Work Orders

To create a new work order in Dynamics 365 for Field Service, follow these steps:

1. **On the black navigation bar at the top of the screen, click the down arrow to the right of the name of the module you're in.**

   The Tile Selector pull-down menu appears.

2. **Click the Field Service tile.**

   The Field Service tile is the blue tile to the right of the orange Marketing tile.

   The menu items and menu item headings change to reflect the choices most closely related to the Field Service module. (Refer to Figure 10-1.)

3. **Click Work Orders, found under the Work Order & Scheduling menu heading, to the far left of the screen.**

   The Work Order view (a list of work orders) appears.

4. **Click the New button to create a new work order.**

   The Work Order form appears. (See Figure 10-4.)

   The next sequential work order number is automatically filled out by the system.

   The System Status field (which is the status of the work order) defaults to Open – Unscheduled.

   Required fields have a red asterisk to the left of the field label.

5. **Click the Magnifying Glass icon on the Service Account look-up menu.**

   You must select a service account.

   The service account is the customer for whom the work is being performed.

   The billing account defaults to the service account, but you can select a different account if the work is being paid for by another account associated with the service account.

   The Primary Contact and Email fields fill in automatically based on the service account.

6. **Click the Magnifying Glass icon on the Work Order Type look-up menu.**

   You must select a work order type.

7. **Click the Magnifying Glass icon on the Price List look-up menu.**

   The Price List field is found in the Settings section, in the General field group. (Again, see Figure 10-4.)

8. **Fill out the Time from Promised and Time to Promised fields.**

   A handy calendar control helps you select when the work is promised to be performed.

9. **Review the address at the bottom of the form, and modify if necessary.**

   The address should populate automatically when you select the service account.

   The address is essential for scheduling the work order in an efficient manner based on the location of your technicians.

10. **(Optional) Add a note or an activity to the work order.**

    In the Summary section in the middle of the screen, you can add activities, such as phone calls and tasks, or type a note to provide information that the technician can view from the field by using the Field Service mobile app.

11. **Click the Save button on the Field Service command bar.**

    The command bar is located directly under the black navigation bar at the top of the screen.

    You need to save the work order before you can add products or services.

    Add the services to be performed and any products (parts) that are required. Clicking the plus sign (+) located on the far right end of the product-and-services grid opens a window to add a new line to the grid, allowing you to specify the products and services.

    You can add service tasks as well, in a similar fashion.

12. **In the Related To field group in the Settings section, you can relate the work order where applicable; doing so is optional.**

    The work order can be related to a parent work order, an agreement, an opportunity, or a case.

    Keep in mind that if this work order were related to an agreement, for example, you could have more easily generated the work order from the agreement, thereby having more information automatically filled out by the system based on the information contained in the agreement.

13. **Click the Close button — the X on the far right side of the command bar — to exit the work order.**

    You're taken back to the view of work orders. Click the down arrow to the right of the View name to see a pull-down menu of built-in system *views* (different ways of filtering the list of work orders). Assuming that you haven't yet scheduled this new work order, switch the view to the Unscheduled Work Orders view to see your new work order appear as a row in the list.

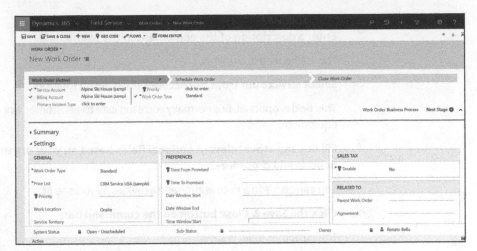

FIGURE 10-4:
The New Work
Order form,
displaying the
Settings section.

Adding a Customer Asset

A *customer asset* is an equipment record; this is the piece of equipment that your technicians will service, so you need to have a record of it and keep track of the work orders related to it; doing so provides your service record for that piece of equipment.

To add a customer asset in Dynamics 365 for Field Service, follow these steps:

1. **On the black navigation bar at the top of the screen, click the down arrow to the right of the name of the module you're in.**

    The Tile Selector pull-down menu appears.

2. **Click the Field Service tile.**

    The Field Service tile is the blue tile to the right of the orange Marketing tile.

    The menu items and menu item headings change to reflect the choices most closely related to the Field Service module. (Refer to Figure 10-1.)

3. **Choose Customer Assets, found under the Service Delivery menu heading.**

    A view (list) of the customer assets appears.

4. **Click the New button to create a new customer asset.**

    The Customer Asset form appears.

    Required fields have a red asterisk to the left of the field label.

5. **Enter a description of the equipment in the Name field.**

   The Name field is required.

6. **Select an Account from the Account (Customer) look-up.**

   This field is optional, but normally you'll indicate the customer who owns the equipment.

7. **Fill out any other relevant optional fields based on your organization's policies and procedures.**

   You can also add a note and/or add activities as you see fit.

8. **Click the Save & Close button on the command bar.**

   The customer asset is saved.

   You're taken back to the view of customer assets.

Transferring Inventory

It often happens that parts are exchanged between locations. Perhaps a part is needed at a particular depot and a driver is able to drop it off, for example. You can enter an inventory transfer to record the movements of inventory items among your warehouses.

To create an inventory transfer in Dynamics 365 for Field Service, follow these steps:

1. **On the black navigation bar at the top of the screen, click the down arrow to the right of the name of the module you're in.**

   The Tile Selector pull-down menu appears.

2. **Click the Field Service tile.**

   The Field Service tile is the blue tile to the right of the orange Marketing tile.
   The menu items and menu item headings change to reflect the choices most closely related to the Field Service module. (Refer to Figure 10-1.)

3. **Click Inventory Transfers, found under the Inventory & Purchasing menu heading.**

   A view (list) of inventory transfers appears.

4. **Click the New button to add a new inventory transfer transaction.**

   The Inventory Transfer form appears.

The next sequential Transfer No. (number) is automatically filled out by the system. Notice that an icon that looks like a lock appears to the left of the number. The Lock icon indicates that this field is locked down — it cannot be edited by the user.

Required fields have a red asterisk to the left of the field label.

5. **Click the Magnifying Glass icon on the Source Warehouse look-up menu.**

   Select the warehouse you're transferring from.

6. **Click the Magnifying Glass icon on the Destination Warehouse look-up menu.**

   Select the warehouse you're transferring to.

7. **Enter the quantity in the Transfer Qty field.**

   Of course, you can only transfer a quantity up to what is on hand.

8. **Click Transfer.**

REMEMBER

You can do so much more with Dynamics 365 for Field Service than I can possibly describe in one chapter. I highly recommend that you ask your administrator to create a sandbox (test) instance and to install the demo data. You can sign in to the sandbox and play around with various scenarios. You'll want to kick the tires, so to speak, and explore the many capabilities that Field Service offers. Be sure to get assistance from your authorized Dynamics 365 solution provider when you consider implementing a new feature, to ensure that you follow best practices.

3

Business Central ERP (formerly Dynamics NAV)

IN THIS CHAPTER

» Getting a bird's-eye view of Dynamics 365 Business Central

» Understanding the difference between the Essentials and Premium editions

» Setting up the books, chart of accounts, and bank accounts

» Generating quotes, orders, and credit memos

» Maintaining your customers, vendors, and inventory items

Chapter **11**

Accounting for Your Business with Business Central

From humble beginnings, in Denmark in 1985, the seed of what is now Microsoft Business Central was sown. A Danish company called PC&C (short for Personal Computing & Consulting) released its first accounting software. Branded as PCPlus, it had only basic accounting features and could be used by only one user at a time. The PC revolution was under way, and literally hundreds of little accounting applications sprung up everywhere. PCPlus was eventually improved and rebranded as Navision, which was a client/server application that could be used by more than one person at the same time. (Imagine that.) From Denmark, Navision spread to Germany, England, and beyond, becoming a popular product throughout most of Europe by the time it was finally released for Windows 95, and thereby gained even more traction. The success of Navision has largely been attributed to its ease of extension and tailoring for individual clients due to its built-in, user-friendly customization tools. Another key selling point was its robust feature set, which included manufacturing capabilities.

By the time Microsoft acquired Navision in July of 2002, the company was a leader in off-the-shelf accounting software for the SMB (small-to-midsize business) sector in Europe. Microsoft had previously acquired Great Plains together with Solomon, which were two of the leading SMB accounting software packages in the United States. Many people believe that Navision was acquired to gain a customer base in Europe to complement the large customer base in the United States. Navision was rebranded by Microsoft as Dynamics NAV, and has had continued success, steadily gaining more market share over the years.

Accounting software — or, as it's commonly known, ERP (enterprise resource planning) software — is a vital mission-critical component of any organization's information technology investment. But ERP is different from many other types of software: ERP tends to become entrenched in organizations because, once it is established, migrating to a different solution is often expensive, time-consuming, and fraught with peril. Therefore, ERP is considered an *anchor* application: Once it goes in, it tends to stay there for decades. Microsoft executives were eager to enter the ERP market through these ERP acquisitions, which included Navision, not only for the profits from selling ERP itself but also because ERP would act as an anchor to help ensure that customers remained on the Microsoft technology stack — the one that includes the Windows operating systems, the SQL Server database, the Office automation suite (Word, Excel, Outlook, and so on), and programming languages such as .NET Visual Basic and C#.

Fast-forward to today's volatile cloud services revolution and you see that for Microsoft to keep its ERP anchors in place, a flexible, user-friendly, easily customizable ERP offering with light manufacturing capabilities that is right-sized for the SMB sector is a necessary piece of the puzzle. Enter Business Central, a cloud ERP for the SMB market. To complement its SMB offering, Microsoft has also migrated Dynamics AX to the Dynamics 365 cloud, branding that ERP package as Dynamics 365 for Finance and Operations; Finance and Operations (AX) is targeted toward larger, mid-market enterprise clients.

Microsoft has done an amazing job in migrating Dynamics NAV to the cloud and offering it as a Software as a Service (SaaS) solution under the Dynamics 365 umbrella, rebranded now as Business Central. For existing users of Dynamics NAV, the software will seem familiar, but much has been enhanced and improved as well. Business Central benefits from all the benefits of SaaS, as well as from the Dynamics 365 common technologies, which include Power BI, PowerApps, Microsoft Flow, and Office 365. Now that NAV is in the cloud as Business Central, an even more powerful, more flexible, and more fully integrated ERP software is available from Microsoft.

TIP

Business Central has two levels: The Essentials version hosts 70 to 80 percent of the total available modules, and the Premium version handles the rest. See Table 11-1 for a guide to what is available in each edition.

TABLE 11-1

Business Central Options

Module	Essentials	Premium
GL / AP / AR	✓	✓
Budgets / Account Schedules	✓	✓
Consolidations	✓	✓
Inter-Company	✓	✓
Multi-Currency	✓	✓
Sales Orders / Invoicing	✓	✓
Purchasing / Purchase Orders	✓	✓
Receiving	✓	✓
Fixed Assets	✓	✓
Jobs (tracking with timesheet)	✓	✓
Dimensions	✓	✓
Workflow	✓	✓
Nonstock Items	✓	✓
Inventory (stock)	✓	✓
Assembly	✓	✓
Distribution / Shipping	✓	✓
Warehousing (with Bins)	✓	✓
Lot / Serial # Tracking	✓	✓
Document Management	✓	✓
Human Resources	✓	✓
Office 365 Integration	✓	✓
Dynamics Sales / CRM Integration	✓	✓
Manufacturing – Requisition Sheets		✓
Manufacturing – Inventory Planning		✓
Manufacturing – Production Orders		✓
Manufacturing – Bill of Material		✓
Manufacturing – Capacity Planning		✓
Service Management – Items		✓
Service Management – Pricing		✓
Service Management – Contracts		✓

REMEMBER

The screen shots shown in this chapter are from the Essentials version; the Premium modules are deeper-level subjects with a great deal of complexity. Consider bringing in a professional-services firm to implement the Premium version and its features. For example, manufacturing and service management, which are both deep-level subjects, are beyond the scope of this chapter.

Getting to Know the Interface

In this section, I cover the interface of Business Central. Before I get there, I must ask: How often have you logged in to a new application and the software designers have greeted you with a message reading something like this:

> Welcome! We have recently improved the user interface to better meet your business needs. Please take a moment to look around, and we hope you love it as much as we do.

A true translation of that welcome message might go something like this:

> Welcome to the new interface update. We have changed everything and moved the essential icons that you are accustomed to using, hiding them deep within obscure menus, which we forgot to convert from Klingon-speak back to easy-to-understand terms. Take a tour by clicking the Help button (which is still under construction). Good luck.

We have all dealt with this kind of frustration when learning new applications, and it's one reason that many of us are afraid to move our ERP system to the cloud. You can rest assured, however, that Microsoft has done an excellent job with this application by laying out the significant sections in an easy-to-use interface. The interface mimics the concepts contained within its previous versions yet simplifies them by reorganizing them into smaller sections to ensure that you can follow the flow of transactions throughout the application.

The major sections of Business Central are briefly described in the following list; then I dive into critical parts of the application to help you get acquainted with their overall functionality so that you can better assess whether Business Central is a fit for your organization.

This list describes the major Business Central sections:

>> **Main Screen:** This fully customizable dashboard allows for common action links (think quick links from Microsoft's Dynamics GP product).

- » **Finance:** This section includes your chart of accounts, general ledger (GL), fixed assets, budgets, reports, currency setup, and more.

- » **Cash Management:** In this section, you configure bank accounts and their statements, global payment terms, cash receipt journals, and more.

- » **Sales:** Here is where you manage customer setup cards, items, quotes, orders, sales invoices, credit memos, and returns.

- » **Purchasing:** Go here to manage vendor setup cards, quotes, purchase orders, purchase invoices, purchase credit memos, and more.

- » **Approvals:** In this section, you manage approval requests and workflows.

- » **Self Service:** Access timesheets and other user tasks here.

- » **Setup & Extensions:** In this section, you'll find hundreds of settings that, taken together, can customize your Business Central Experience to precisely fit your organization's requirements.

TECHNICAL STUFF

Some powerful API (*application programming interface*) connections are built into Business Central that allow you to import data, convert it, and process it. Examples of these are tools for sales and inventory forecasting, QuickBooks online standard data migration (inclusive of customers, vendors, items, and accounts), PayPal payments, Microsoft Pay, Dynamics GP Data Import, and a bank feed tool that can help you quickly reconcile payments made to and from your bank accounts. Many of these can be found by choosing Setup & Extensions ➪ Extensions from Business Central's main menu.

Making Your Way Around the Home Screen

One of the best features of Business Central is the capability to customize the home screen based on the role of the user. Unlike in many applications, these role types are already predefined and provide access to users based on their roles within the organization. This feature allows for easy setup with minimal administration. You can customize these screens to suit the user roles that you have within your organization. A built-in tool called Designer allows for the customization of specific screens throughout the application (such as the customer card), which globally adjusts the fields visible for all users.

This home screen is entirely clickable, and you can drill into the data presented onscreen. For example, if you click the Sales This Month number, the system takes you to a report of all paid invoices that make up your total sales. To exit any screen, click anywhere on the screen and press the Esc button on the keyboard. You can also click back in your browser in many areas.

To customize almost any screen within Business Central, follow these steps:

1. **Click the Gear icon in the top right corner of the Business Central screen.**

A pull-down menu appears, with the following choices:

- Personalize
- My Settings

2. **Click Personalize.**

Doing so brings up the Personalizing task box (indicated by red outlines that appear on the frames onscreen).

3. **Hover the mouse over that section of the interface you want to move, and then click.**

The item you select is outlined by a red box, as shown in Figure 11-1.

You can also click the Ellipse button — the one with the three periods (. . .) at the top right corner of a section — to reveal custom settings related to a specific screen module.

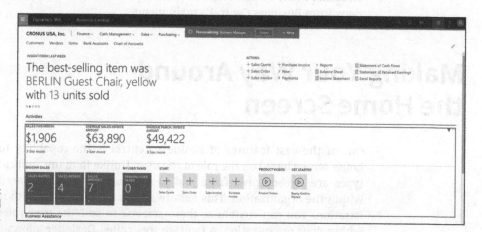

FIGURE 11-1: Business Central Designer.

4. **To finish editing the screen, click the Done button at the top of the screen.**

Your changes are saved.

TIP

You can also customize most other screens within Business Central Design. This includes the ability to customize any lists. You save these as *extensions* (another word for personal customizations) that you then apply to specific groups of users and screen setups. This saves you time and money by not requiring you to hire expensive user interface (UI) developers to customize your interfaces to have useful information on common screens. You can then upload these extensions to other environments and even across different companies within your environment.

WARNING

Even with high-resolution monitors, you may have a hard time seeing some of the information on the Business Central Designer screen. Microsoft has included an Expand button on the interface to alleviate this problem. (See Figure 11-2.) Clicking this button initiates Full Screen mode, which expands the window to the corners of the web browser screen. I also recommend maximizing the browser within your computer's operating system.

The Full Screen Mode button

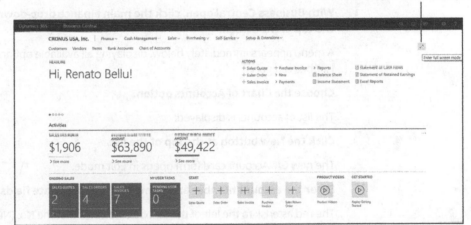

FIGURE 11-2:
Full Screen
Mode button.

Setting Up the Books

Time to look at some core settings and features of Business Central as it comes out of the box. I start by guiding you through setting up your books by adding accounts to the chart of accounts, and then move to defining general ledger (G/L) account categories (different from the previously used segments). Lastly, I have you take a look at specifying bank accounts for those accounts.

REMEMBER

Fortunately, Business Central does not define the account number master record as a fixed string inclusive of all segments, like some other Microsoft ERP products do (Dynamics GP, for example). Instead, Business Central defines the account number master record as just the natural account number. Segments can be defined separately and are referred to as *dimensions*. You first specify the natural account (sometimes referred to as the *main*, or *root*, account) and then add dimensions later. You do this because many charts of accounts end up with astronomically high account counts (sometimes in the hundreds of thousands). With dimensions, Business Central is able to tag transactions in ways that not only define which business unit or geographical area a transaction affects but also include data such as what was sold, who sold it, and the category of customer(s) that bought it. This allows for a smaller chart of accounts and an extremely powerful business intelligence (BI) integration on the back end that will both qualify and quantify transactions.

Adding accounts to the chart of accounts

To add a natural account (the only kind that exists in Business Central) to a chart of accounts, follow these steps:

1. With Business Central open, click the main Finance drop-down menu, at the top of the screen.

A menu appears immediately below, displaying all available options within the Finance category.

2. Choose the Chart of Accounts option.

The list of accounts is displayed.

3. Click the New button at the top of the list.

The new G/L Account card form opens in Edit mode.

4. Enter the account number and name in the appropriate fields.

The red asterisk to the left of the text box indicates that the No. (Number) field is a required field.

5. Select the account category.

When you select this category first, the Income or Balance option automatically defaults to the most likely category.

6. Assign the account subcategory.

This step helps for reporting purposes, to further break down subsets of accounts and dimensions of those accounts.

7. Define the default entry type (Debit/Credit) for the account.

This refers to whether the transactions posted to this account are typically credit, debit, or both (such as a clearing account) by default.

8. **Select the account type.**

Select one of these types: Posting, Heading, Total, Begin-total, or End-total.

9. **If the account is set to a totaling account, define the totaling accounts.**

The totaling accounts are a list of the account's whole totals sum to the balance of the account. Separate account numbers by using the pipe (|) symbol. Click the Ellipse button on the page to bring up a selection of accounts. To select multiple accounts, hold down the keyboard's Ctrl button while clicking each account.

Some sample text input for this field is

```
10200|10500|10800|10940|20400
```

After you enter the account numbers on this screen, the Balance field on the account setup automatically updates to reflect the selected accounts.

10. **Select the appropriate boxes in the General section to specify whether this is a reconciliation account, a direct posting, a blocked account, or another option.**

A blocked account specifies that the related record may not be used in posting a transaction while it remains blocked.

11. **Fill out the rest of the account information on this screen.**

If you hover the mouse over the label of a field, a pop-up Help box appears that describes the field.

12. **Finally, use the top bar above the card to select dimensions (if these have been defined) to tag transactions reflected within this account.**

You can view the account balance, view the account balance by dimension, and modify the posting setup. (That last step is important if you're working with accounts with different sales and purchasing accounts associated with them).

13. **Click the Edit button on the Home tab of the menu at the top of the screen to save your changes.**

Clicking the Edit button moves the account from Edit mode back into View mode.

There's no Save button on this screen, even for new accounts.

14. **Click the X to leave that account card (or press Esc on the keyboard).**

To edit an account already in place on the chart of accounts, click the Ellipse button next to its name and choose Edit from the menu that appears. (See Figure 11-3.)

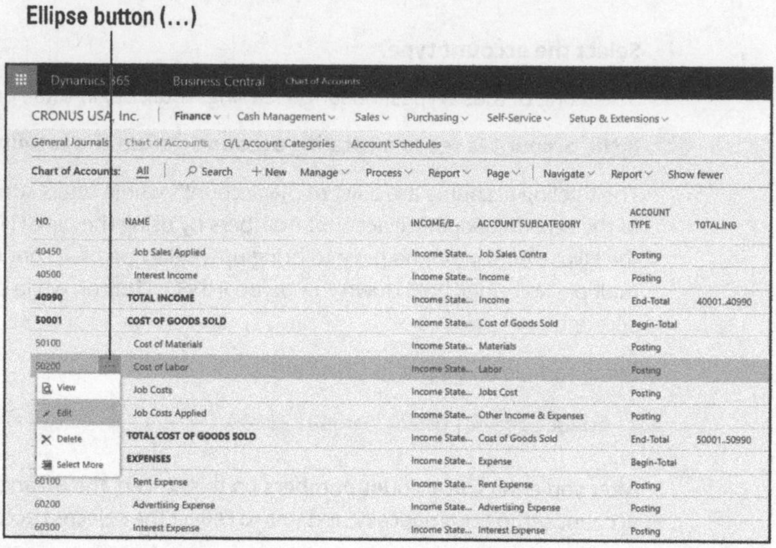

Ellipse button (...)

FIGURE 11-3:
Chart of accounts
Account Edit
button.

TIP

When you're viewing the chart of accounts, you'll notice accounts displayed in bold, which typically indicates whether an account is a totaling account for the accounts rolled up within it (refer to the Totaling column). When editing an account, notice that a) the pipe symbol (|) allows you to input specific pipe-delimited accounts in a list and b) if you click the Ellipse button, you're presented with a menu where you specify a series of accounts. For example, in the sample data, the total income account has 40001..40990 as the setting in the Totaling column (indicating that any account between 40001 and 40990 is included in the total). You may, however, instead specify a discontinuous range of accounts — the 10200, 10500, 1800, 10940, and 20400 accounts, for example — by using the text 10200|10500|10800|10940|20400.

Defining G/L account categories

Business Central has a simple yet effective way of setting up account categories. These categories make it easy to map general ledger (G/L) accounts to specific categories. You can also create subcategories and assign those categories to existing accounts. Each group shows you the total balance of the accounts within those categories within the different financial reports available throughout Business Central. These categories are a handy way to quickly specify the totaling on your financial statements. You may change these on the fly, making account categories a robust way to categorize your financial data. For example, a department may change its basic functionality from one year to the next. Account categories allow you to create and maintain financial reports more easily.

REMEMBER

Account categories determine how accounts roll-up to calculate totals used on financial reports. For example, Current Assets is an account category with no specific G/L accounts explicitly defined on the account number level. However, Cash, Accounts Receivable, Prepaid Expenses, and Inventory are all account categories that roll-up within the Current Assets category. This means that the Current Assets category reports the total of all G/L accounts represented in those four categories.

Check out the main screen for G/L account categories. On this screen, you see a list of every account category. To get things started, go ahead and make a new item. The following steps show you how:

1. With Business Central open, choose Finance ⇨ G/L Account Categories from the menu bar at the top of the screen.

The list of G/L account categories appears.

2. Choose Manage ⇨ Edit List from the menu that appears, immediately above the list of G/L account categories.

You're now in List Edit mode, where you can add new G/L account categories or edit existing ones.

3. Select a G/L account category from the displayed list, and then click the New button on the Home tab of the menu at the top of the screen to create a new category immediately below the selected category.

4. Use the Move Up and Move Down buttons to place the new G/L account category where you want it to fall within the list.

5. Under the G/L Accounts in Category column, specify the G/L accounts that pertain to the new G/L account category.

The Additional Report Definition column is used to determine where the G/L category would appear within a statement of cash flows (called the *cash flow statement* in Business Central), so be sure to specify that setting if you intend to use the cash flow statement.

WARNING

Business Central has no concept of roll-ups or subcategories: Instead, it has account categories that are "indented" to become part of another category above them in the structure. Neither does Business Central display how "deep" within a hierarchy an account lies on all forms, which can be troublesome when you're trying to ensure that you have properly assigned an account in the proper level of a roll-up. If you moved an account accidentally on the category screen and are having trouble restoring it in the correct part of the hierarchy, use both the Indent and Outdent buttons, as well as the Move Up and Move Down buttons, to reposition it.

Specifying bank accounts

Business Central lets you link bank accounts by way of a secure interface — definitely one of the nicest features of this cloud-based application. One thing, however, that is not so easily discovered, is how to set up API connections between your bank and the Business Central system, to drastically help with the reconciliation of bank accounts. In this section I discuss how to

>> **Set up and link bank accounts**

>> **Enable automatic bank imports using Envestnet Yodlee Bank Feeds (the connection Microsoft has authored, installed, and enabled by default)**

>> **Match transactions within the interface to bank transactions**

>> **Reconcile your bank accounts**

REMEMBER

This section covers automatic bank reconciliation and the import of transactions. You can do all this manually, but one of the many benefits of this application is that you can import transactions automatically and reconcile them within an easy-to-use interface. The system even attempts to automatically reconcile and gives you a match-confidence score based on a few unique matches, such as amount and date and other information related to that transaction.

Follow the next set of steps to set up all these features, and you'll be on your way to saving time when the time comes to reconcile your bank accounts.

To link a bank account to an account set up in Business Central, follow these steps:

1. **Choose Cash Management ⇨ Bank Accounts from Business Central's main menu at the top of the screen.**

    Doing so displays a list of available bank accounts.

    You can create a new bank account by clicking the New button and filling out your bank account information.

    In this example, you use an existing bank account.

2. **Click the Ellipse button — the one in the second column, immediately to the right of the name of the bank account — on the row for the bank account you want to edit.**

    A small drop-down menu appears.

3. **Select Edit from the drop-down menu.**

    The Edit Bank Account Card form appears.

4. **Click the Link to Online Bank Account button in the Home ribbon.**

The Link to Online Bank Account form appears.

5. **When prompted, ensure that you're on a secure connection, enter your banking information, click Next, and then click OK.**

A new screen appears, displaying the accounts already linked.

6. **Click OK.**

Doing so brings you to the next section, where you set up automatic bank imports.

7. **Click to select the account name for which you want to set up automatic bank imports, and then click the Automatic Bank Statement Import Setup button.**

You configure this on the bank account card, which tells you the bank account linking status in the top right corner of the general section.

8. **In the Import Setup window, select the number of days to include in the import and then select OK.**

The specified transactions are imported into your payment journal.

After these transactions have been imported, you're ready to reconcile. *Reconciling electronic transactions* refers to the act of ensuring that the transactions within the system for any given bank account match the transactions listed on the bank ledger. You must regularly reconcile your bank, payable, and receivables accounts by applying your payments recorded in the bank to associated credit memos, unpaid invoices, and open entries in Business Central. You can do this in the Payment Reconciliation Journal window. (See Figure 11-4.)

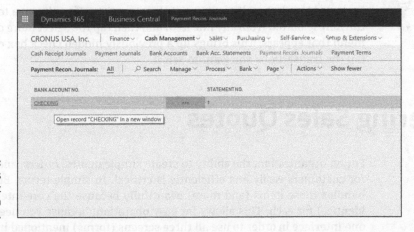

FIGURE 11-4: Business Central's Payment Reconciliation Journals window.

REMEMBER

You can use the Bank Account Payment Reconciliation Journal form to import bank transactions manually via a bank file transaction download. The automatic import simply saves you the trouble of having to download a file daily or weekly from your banking institution.

The Bank Account Payment Reconciliation Journal form lets you execute these actions on a transaction:

>> Have the system apply payments automatically

>> Post payments only

>> Transfer the difference to another account

>> Apply payments manually

>> Remove specific applications already made

>> Post payments only

After you have applied the transactions, click the Post Payments and Reconcile Bank Account button and your bank account will be reconciled.

As you can see, Microsoft Dynamics 365 Business Central makes bank reconciliation a much swifter process by using intelligent algorithms to match payments to outstanding invoices, credit memos, and accounts. This makes the month-end closing procedures much more efficient, with fewer manual entries being required for bank reconciliation. This kind of automation is a tremendous time-saver for you and your staff.

TIP

When selecting anything from a list (including transactions on the Bank Account Payment Reconciliation Journal form), you can hold down the Ctrl button on the keyboard to select multiple items at the same time. If you're on a touchscreen, tap the Ellipse button from any line item and then tap the Select More option from the menu that appears. This brings up a previously hidden check box column. Simply tap the transactions you want to select.

Entering Sales Quotes

For an organization, the ability to create simple quotes, orders, and credit memos for customers easily and efficiently is critical. In simple terms, Business Central handles these items (and more) beautifully because the core interface is almost identical for each. This allows for easy operation, because you need to learn only one interface in order to use all three screens (forms) mentioned in the preceding section. I have selected a few key pieces for you to work through in this section in order to make you comfortable with creating the aforementioned items. First on the list: sales quotes.

Some key pieces of information are required before entering a sales quote, including the ones described in this list:

>> **Customer:** To create a sales order, you don't have to set up the customer card ahead of time; however, note that it saves a good deal of time when you're working with quotes, because the contact information for that customer will already be in place. (I cover how to create customers shortly.)

>> **Line Items:** For sales orders, I recommend that you set up items in the system ahead of time. However, the full Item Creation screen comes up if you try to enter a new item and it sees that no such item exists.

>> **Invoice Details:** You must specify invoice information on this sales quote so that it can convert into an order or invoice. This includes payment terms, ship-to and bill-to information, and contacts.

It's time to take a closer look at the interface to find out how to manage this simple yet powerful functionality. To create a new sales quote, follow these steps:

1. **Choose Sales ⇨ Sales Quotes from Business Central's main menu at the top of the screen.**

   Doing so brings up a filterable, comprehensive list of all outstanding sales quotes so that you have a single dashboard to see what's in the pipeline.

2. **Click the New button found above the list of quotes.**

   The New Sales Quote form displays.

3. **Enter the name of the customer from the list from Step #1.**

   Business Central has a swift name-search feature. You can even enter the customer number and it filters accordingly.

TIP

4. **After you have selected a customer from the list, follow the red asterisks and fill out the required lines.**

   The easiest way to select an item is to click the Ellipse button next to the Item Number text field to open a drop-down menu. Choose an item from that menu, and then fill in a quantity for this item. The rest of the quote automatically fills out.

5. **Fill out all other appropriate information on this screen, and ensure that you select a payment service if you have electronic services (such as PayPal) enabled.**

   This step ensures that the customer receives a payment link when you create an invoice from this quote, allowing them to pay via PayPal or a credit card.

At this point, either a workflow triggers, sending out approval emails, or the system allows you to email the quote directly to the customer email address on file.

REMEMBER

If Business Central has the logic set up properly, it will tag sales quotes that include specific items or involve specific customers with a dimension at the beginning of the sales process — as opposed to categorizing those transactions later. Again, this is how Business Central is able to qualify the financial data coming in without the need to break out the G/L accounts into different segments (for things like offices and business units, for example.) This helps greatly with reporting. Explore the other sections of the Sales Quote menu as shown in Figure 11-5 (in the following section)— it has tools that can help you identify the profitability of a quote and tools to help you easily modify the quote.

Creating Sales Orders and Invoices

The hope is always that a sales quote converts to an order or an invoice. To have Business Central do this for you, click either the Make Order button or the Make Invoice button on the Sales Quote top bar menu. (See Figure 11-5.) This takes the information from the original sales quote and generates a sales order or sales invoice based on that information.

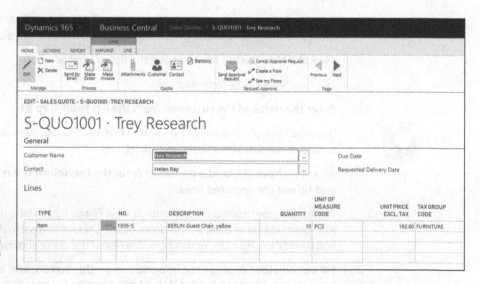

FIGURE 11-5:
The Business
Central Sales
Quote form.

So then, which one should you choose — order or invoice? A few scenarios can help you determine when you would choose one or the other, but I have baked it down to these two easy points:

» **Order Instead of Invoice Reason #1:** Select Make Order if you need to distribute only part of an order because you don't have the entire inventory on hand. This is because there's a Quantity to Ship field on a sales order. If you need to ship out less than the entire amount, only that portion will move to the Quantity field to invoice a portion of the order. Essentially, use this if you're breaking down a shipment from different parts on an order.

» **Order Instead of Invoice Reason #2:** If you're running a drop shipment for a portion or all of an order, select Make Order. In other words, if you sell items delivered directly to your customer from one of your vendors, use a sales order.

To be clear, you can have multiple invoices for the same sales order, so this allows you to break down the quote. If you create the sales order at the beginning of the sales process, you can have multiple invoices for different parts of the order that ultimately pay down the tracked balance from the paid invoices. Business Central also allows you to recognize the sales revenue in different steps throughout the order. If the customer cancels the order mid-delivery, you can issue a credit memo to refund payments that have already been received and that are associated with the sales order; then you can cancel the sales order altogether.

It works best to use sales invoices in a buy-and-pay type of business. It is more simple and direct because it removes the shipping and invoicing steps of the sales order process. If you need to cancel an order, you can simply use the sales return order function.

After you have made your decision and clicked either the Make Order or Make Invoice button, follow along to the next screen. To speed things along, I cover only how to post a sales invoice from a sales quote — the Make Order process is quite similar. Follow these steps:

1. **Click the Make Invoice button on the command bar in the Edit Sales Quote form.**

   A dialog box appears, asking whether you want to convert the quote to an invoice.

2. **Click Yes.**

   The quote is converted to an invoice with the information from the quote, including all line items.

   You can adjust any line items here for various reasons; for example, you may want to substitute another item for out-of-stock items.

3. **On the invoice that has been created, fill out or edit fields based on the business rules and policies of your organization.**

Every organization is different, and your organization will undoubtedly have certain fields to verify and modify to ensure that the invoice is properly keyed and annotated for various scenarios.

4. **Toggle the Show More/Show Less button to make visible or hide fields in the Sales Invoice header.**

   The Show More/Show Less button is located to the far right of the screen, above the General section at the top of the sales invoice.

5. **(Optional) Clicking the Attachments button lets you add any attachments you may need to include.**

   This step allows you to include documents along with an invoice (such as price sheets, contracts and agreements, and images).

   Be sure to select the Flows to Sales TRX check box on the Attachment screen if you want these attached items to follow the transaction through the system.

6. **After all information has been supplied, updated, and double-checked for this invoice, click the Post or Post and Send button on the Home tab of the command bar in the Posting section.**

   This action delivers this invoice to the internal accounts associated with this transaction (Accounts Receivable, for example) and delivers the invoice to the customer according to their customer contact settings.

   This step moves the invoice to posted sales invoices. It's now available for you to match it to a payment received from the customer.

REMEMBER

Sales quotes, orders, and invoices are a simple yet powerful part of Business Central. Be sure to study the screens within each category; many menus and options available to you. If you're unsure what a menu item does, simply hover the mouse over that button. A short description pops up to explain the functionality behind the button.

Creating Sales Credit Memos

Sales credit memos are an important part of Business Central and are likely a vital part of any organization. You typically issue these memos whenever a customer returns an item or to correct an incorrect invoice that was already paid if you need to make an adjustment against that invoice.

Just as you must determine whether you're going to use a sales order or a sales invoice, you must also determine whether you want to use a sales credit memo or a sales return order. This section covers sales credit memos because they function like sales invoices in that they're simple transactions that don't require a lot of item handling or warehouse documents.

In the following list, I briefly describe the difference between a sales credit memo and a sales return order:

>> **Sales credit memo:** Use a credit memo for straightforward returns or reimbursements against a specific sales document (like an invoice). After being posted, a reversal occurs that adjusts the original sales document (likely an invoice) for that amount. Doing so also allows you to make a refund payment to the customer.

>> **Sales return order:** Sales return orders give you control over the sales return process. Use a sales return order to automatically issue a sales credit memo and other return-related documents (such as replacement sales orders) when a customer wants to return items that they have already paid for.

With that comparison out of the way, it's time to create a sales credit memo. Follow these steps:

1. **Choose Sales ⇨ Sales Credit Memos from Business Central's main menu at the top of the screen.**

   Doing so displays the list of all available sales credit memos. It also allows you to create a new one.

2. **Click the New button.**

   A new sales credit memo appears onscreen, as shown in Figure 11-6.

   You can create a credit memo based on an invoice (to quickly "reverse out" the invoice, so to speak), or you can create one completely from scratch.

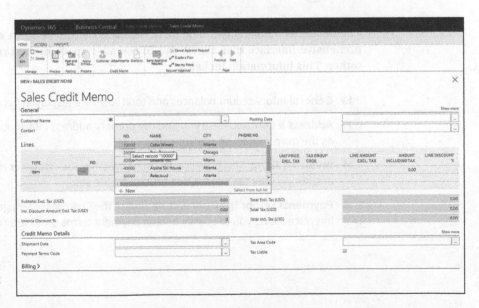

FIGURE 11-6:
The Sales Credit Memo screen.

3. **From the Customer Name drop-down menu, select the customer to which you want to issue a credit memo.**

    The red asterisk next to Customer Name indicates that the field is required.

4. **Fill out the fields as required by your organization's business policies and procedures for issuing credit memos.**

    The fields you need to fill out depend on the standards your organization has adopted as well as on the general circumstances of the transaction.

5. **Review and correct any items on this document.**

    When reviewing, you may notice a banner at the top that appears when a customer has an overdue account. It does this to ensure that you know the account is overdue, to help you in deciding whether to issue this credit memo.

6. **If you want to see where the distributions will affect different accounts within your general ledger upon posting this memo, click the Preview Posting button, found in the Postings section of the Actions tab.**

    Do this the first few times you issue credit memos to this customer, to ensure that you have properly mapped your general ledger accounts.

7. **After you complete the review, click the Post button.**

    Doing so converts the credit memo into a posted sales credit memo. You have successfully posted the credit memo.

Maintaining Customers

The Customer Management module in Business Central boasts a simple but comprehensive interface that allows you to see all-important data related to a customer. This information includes:

>> **General Info:** Account balances and total sales are displayed here.

>> **Address & Contact:** Here you find the primary address information as well as the main contact on the account.

>> **Invoicing Setup:** This is where you mark whether the customer is tax liable and supply their tax information and corporate setup.

>> **Payments Setup:** The Payments section of the Customer Management interface allows you to specify default payment terms on all future invoices.

>> **Shipping:** This is where you specify a location code for that customer (which is important if you're using warehousing).

You can also set up reserve options for the customer.

>> **Top Bar Tasks:** You can use the toolbar at the top of the page to create a sales quote, invoice, credit memo, sales order, and reminder and to add more account details for that customer.

The best way to get started is to create a customer record. To begin, follow these steps:

1. **On the Business Central home page, choose Sales ⇨ Customers ⇨ New from the main menu.**

   Doing so brings up a prompt to help you define the customer type. You can select Business-to-Business Customer (typically used for a bank relationship) or Cash-Payment / Retail Customer (cash relationship).

2. **For a basic customer, select the Cash-Payment / Retail Customer option.**

   The New Customer Card form displays.

3. **Follow the prompts and enter the proper customer information.**

   Required fields are indicated by a red asterisk.

4. **After completing the data entry for the customer record, click the Edit button (which has a Pencil icon) in the top left corner of the window to save the customer record.**

   You're taken out of Edit mode.

   The fields appear gray to indicate that they're no longer editable.

The more time you spend setting up customer master records properly, the less time you spend configuring each order. The time it takes to process an order is longer if you don't specify the customer's default settings ahead of time.

TIP

Selecting a customer on the Customer Selection screen opens the summary screen associated with the customer card for that customer. (See Figure 11-7.) This allows you to see all major documents associated with the customer, inclusive of sales quotes, sales orders, sales credit memos, posted sales shipments, and more. You can use this handy overview to see which documents may be pending for the customer. Clicking the square tiles automatically navigates you to a list of those documents, so the summary screen acts as a navigation tool as well. This tool helps you maintain good relationships with your customers as you access their financial data on the fly.

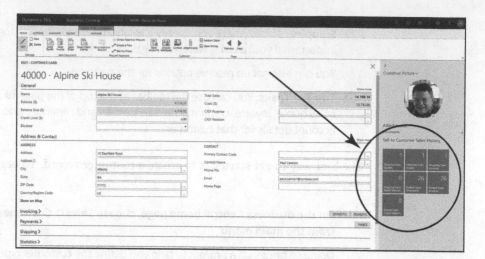

FIGURE 11-7:
Customer Quick
Navigation tiles.

To see a comprehensive list of the customer transactions associated with a single customer, click the Navigate tab in the top left corner of a customer card. This brings up a list of available documents for a customer, including the ones described in this list:

>> **Quotes, invoices, orders, and return orders:** Here you see a full history of all documents, easily sortable by date. This includes a comprehensive list of each item and all customer transaction types.

>> **Ledger entries:** This is a full history of every single general ledger transaction that has ever posted related to this customer. You can filter this list based on document type, date, amount, and more.

This overview is a powerful feature for showing how this customer is affecting balances throughout your chart of accounts.

REMEMBER

>> **Issued documents:** Here you can find reminders and finance charge memos.

>> **Recurring sales lines:** This screen displays all recurring items.

>> **Document layouts and special prices or discounts:** On this screen, you can configure custom pricing on a customer-by-customer basis.

>> **Dimensions:** You can set and configure dimensions on this screen, which tags transactions associated with that customer, with various categorizations for reporting purposes.

One advanced technique within this Customer Management screen involves using the tools on the Actions tab within a customer card. Within this screen, you see a button labeled Save As Template and another labeled Apply Templates. These commands allow you to save this customer as a template and to apply those same settings to another customer or another new customer. Savable information includes address and contact, invoicing preferences, price groups, default discounts, payment methods, codes, statement settings, and more.

Maintaining Vendors

Maintaining vendors in Business Central is similar to maintaining customers. Most of what you see on these screens is similar from an interface perspective, but they obviously will have different business implications. The available screens include the ones described in this list:

>> **General Info:** This includes basic information about vendors, including account balances.

>> **Address & Contact:** Here you find the primary address information and main contact for the vendor.

>> **Invoicing Setup:** Mark whether the vendor is tax liable, their bank communication preferences, and more options related to invoicing.

>> **Payments Setup:** This section allows you to generate default payment terms on all future invoices.

>> **Payments:** This is where the vendor setup screen differs from the customer screen. Here you can specify default payment information, such as method, terms, check date formats, bank account codes (BAC), and the Federal ID number for that vendor.

>> **Top Bar Tasks:** At the top of the page, you create purchase invoices, purchase orders, purchase credit memos, and more.

Some extra features on the Actions tab allow you to view 1099 information, apply templates to the vendor, and run a balance report on their current documents. Another tab you'll want to visit is the Navigate tab. Here you'll find a critical screen labeled Cross References. (I cover that screen a bit later in this chapter.)

REMEMBER

Cross references — commonly referred to as *vendor item numbers* — allow you to create a reference between your system and your vendor's system to replace item numbers that you use with item numbers they use at the time of document issuance. This affects all items on the purchasing invoice (or sales documents for customers) sent over to them. This allows you to maintain the item codes in your system, but present the purchasing or sales items using codes that are in their system.

To set up a cross reference for a vendor, follow these simple steps:

1. **On the Vendor Card screen, click the Navigate tab on the command menu.**

   The command menu changes so that you now see a Vendor, Purchases, and History section with a variety of command buttons.

2. **Click the command menu's Cross References button — the button with two green arrows.**

   The Edit Item Cross References window displays, showing a list of cross-referenced items; this list may be empty if you haven't yet created any cross-referenced items.

3. **Enter the vendor's item reference number into the Cross-Reference No. (Number) field on a new line.**

   This, again, is how the vendor refers to the item within their system.

4. **Now enter the item number in the Item No. field; or click the Ellipsis button from the item number field on that same line and select from your system the item for which you want to set up a cross-reference.**

   This is, again, what you call the item in the Business Central item card.

5. **Lastly, select the unit of measure and enter a description.**

   This may differ completely from the actual item unit and description, and it won't affect the master Item Card setup. Entering information in these fields affects only what the vendor sees on the documents you issue to them, such as purchase orders.

TIP

The Description field is a helpful way for you to keep track of the actual cross-reference.

When you choose Purchasing ⇨ Vendors from the main navigation bar, you see a visual representation of all your vendors in card form, as shown in Figure 11-8. You can highlight and select these vendors. To change a selection, you could click them, but that would bring up the whole vendor card. To cycle through the vendors, use the arrow keys on the keyboard and move your selection around. After you've selected the vendor you want to work with, you can use the New Document drop-down menu to create a document from the list (purchase invoice, order, and credit memo). (Again, see Figure 11-8.) This action starts off the new document with the information from whichever vendor you had selected when selecting an already filled-in document.

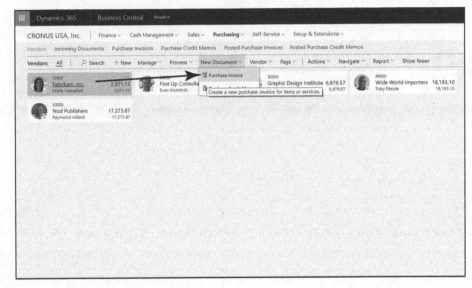

FIGURE 11-8: Vendors screen, with the New Document shortcut menu displayed.

IN THIS CHAPTER

» **Migrating from Dynamics NAV to Business Central**

» **Navigating in Business Central with menus, actions, role centers, and page or report searches**

» **Setting up Business Central with manual setup options, user groups, permissions, and roles**

» **Defining a number series to apply sequential numbering schemes to transactions and cards**

» **Touring the inventory item setup**

Chapter **12**

Setting Up Business Central for Optimal Results

Business Central is one of two on-premise ERP packages that Microsoft has revamped and migrated to the Dynamics 365 cloud, where it's offered as a Software as a Service (SaaS) monthly or annual subscription. The other package is called Finance and Operations. (Business Central was previously branded as Finance and Operations Business edition, whereas Finance and Operations was previously branded as the Finance and Operations Enterprise edition.) Business Central is based on Dynamics NAV (formerly Navision). The project to port (migrate) Dynamics NAV to the Dynamics 365 cloud (thereby creating Business Central) was code-named Tenerife. Finance and Operations was based on Dynamics AX (formerly Axapta), a more heavy-duty application than NAV. Business Central (NAV) is geared toward small and midsize organizations, whereas Finance and Operations (AX) is geared toward larger enterprise clients. That being said, Business Central is no rinky-dink application: It's a full-featured ERP offering, jam-packed with functionality, that comes in two flavors: Business Central Essentials and Business Central Premium.

This list specifies some sample modules that are included with both Essentials and Premium:

» **Financials:** Handles general ledger, budgeting, cash management

» **Supply Chain:** Manages inventory, sales orders, purchase orders

» **Project Accounting:** Handles jobs, timesheets, resources

» **HR:** Manages employees, employee expense reports

» **CRM:** Deals with prospects, opportunities, campaigns

And this list specifies some sample modules that are available only with Premium:

» **Service Orders:** Handles field service contracts, dispatching

» **Manufacturing:** Deals with demand forecasting, capacity planning

TIP

Though Business Central includes customer relationship management (CRM) functionality, keep in mind that a big part of Dynamics 365 is Dynamics CRM (now called Dynamics 365 for Customer Engagement), so the CRM part of NAV is redundant functionality in the sense that the more robust CRM capabilities are found in Customer Engagement (Sales, Service, and Marketing, for example). Fortunately, the CRM features of Business Central integrate to some extent with Dynamics 365 for Customer Engagement, so it's possible to set up a hybrid CRM environment, using a mix of functionality from both applications. That being said, if your organization is a Dynamics NAV site and you're migrating to the cloud with Business Central, it may make more sense to convert your NAV CRM to the more robust Customer Engagement CRM.

The on-premise Dynamics NAV ERP system is widely adopted — admittedly, more so in Europe than in North America. NAV is praised for its ease of customization, and its manufacturing capabilities, which are quite powerful for an SMB (small to midsize) ERP package. Keep in mind, though, that Business Central is not NAV. It's based only partly on NAV and on other aspects of Dynamics 365 in general, and it doesn't contain exactly the same functionality of the on-premise Dynamics NAV ERP package; nonetheless, if you can do it in NAV, in all likelihood you can do it in Business Central. Furthermore, as time goes by, Microsoft will keep adding new, exciting features and capabilities to Business Central. A huge advantage of Business Central over NAV is its tight integration with other Microsoft technologies, such as Office 365, Power BI, PowerApps, and Microsoft Flow.

Furthermore, an ecosystem of third-party developers has created (and will create more) add-on apps (now called *extensions*) for Business Central. The way of the future is to allow organizations to choose the apps they need from an app store that sells solutions from thousands of vendors. Many of these extension apps provide interfaces to various kinds of Internet services, such as PayPal. The concept is to loosely couple the Internet's power with other apps and services inside and outside the organization, building a tailored solution rather than a single large monolithic ERP. Business Central is designed to work with extensions that foster a loosely coupled best-of-breed approach rather than a single closed proprietary model.

Migrating from Dynamics NAV to Business Central

Microsoft isn't forcing existing users of Dynamics NAV to move to Business Central — though it certainly encourages it and its long-term strategy seems to point to the eventual replacement of Dynamics NAV with Business Central. However, many organizations still prefer the on-premise software and aren't quite ready to move to the cloud. Before Dynamics NAV became Business Central, Microsoft had already created a web user interface for NAV, so the application had a head start as far as porting it (reprogramming it) to become a true multi-tenant SaaS offering. If you're used to using the Dynamics NAV's web user interface, coming up to speed on Business Central should be a snap. Many organizations have been running Dynamics NAV in a hosted cloud environment and using the web user interface, so in that sense, NAV cloud sites already existed before the introduction of Business Central. However, its introduction provided a new, subscription-based pricing model as well as hosting by Microsoft in the Azure cloud and full integration with all the other Microsoft cloud technologies.

To upgrade your ERP system from Dynamics NAV to Dynamics 365 Business Central, you cannot simply run a setup program, click your way through a wizard that makes you click the next button over and over again, and magically be on Business Central. In fact, the migration from NAV to Business Central is technically referred to as a product line *transition*, not an upgrade. You're encouraged to confer with your authorized Dynamics 365 solution provider, who should be able to author a detailed migration project plan to accomplish the product line transition from NAV to Business Central for your organization.

TECHNICAL
STUFF

The original Dynamics NAV, called Navision, used a proprietary programming language called C/AL (Client/server Application Language) which was based on Pascal. To customize Dynamics NAV, you program in AL using the NAV Development Environment. To customize Business Central, you program in Visual Studio Code and the AL language extension version 2.0 or higher. If you plan to migrate from Dynamics NAV (on-premise) to Dynamics 365 Business Central (cloud), you can convert your previous AL customizations to a new extension app for Business Central. The syntax hasn't changed that much, so a Dynamics NAV programmer can get up to speed relatively quickly in coding customizations for Business Central.

TIP

Simple user-interface changes, such as making a field invisible, can be made in Business Central using the Business Central Designer — a drag-and-drop design tool that doesn't require any knowledge of how to program in AL (or in any other low-level coding language, for that matter).

In the move from NAV to Business Central, you will be, in essence, re-implementing your ERP system using a similar but new software. In other words, you need to perform the manual setup for Business Central, not simply have all your old settings in NAV automatically appear in Business Central. In addition, you need to carry out a data conversion for which you must decide which data should be imported from NAV to Business Central. You can purchase many helpful tools to perform this data conversion as Microsoft is helping to make the product line transition as simple as possible. The code base and the underlying SQL database data model are similar between NAV and Business Central, but you have many factors to consider, including:

>> How best to convert NAV AL customizations to Business Central extensions

>> How best to repoint or replace custom reports written in other non-Microsoft reporting tools, such as Crystal Reports

>> How to repoint existing on-going data integrations

>> How many years of history to bring over (an opportunity to purge obsolete data)

>> How best to leverage Microsoft Office 365; for example, tighter Outlook email integration such as automated email delivery of quotes and invoices

>> How to deal with licensing issues

Navigating in Business Central

In describing how to navigate software, the terminology is often inconsistent; this point may be a bit confusing, but the most commonly used terminology can be easily demystified. For example, the term *page* in the phrase *search for page or report* refers to a web page, or screen. In fact, many terms have popped up over the years as a substitute for *screen* because *screen* tends to make someone picture the entire screen (as in an old-fashioned character-based green screen application). The newer terms *window* and *form* indicate that you can have multiple windows (forms) open at the same time and toggle between them. However, *window* makes you visualize the Windows operating system, whereas many apps now run on Android, and the term *form* is a generic and nebulous word. The terms *page* and *web page* came into vogue because nowadays applications run on the Internet (the World Wide Web); however, as more apps now run on mobile devices, that term too is falling into disfavor. The term *dialog box* or *dialog window* is used for small windows that pop up and prompt the user for information. The term *card* is used to denote a Master Record Maintenance window, such as the form you would use to add or update a customer, vendor, or inventory item. Well, let there be no confusion: In this book, I use these terms interchangeably: *screen, window, form, card, dialog box, page* and *web page*.

Searching for screens and reports

Microsoft has sought to make navigation within Business Central as easy and intuitive as possible. One of the most frustrating experiences of working with software applications is not knowing how (or not being able to remember how) to get to a certain screen. You have to keep fishing through a hierarchy of menus, searching deeper and deeper into the rabbit hole, only to come up empty-handed. At last, in desperation, you resort to reading the documentation you find on Google or another search engine, but that documentation forces you to complete a long series of steps to get to the screen, and then you still have the frustrating experience trying to navigate from the steps listed in the documentation to the actual menu items in the application, which don't always agree because the documentation may be somewhat out-of-date or pertain to a slightly different version of the software.

In Business Central, Microsoft has devised a better way to find any screen in the application, in the form of a global menu search available for the application: the Search for Page or Report feature. This search doesn't look for individual records (such as a particular vendor or customer) but rather for links to screens (such as the Vendor or Customer Card Maintenance screen). The Search for Page or Report feature is accessed by clicking the Magnifying Glass icon, found on the right side of the top black navigation bar. (This navigation bar is also referred to as the *address bar.*) Using the Search for Page or Report feature, you can find your way around Business Central without having to memorize where menu items are located within a cascading maze of menus. The bonus plan here is that this same feature can be used to find both screens and built-in reports; by the way, many reports are more often printed to the screen, rather than on hard copy (paper), and can therefore, in essence, be thought of as screens as well).

TIP

The Escape (Esc) key on the keyboard is important in Business Central because some of the screens don't display Exit or Close command buttons. Instead, use the Esc key to close a window and go back to the previous screen. Alternatively, to close the window, you can click the X icon (for eXit), located at the far right end, on top of a window (if one is available). Typically, screens in Business Central don't have command buttons labeled Save, Close, or Save & Close (as you might see in Dynamics 365 for Customer Engagement), but don't worry: Conveniently, your changes are saved on or before exiting, without your having to click a Save button.

As an example of navigation by means of the Search for Page or Report feature, see Figures 12-1 and 12-2. In this example, I search for the Vendor Maintenance screen. Keep in mind that navigating to the vendor card is easy enough by simply using the menu navigation; however, for many screens that are harder to find, you can locate them by using the Search for Page or Report feature.

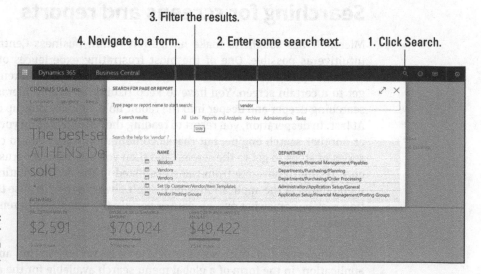

FIGURE 12-1:
Searching for page or report in Business Central.

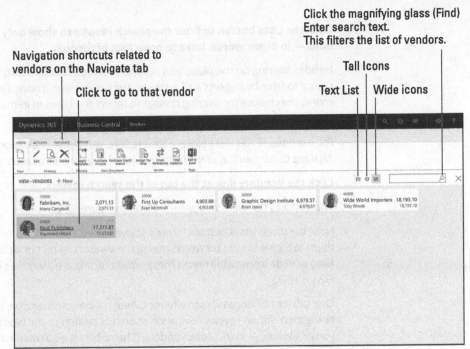

Navigation shortcuts related to
vendors on the Navigate tab

Click to go to that vendor

Click the magnifying glass (Find)
Enter search text.
This filters the list of vendors.

Tall Icons

Text List   Wide icons

FIGURE 12-2:
Navigating within
the list of
vendors.

To navigate to the Vendor Maintenance screen using the Search for Page or Report feature, follow these steps:

1. **Click the Magnifying Glass icon on the address bar.**

The Magnifying Glass icon on the address bar (the black navigation bar at the top of the web page) launches the Search for Page or Report feature.

The Search for Page or Report dialog box displays.

Refer to Figure 12-1.

2. **Enter a page or report name. (For this example, type** vendor.**)**

The search will include items that begin with the search text you enter.

With each letter you type into the search box, the list of page and report links below it changes to reflect the change in search criteria.

In the Name column, you see the name of the page or report.

In the Department column, you see the navigation path for that page or report (where it's located within the hierarchy of menus).

3. **Click the Lists button to filter the search results to show only list-related links — in other words, links to open lists of records.**

Besides filtering on the pages and reports that are related to lists, you have the choice to filter by Reports and Analysis, Archive, Administrative, Tasks, and more. The choices for filtering change to reflect the types of items that have shown up in the search results.

For example, if you were looking for a report, you would click Reports and Analysis to narrow the search results to display only links to reports.

4. **Click the Vendors link at the top of the search results.**

The Vendors List window appears. (Refer to Figure 12-2.)

Note the three small buttons located above the list to the right. You can use them to toggle the list between viewing the vendors as text or as tall icons (tall tiles) or wide icons (wide tiles). (These small buttons are identified earlier, in Figure 12-2.)

One tab (or ribbon, as it's sometimes called) is labeled *Navigation;* clicking the Navigation ribbon reveals navigation shortcuts related to the type of record you're viewing — in this case, vendors. (The ribbon is also referred to as a FastTab.)

The Magnifying Glass icon located to the far right above the list of vendors allows you to filter the list of vendors (vendor tiles) displayed; as you type in the search box, the vendors are instantly filtered by each letter as you key them in; filtering is based on vendor name. The asterisk (*) may be used as a wildcard character.

5. **Click any Vendor icon (tile) to open the Vendor Card (Maintenance Window) for that vendor.**

The vendor card displays.

Navigating by menu

Navigating by menu in Business Central is straightforward. You'll find a Navigation area near the top of the screen located directly under the black navigation (address) bar, with top-level menu choices for each module of the application as well as a self-service menu and a settings menu. (See Figure 12-3.) When you click a top-level menu choice, a second level of menu choices related to what you clicked appears immediately below in a row of choices. Clicking one of the second-level choices opens a screen, which is usually in List view.

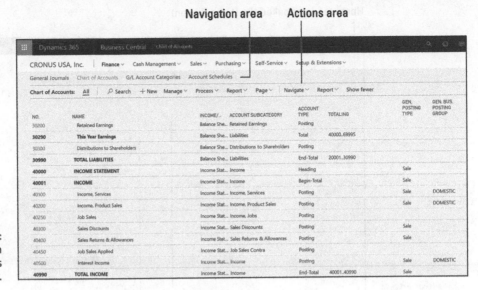

Navigation area   **Actions area**

FIGURE 12-3:
Menu navigation
in Business
Central.

For example, Figure 12-3 shows that if you choose Finance ⇨ Chart of Accounts from the module's main menu/navigation area, the chart of accounts is displayed in a list. When the list appears, you see a command bar in the Actions area with command buttons (a button you click that opens another window or performs a command) and pull-down menus (a button you click that causes yet another little menu to drop down from the button, giving you more selections). The buttons that have pull-down menus can be identified by the down arrow immediately to the right of the menu item name.

If you take another look at Figure 12-3, you can see that the + New Button has no down arrow to the right of it. Clicking the New button opens the G/L Account Card window. On the other hand, the Process button does have a down arrow to the right of it. When you click the Process button, no command is issued right away, but instead a pull-down menu appears, giving you more menu choices. When you click a menu choice on the pull-down menu, the command is issued. The commands on the command bar pertain to the list of records you're viewing, and specifically to a particular record or records you have selected in the list.

REMEMBER

For simplicity's sake, to describe navigation in this chapter, I use the following convention: The command arrow (⇨) is used between menu choices to indicate the sequence of menu items selected from top level to second level and so on.

For example, to add a new G/L Account card to Business Central, the navigation is shown here:

Finance ⇨ Chart of Accounts ⇨ New

The G/L Account Card window displays. (See Figure 12-4.)

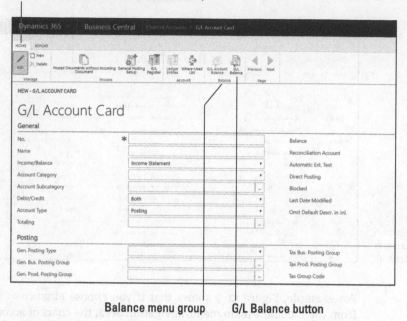

Home tab (also called the Home Ribbon)

FIGURE 12-4:
A G/L Account
Card in Business
Central.

Balance menu group   G/L Balance button

Notice that more menus appear at the top of the window; in fact, menu ribbons are located at the top of most windows. In this example, the Home tab and Report tab that you see along the top of the menu can be clicked to cause the menu ribbon to display another set of related buttons (menu choices). The buttons found on a ribbon are further organized into menu groups. Figure 12-4 shows what I mean. Note that the Balance menu group has two buttons: the G/L Account Balance button and the G/L Balance button. When you hover the mouse over any one of these buttons, a pop-up Help balloon appears, to describe what the button is meant to be used for.

Feeling at home in your Role Center

The home page when you sign in to Business Central is called a Role Center. The Role Center concept was introduced as part of a user-centric design philosophy embraced by the Microsoft design team as a core principle in moving Dynamics NAV to the cloud as a SaaS offering and rebranding it as Dynamics 365 Business Central.

A *user-centric* design means, among other things, that the menus, buttons, and information that are displayed when you sign in reflects what is important to you, not just a standard menu structure that everybody, regardless of their job title, has to live with. Rather than struggle to learn how to navigate a maze of menus, you're presented with only the menu items, quick-access command buttons, actions, and links that take you to the functions and features that matter most to you. Your Role Center page may appear different from those of other users, depending on your role in your organization. Your user profile in Business Central determines your Role Center home page. Default profiles can be specified for each user group. Every user who has the same profile starts out with the same Role Center.

A great feature is the ability to customize any Role Center to fit the specific needs of any individual user; this means that your home page can be completely unique, tailored to your precise preferences. The Business Central user interface can be customized by way of personalization and configuration. As a user, you can tailor your own home page (an example of customization through personalization); as a Business Central system administrator, you can set up and modify Role Centers (an example of customization through configuration).

The Role Center provides yet another important way to navigate throughout Business Central. In fact, if your Role Center is tailored just right, it pretty much takes care of all your navigation needs, because all the links you use daily are at your fingertips.

Role Centers may include many different types of elements, such as the ones described in this list:

>> **Standard (top-line) menus:** These menus, which are organized mainly by module or functional area, are directly under the address bar (the black navigation bar at the top).

>> **Actions:** Actions are, in essence, command buttons — a link you click that executes an action. Actions that normally appear in menu navigation ribbons (tabs) across the top of various windows can also be displayed on the Role Center. In other words, you can take menu items (actions) from anywhere in Business Central and have a shortcut link to that menu item on a Role Center page.

>> **Insights:** Insights are prebuilt queries that refresh every ten minutes; they find interesting facts within your organization's data and display them as headlines, similar to a news feed.

Your system administrator must install the Essential Business Insights Extension for Business Central before Insights can be displayed on your Role Center home page.

>> **Cues with drill-down:** Cues are tiles that show a number, such as the number of unposted (pending) sales invoices.

You can then click the tile to drill down into the details. For example, you can drill down to display a list of unposted sales invoices.

TIP

>> **Power BI visualizations:** Graphs and reports developed using Power BI (Microsoft's report writing tool).

Download and install Power BI Desktop if you want to create your own Power BI reports.

Business Central comes with the following prebuilt Role Centers, which you can use as is or tailored to your organization's precise requirements by your system administrator or Dynamics 365 solution provider:

>> Default

>> Business Manager

>> Accountant

>> Order Processor

>> Relationship Manager

>> Team Member

>> Project Manager

>> Administrator

REMEMBER

Personalizing your Role Center is as easy as clicking the Gear icon, which brings the screen into Edit mode. However, your system administrator may want to control the level of Role Center customization, so that person may limit access to the Designer feature. Creating a new Role Center or modifying an existing Role Center requires some fairly advanced technical knowledge. Please confer with your Dynamics 365 system administrator or authorized Dynamics 365 solution provider for more details.

TIP

The quickest way to navigate back to your Role Center home page is to click your company name in the upper left corner of the screen. Alternatively, you can click the Magnifying Glass icon on the address bar (the black navigation bar at the top of the web page), which launches the Search for Page or Report feature. Type **home** in the search box, and then click the Home link when it appears in the search results.

TIP

To navigate to a previous window in Business Central, you can use the Go Back arrow (the left-pointing arrow) as you would in any typical web application; browsing back is yet another way to navigate in Business Central.

Setting Up Business Central

As with any ERP system, the software works only as well as the way it's configured. Changing settings is essential to optimize performance.

The settings in Business Central are organized into these four major areas:

>> **Assisted Setup:** Here you find a handful of wizards (automated programs that lead you through a process step by step).

These wizards can help you with a variety of setup tasks, including converting data from commonly used ERP systems such as QuickBooks, making Business Central data available for reporting in Power BI, configuring email, and more.

>> **Manual Setup:** The Manual Setup area is the heart of the Business Central setup, where the majority of the configuration settings of Business Central are located.

These are the settings that you, as an ERP user of Business Central, will be primarily concerned with in setting up your accounting software to work the way you want.

>> **Service Connections:** Here you find connections to services of various kinds, such as the Microsoft Pay Merchant services (for credit card processing).

WARNING

Microsoft Pay Merchant is quite a technical area. Consult with your IT department and your authorized Dynamics 365 solution provider regarding these connections.

>> **Extensions:** Extensions used to be called third-party *add-on* or *bolt-on* products; *add-ons* are applications that provide extended functionality and work inside of or connected to the main Business Central application.

Some of these add-ons were designed specifically for Business Central; others are more generic and work with other applications as well, albeit in different versions of the same app.

Many extensions simply provide a bridge between Business Central and an existing, widely adopted Internet service such as PayPal.

REMEMBER

An ecosystem of third-party companies, often referred to as *independent software vendors (ISVs)* are always creating new add-ons for Dynamics 365 in general and for Business Central specifically; for example, Business Central has a sales commissions calculation app from a third-party company called NAV-X.

Microsoft itself publishes many of the add-on apps (extensions) for Business Central; for example, Microsoft Image Analyzer can be installed as an extension within Business Central. This extension uses Microsoft Cognitive Services to add the capability, among others, to analyze images of customer contacts and to assign attributes such as age and gender.

To search for additional extensions for Business Central, follow these steps:

1. Choose Setup & Extensions ➪ Extensions from the main menu.

Choosing Extensions displays the list of extensions that have been added to your Business Central system, as shown in Figure 12-5.

The list shown in Figure 12-5 is displayed as tall tiles, but you can toggle to Text List view or to Tiles (Smaller Tiles) view using the View Layout Option button (which resembles a computer monitor when set to Tall Tiles) located in the top right corner of the web page, immediately to the left of the two arrows. (The icon changes as you change the view option.)

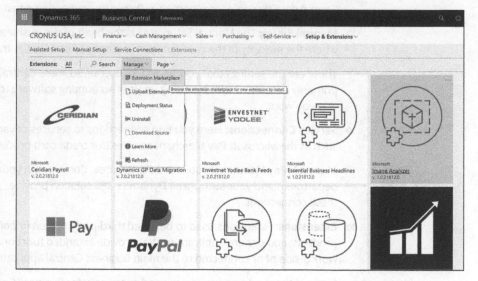

FIGURE 12-5:
Extensions and menu item for the Extension Marketplace in Business Central.

2. In the Actions area, click Manage.

A drop-down menu appears.

3. Select the menu's Extension Marketplace item.

Microsoft AppSource opens. The apps — displayed as long tiles — are filtered to display apps for Business Central.

AppSource is Microsoft's central portal for users to find cloud apps of all kinds that work with and enhance the Microsoft cloud offerings.

4. In the search box located on the far right side of the AppSource window, enter the word bank **as the search criteria.**

Alternatively, you may enter any search term you want.

The list of extensions is automatically filtered to show only apps that are named with the search term you entered.

The asterisk (*) can be used as a wildcard character.

5. **To install the extension, click Get It Now.**

Some extensions may have links other than Get It Now, such as Free Trial or Contact Me.

Alternatively, you can click the top part of the tile of the extension to open a web page that tells all about the extension you clicked. The web page usually has a Get It Now button; click < Apps to go back to the list of extensions.

After you click the Get It Now link, a dialog box appears. It guides you through the installation process; you may be prompted for additional information. Different apps may have different installation wizards to guide you through the installation.

WARNING

Configuring an ERP system requires an expert who is trained in (and very experienced with) ERP packages in general and in the software you're implementing specifically, and who is knowledgeable of general accounting principles and common business practices. I highly recommend that you work with an authorized Dynamics 365 partner (solution provider) when implementing Business Central for your organization.

Working with manual setup

To display the Business Central Manual Setup options and then open the Company Information Setup window, follow these steps:

1. **Choose Setup & Extensions ⇨ Manual Setup from the main menu.**

The list of manual setup options appears.

2. **Using the View Layout Option button, change the View Layout option to List view. (See Figure 12-6.)**

The View Layout Option button is located in the top right corner of the web page. Click this button to toggle the display to List view.

List view comes with four column headings: Name, Description, Area, and Keywords. The entire list can be sorted by column heading; for example, click Area and then select Ascending from the menu that appears. The list is sorted by area (module).

REMEMBER

To open any setup window, click the name of the setup option in the Name column. For example, Figure 12-6 shows where to click to open the Company Information page.

Click here.   View Layout Option icon

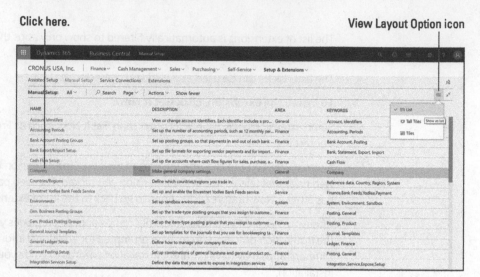

FIGURE 12-6:
Manual setup
options in
Business Central,
displayed in List
View layout.

3. **Click Company in the Name column.**

The Company Information page appears, as shown in Figure 12-7.

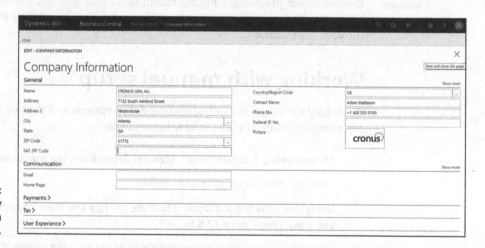

FIGURE 12-7:
Editing company
information in
Business Central.

4. **Edit any fields that require updating.**

For example, edit the email address, if necessary.

5. **Click the X in the top right corner of the web page.**

In Figure 12-7, near the X, notice that the bubble Help text (which appears if you hover the cursor over it) says "Save and close the page."

The Company Information page closes.

Your changes (if you made any) are saved and you return to the list of Manual Setup options.

Setting up number series (sequence numbers)

A *number series* is a sequential numbering scheme that is used as an ID number for a master data record (such as a customer or vendor) or a transaction record (such as an invoice or a journal entry). The number is always an integer. From the starting number to the ending number, the length remains constant because it contains leading zeros; for example, the number series for a draft invoice transaction might run from a starting number of 00001 to 99999. The lead zeroes are added by the system to retain a consistent length for the ID number. You're allowed to include an alphabetic prefix on a number series; for example, the number series for a sales invoice might be INV-0000001 to INV-9999999 or IN0001 to IN9999; dash characters are optional. As another example, for the vendor ID, you might use this series: V10000 to V80000. No rule applies to the starting and ending numbers other than that the starting number must be less than the ending number, for obvious reasons, and the number of digits should, ideally, be consistent.

This list describes the columns you see in the Number Series Setup window. Each column is important in helping define and organize your number series codes.

>> **Code:** The unique ID that identifies the number series. The code is a short alphabetical name you give to the number series to identify it. Each number series must have its own, unique code.

>> **Description:** A free-form text field that assists in identifying what this code does.

>> **Starting No.:** Defines the first number, or combination of numbers and letters, in the sequence.

>> **Ending No.:** Defines the last number, or combination of numbers and letters, in the sequence.

>> **Last Date Used:** Identifies the last time a number from this series was assigned.

>> **Last Number Used:** The last number used in the production system, which can help when creating new and related number series.

For example, you may be retiring one invoice number series and moving to another with a different code.

>> **Default Numbers:** Enables you to control whether the number series automatically assigns numbers to the entity (transaction type or master record type) it's assigned to.

>> **Manual Numbers:** A check box that gives you control of whether a user is allowed to manually assign numbers outside the number series when manually keying in a new transaction or a new master record.

This column can be useful for when you have special item types; for example, with inventory items that you normally want to auto-increment, but not 100 percent of the time. This would allow a user to assign a special inventory item ID during item creation that doesn't follow your standard sequential numbering convention.

>> **Date Order:** Enforces a requirement for the number series to sequence chronologically. (Be careful. It's tricky.) For example, an invoice posting on August 2 of a specific year and a number within a series of 0005 could not then be followed up by an invoice on June 15 of that same year with a sequence number of 0006, because June 15 would have occurred, chronologically, before August 2.

Enable the date order on a number series only if the organization is within a jurisdiction or industry that requires it by law. Otherwise, you may run into costly and time-consuming complications.

To set up a number series, start by seeing what numbers series are available. You do that that by choosing Setup & Extensions ⇨ Manual Setup ⇨ Number Series from the main menu in order to display a list of all number series codes contained within the system.

To specify the use of a number series for an entity, such as vendors, you must navigate to the setup screen where that specific setting is found. (For example, the number series for vendors is found in the Purchases & Payables setup screen.)

To assign a number series in the Purchasing & Payables setup, do the following:

1. **Choose Setup & Extensions ⇨ Manual Setup ⇨ Purchases & Payables Setup from the main men.**

   The Purchases & Payables Setup window displays, as shown in Figure 12-8.

2. **Select the number series you want to use for the vendor, invoices, posted invoices, credit memos, and posted credit memos.**

   Select these items by clicking the Ellipsis button (the three dots) next to the text box where you can enter a number series. Doing so displays a drop-down menu of all number series codes that have been set up in your instance of Business Central.

After you have selected the number series you want to use, you can close the window by clicking the X, or press the Esc key on the keyboard to close the Purchases & Payables Setup window.

Your changes are saved on exit.

Select the number series.

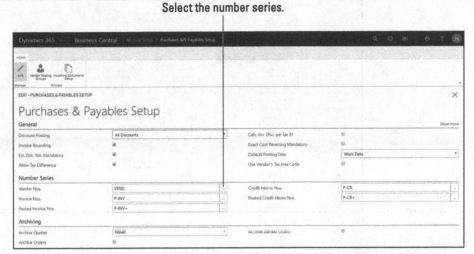

FIGURE 12-8:
The Purchases &
Payable Setup
window in
Business Central.

Defining number series relationships

The number series relationship is an important feature of Business Central. To help you understand what a number series relationship does, let's take a look at a practical example. All the invoices you create in your Business Central system are numbered with a sequence numbering convention that you define. Suppose, however, that you want to have separate sequence numbers for domestic invoices as opposed to international invoices.

To accomplish this task, you can create two number series codes, one called INV-D (domestic) and another called INV-I (international). You should ensure that you set up each number series in a way that makes them distinguishable by using a different prefix or a different number range or both. With that prep work done, you're ready to define the relationship between the two number series.

Follow these steps:

1. Highlight the first number series (in this case, INV-D) by selecting that row in the list of number series codes.

2. **Click to select the Home tab on the ribbon, and then click the Relationships button, as shown in Figure 12-9.**

The Edit No. Series Relationships window displays.

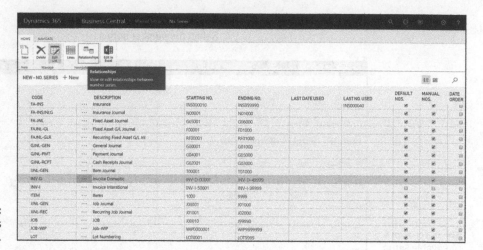

FIGURE 12-9:
Number Series
List overview.

3. **Click the New button to add a relationship.**

In this case, you would add the INV-I to the list so that the two number series codes become related. Then, when assigning a number sequence to invoices from its configuration screen, you can assign the INV-D number sequence. That way, whenever you create an invoice, you can select which number series you want to use (domestic or international). In this example, the number series relationship helps to differentiate the invoice history by a domestic and international classification for reporting and filtering purposes.

Managing users and permissions

Managing users in Microsoft Dynamics 365 Business Central is important, especially in today's world of ever-increasing sensitivity to privacy and security issues. Business Central provides a user-friendly and powerful way to control access to different functions within the application with just a few clicks.

Before you get started with the security concepts, you need to be aware of a few steps that must take place to get a user signed in to your instance of Business Central:

» **User creation in Office 365 Admin Center:** This is a required first step. You must contact your Office 365 administrator and have that person create users in the Office 365 Admin Center. After users are created, they're available for import into the Users section of Business Central.

» **User import using the Get Users command from Office 365 action:** This feature is available on the user administration screen that allows you to import users from your Office 365 instance.

Run the import by following these steps:

1. **Choose Setup & Extensions ⇨ Manual Setup ⇨ Users from the main menu.**

The Edit Users window appears, displaying a list of the Business Central users.

2. **Choose New ⇨ Get Users from Office 365 from XXX.**

Ensure that you have permissions to bring in users, and then wait for the import to take place.

After the users have been imported, you have the ability to edit the user's username, full name, state (enabled or disabled), and authentication email.

Permission sets (also referred to as *role IDs*) are a primary means of controlling security in Business Central. Permission sets allow you to configure specific access requirements for specific user types. At their core, these permission sets define which database objects and system resources the user has access to, which ultimately determines which windows they can gain access to. Business Central defines and controls access on a per-company basis, so if you're accounting for multiple companies with Business Central, the permissions a user has can vary from company to company.

Business Central comes preloaded with several well-defined permission sets, which you're free to make use of. You can use them as is, modify them, or define completely new permission sets.

TIP

There's no need to create or even modify a permission set; you can simply use the permission sets that come with the system. I recommended that you avoid modifying the built-in permission sets, because you might create an administrative headache by overcomplicating the security setup. If you find you need to set permissions in a more customized fashion, instead of modifying any of the built-in permission sets, create extra permission sets (where needed) that are clearly named in such a way as to differentiate them from the built-in permission sets.

To assign permission sets to users, follow these steps:

1. **Choose Setup & Extensions ⇨ Manual Setup ⇨ Users from the main menu.**

The Edit Users window appears, displaying a list of the Business Central users.

2. **Click to select the ribbon's Navigate tab.**

The command buttons (actions) change to reflect those associated with the Navigate tab.

As part of the Permissions menu group, you find the Permission Set by User button, as shown in Figure 12-10.

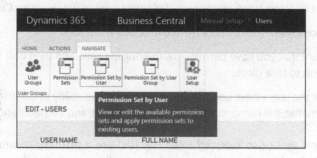

FIGURE 12-10:
Assigning
permission sets
by user in
Business Central.

3. **Click the Permission Set by User button.**

The Permission Set by User window appears.

The role IDs (permission sets) are listed in rows, and the users are listed in columns, creating a grid, or matrix, with check boxes. You simply select the check box in the appropriate cell to assign a role ID to a particular user or to all users.

Note the All Users column, for the convenience of assigning a role ID (permission set) to every user in the system with just one click.

4. **Click X to save and close the page.**

Doing so assigns the specified users their permissions sets.

Assigning the permission set called Super to a user gives that person complete and total access to every resource within Business Central. This is a root, or admin level, role. Make this assignment *only* to users who are allowed to see all data within the system and to make settings changes at the system administrator level.

REMEMBER

You can set permissions by user group as opposed to individual users, and there's a window to do that as well; the window is accessed from the User Groups button on the same Navigate tab. (User groups are associated with one or more permissions sets and are managed with the help of the User Group window, shown in Figure 12-11.)

FIGURE 12-11:
Permission sets for user groups in the Business Central user security setup.

In Figure 12-11, the D365 FINANCE user group is selected; on the right side of the web page, you see the list of permission sets (role IDs) associated with (assigned to) that user group; for example, D365 CASH FLOW is one of the permission sets assigned to the D365 FINANCE user group.

Well, here's how it works: You put the user in a user group, and the user group in turn is associated with one or more permission sets (role IDs), with each permission set giving access to various tables and other resources in the system. This approach is highly recommended for assigning security in an application, because, if a new employee comes aboard to replace someone who has left your organization, you only need to put that person in the proper user group and their security should be all taken care of.

Setting up inventory

The first thing you must do when defining how inventory works within Business Central is to configure your core inventory setup, which includes the actions described in the following list:

>> **Inventory Setup:** Define the default cost method and the number series for your inventory, among other settings. (See Figure 12-12, at the end of this list.)

>> **Inventory Units of Measure:** Units of measure are how you measure a quantity, such as by the hour or by the box.

>> **Inventory Periods:** Ensure that backdated transactions or cost adjustments involving inventory items don't affect balances during a given accounting period.

After you close a period, the value of inventory cannot be changed, nor can you post transactions in the closed period.

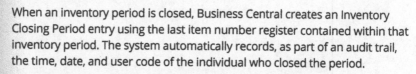

When an inventory period is closed, Business Central creates an Inventory Closing Period entry using the last item number register contained within that inventory period. The system automatically records, as part of an audit trail, the time, date, and user code of the individual who closed the period.

You can reopen an inventory period if you need to. This feature exists to help you avoid the accidental changing of inventory values in a backdated transaction.

>> **Inventory Posting Groups:** Inventory posting groups determine the mappings to general ledger accounts.

You can assign different inventory items to different inventory posting groups, to help ensure that the correct G/L accounts are used during inventory transaction posting.

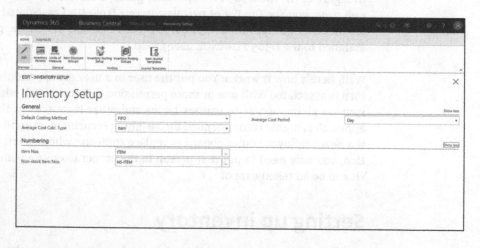

FIGURE 12-12:
Inventory Setup screen in Business Central.

To adjust manual setup for inventory in Business Central, follow these steps:

1. **Choose Setup & Extensions ➪ Manual Setup ➪ Inventory Setup from the main menu.**

The Inventory Setup window displays. (Refer to Figure 12-12.)

2. In the General section, select the default costing method.

Your choices here are FIFO, LIFO, Specific, Average, and Standard.

3. In the Numbering section, select the item number series assigned to inventory items (Item Nos.) and nonstock items.

4. To set up a new unit of measure, click the Units of Measure button on the Home tab at the top of the Inventory Setup window.

The list of Units of Measures appears.

5. Put the list in List view (if it isn't already), using the Show as List button on the right side of the screen (on top of the list).

The columns in this list are Code, Description, International standard (ISO) code, and SAT UofM classification.

Code is a required field, and I recommend that you include a description. The ISO and SAT (which pertains to the Mexican tax authority) are optional and provide a way to display the unit of measure on documents that require a standard spelling for unit of measure.

6. Click X to close the window and save your changes and go back to the Inventory Setup window.

7. To define an inventory period, click the Inventory Periods button on the Home tab at the top of the Inventory Setup window.

The list of inventory periods appears.

8. Select the check box in the Closed column to close the period.

9. Click X to close the window and save changes and go back to the Inventory Setup window.

10. To set up the inventory posting groups, click the Inventory Posting Groups button on the Home tab at the top of the Inventory Setup window.

11. Click New to add an inventory posting group.

12. Enter the code and description.

13. Create an inventory posting group for each group of inventory items that will have different G/L account mappings.

If all the inventory items map to the same G/L accounts, you may need only one inventory posting group.

14. Click X to close the window and save changes and go back to the Inventory Setup window.

15. To specify the inventory posting setup, click the Inventory Posting Setup button on the Home tab at the top of the Inventory Setup window.

16. For each inventory posting group, specify the main inventory G/L account, the interim inventory account, and the WIP (work in process) account, if required.

WIP accounts are typically only required for project accounting or manufacturing where the inventory or project is partially complete; this is often not required for a wholesale distribution business.

17. Click X to close the window and save changes and go back to the Inventory Setup window.

18. Click X again to close the Inventory Setup window.

19. Finally, to add inventory items, choose Sales ⇨ Items ⇨ New from the main menu.

A dialog box appears, prompting you to select a template for the inventory item you're creating. The template fills out default fields and helps ensure that items are configured correctly.

20. Select an item template.

The Item Card window appears

21. Fill out the fields as required by your organization's policies and procedures.

22. Click X to close the window and save changes and go back to the Inventory Item List window.

TIP

Context-sensitive help is available online within Business Central. Within any screen in Business Central, you can call up the Microsoft documentation for that screen by clicking within the screen and pressing Ctrl+F1 on the computer keyboard. Doing so launches a new web page showing the most recent official documentation about that section of the application from the official Microsoft online documentation. This is a convenient way to learn more about the new features of Dynamics 365 Business Central.

4

Finance and Operations ERP (formerly Dynamics AX)

Chapter **13**

Going Beyond Crunching Numbers with Financial Management

Dynamics 365 for Finance and Operations (D365O) is Dynamics AX (formerly Axapta) for the cloud. It's exciting to have Microsoft's most scalable, powerful, and full-featured ERP system, Dynamics AX, available as a true multi-tenant Software as a Service (SaaS) offering. The term *enterprise resource planning* (or *ERP*) is a fancy way of saying back-office finance, accounting, and operations software. Though Dynamics AX, now revamped and rebranded as Dynamics 365 for Finance and Operations, is the subject of this chapter, it would be a good idea (before tackling that task in earnest) to look at how D365O fits into Dynamics 365 as a whole.

Dynamics 365 is an umbrella of different applications and technologies that have been migrated to, or built especially for, the Microsoft Azure cloud, and can be licensed together by paying a monthly or annual per-user fee. You can think of Dynamics 365 as your CRM (front-office, as in customer relationship management) and ERP (back-office accounting) together with Office 365 (Outlook, Word,

Excel, and SharePoint), all living happily together in the Microsoft Azure cloud. Because the licensing is flexible, your organization could choose to use only the ERP or only the CRM or both. You can choose from two ERP sizes: Finance and Operations (AX) designed for larger organizations, and Business Central (NAV), designed for smaller organizations.

The different areas or branches of Dynamics 365 were created over many years by different teams of programmers. In other words, the software has slowly evolved — in many cases, over the course of decades. Some of these applications were acquired by Microsoft, and some were created in-house by Microsoft's own programmers. In many instances, the acquisition of a software development company by Microsoft includes retaining the programming talent. When that happens, the original developers are often the people who are still coding the recent releases, now sold under the Microsoft brand.

The Dynamics 365 tree has these four main branches:

>> **AX:** Dynamics AX has been rebranded as Dynamics 365 for Finance and Operations (D365O). Finance and Operations is a highly scalable mid-market enterprise ERP system with global capabilities, such as *localizations* (adapting the software to specific locale) and robust multicurrency features. AX includes modules for project accounting, manufacturing, warehouse management, advanced supply chain, and much more.

AX goes all the way back to 1986, when two Danish brothers, Preben and Erik Damgaard, released an accounting software called Concord Finance. At one point they were partnered with IBM. Eventually Concord became Axapta, which was later acquired by Navision, another software developer from Denmark. Navision was acquired by Microsoft in the year 2002, and that's how Microsoft ended up with Axapta, which it rebranded as Dynamics AX.

Microsoft has reprogrammed and enhanced the original Axapta almost beyond recognition. Today's Finance and Operations is largely the work of Microsoft's rather colossal army of programmers.

Talent is a human resources (HR) application that is part of the AX family of applications.

Retail is a point-of-sale (POS) application that also emerged from the AX development area.

>> **CRM:** Microsoft CRM Online has been rebranded as Dynamics 365 for Customer Engagement.

The Dynamics 365 for Customer Engagement applications (or you can think of them as modules) include Sales (sales force automation), Service (customer service), Marketing (marketing automation), Voice of the Customer

(customer survey automation), Project Services (professional services automation), Field Services (technician management in the field), and Schedule Board (dispatch).

Microsoft built CRM in-house from the ground up. The exception is the Field Services application, which was originally an add-on for CRM developed by a company called FieldOne Systems, LLC. Microsoft later acquired FieldOne and rebranded its software as Dynamics 365 for Field Services.

>> **NAV:** Dynamics NAV (formerly Navision) was originally rebranded Finance and Operations Business Edition, which caused confusion because the name was too similar to the rebranded name for Dynamics AX. As a consequence, NAV has been more recently rebranded again, this time as Dynamics 365 Business Central. The name Business Central differentiates NAV from AX.

Business Central is Microsoft's cloud ERP offering for the small to midsize business market (the SMB market).

Business Central is much easier to set up, configure, and implement than Finance and Operations, but it has far less capabilities and depth of features. Though Business Central is more robust than entry-level ERP packages such as QuickBooks, it does have its limitations. If you're trying to decide between the two Dynamics 365 ERP offerings, Finance and Operations is the clear choice if your organization is a large enterprise with many users, international requirements, and highly complex business processes. (For more on Business Central, see Chapters 11 and 12.)

TIP

Normally, you would choose either Business Central (NAV) or Finance and Operations (AX) as your ERP system, not both; though you could use both if your organization has different subsidiaries that are of different sizes. Potentially, each subsidiary could run a different ERP system, though generally speaking, it's more convenient for all your subsidiaries to run the same ERP system.

>> **Microsoft Cloud Technologies:** Dynamics 365 runs in Azure — the Microsoft cloud. Microsoft is the *cloud provider:* When you sign in to a Dynamics 365 application, you're signing in to (logging in to) a Microsoft data center. Microsoft is handling the hardware, operating system, network security, user access, data permissions, SQL database, application instances (development, testing, and production environments), backups, and failover, for example.

In addition, Dynamics 365 is tightly integrated with Office 365 (most notably, Outlook, Word, Excel, and SharePoint). The Office 365 tie-in is a major advantage of Dynamics 365.

Lastly, many other key Microsoft cloud technologies are available that greatly enhance the power of Dynamics 365; these include Power BI (for business intelligence reporting and analytics), PowerApps (for building custom apps to extend capabilities and connect to other cloud services such as PayPal,

Dropbox, and DocuSign), Microsoft Flow (for creating custom workflows), Microsoft Common Data Service for Apps (which can be thought of as a prebuilt data warehouse that provides a consistent approach for defining standard data entities), and the Unified Interface for Apps (a way to ensure a consistent look and feel across different Dynamics 365 applications).

Getting a Bird's-Eye View of D365O Capabilities

Dynamics 365 for Finance and Operations (D365O) has dozens of modules, and each one is packed with tons of features. The module list is comprehensive, to say the least. I have organized the list of modules into the following logical areas to give you a feel for what's available:

Financial modules

>> General ledger

>> Budgeting

>> Cash and bank management

>> Fixed assets

>> Accounts payable

>> Accounts receivable

>> Credit and collections

>> Tax

Supply chain modules

>> Procurement and sourcing (purchase orders)

>> Sales and marketing (sales orders and billing)

>> Inventory management

>> Transportation management

>> Warehouse management

Manufacturing modules

» Cost accounting

» Cost management

» Master planning

» Product information management

» Production control

HR modules

» Human resources (HR)

» Organization administration

Miscellaneous modules

» Project management and accounting (professional services automation)

» Service management (field services)

» Time and attendance (time & billing)

» Expense management (employee expenses)

» Retail (point of sale)

System module

» Questionnaire (surveys)

Raising the Flag on Microsoft's Flagship ERP

With Dynamics 365 for Finance and Operations (D365O), Microsoft has created its flagship ERP system, a system meant to compete with the likes of the big boys: SAP and Oracle. D365O can scale to any organization size. D365O can also handle any kind of business, whether it's professional services, government sector, not-for-profit, retail, wholesale distribution, or even manufacturing. It's great to know that D365O has all the modules to handle any kind of organization; however, being a jack-of-all-trades has a downside: The system does everything, but is it done at the level demanded by large enterprise clients in a particular industry niche? For example, though you might run a dairy farm or a brewery using D365O, most large dairy farms and large breweries use industry-specific ERP systems that have advanced features specific to those particular industries. As another example, D365O has manufacturing features, but a huge difference exists between making airplanes (an example of discrete manufacturing) and making toothpaste (an example of process manufacturing). Though many manufacturing systems are designed for a specific type of manufacturing, D365O manufacturing is more generic than that.

The ERP requirements of large, complex organizations in technical industrial sectors are much more exacting than the requirements of a small business or even midsize business in the service industry, such as a start-up investment company. Think of the difference between what you would need in order to run a small ad agency in Manhattan, compared to what you would need to run a global shipping conglomerate that builds ocean liners with locations in 42 countries. A Swiss army knife like D365O can do many things, yet it doesn't have the industry-specific features that are essential to many larger companies.

Microsoft is counting on the fact that independent software vendors (ISVs) will use D365O as a generic base package — a development platform, so to speak — to create industry-specific customizations. This has already been happening with Dynamics AX, and the ISV ecosystem is continuing to grow with D365O. D365O has all the basics of accounting software, such as general ledger, accounts payable, and customers. Building an industry-specific ERP completely from scratch doesn't make much sense these days; you would be reinventing the wheel in creating all the basic debit and credit stuff, which would be a huge waste of time. It makes a lot of sense to use D365O as a base to create industry-specific ERP systems or, alternatively, to use D365O to create a completely unique ERP for your own organization.

REMEMBER

The benefits of using D365O are enormous. Microsoft is in the unique position of being one of three major cloud providers, the number-one office automation provider with Word, Excel, Outlook, and SharePoint, and in the top three of SQL database vendors, not to mention the operating systems, the reporting tools, the programming languages, and on and on. So much of the software that most businesses rely on every day comes from Microsoft, so it makes a lot of sense if you can build your ERP on the Microsoft technology stack, because your ERP is the backbone of your organization, and Microsoft is the backbone of the IT infrastructure in most organizations.

D365O is a huge application with many modules, features, and capabilities —
similar to SAP R3 and Oracle E-Business Suite (EBS), but not quite as immense as
those two well-entrenched, top-tier systems that have captured much of the Fortune 500 market. The problem with SAP R3 or Oracle EBS and big ERP systems like
them is that although they may be quite powerful because they have numerous
features, they're so complicated that they may require an army of consultants to
set up — and they often take forever and a day to get up and running. On the con-
trary, Microsoft, with Dynamics 365 for Finance and Operations, has built a truly
robust ERP with a deep feature set while managing to create an application that
can be implemented relatively quickly. Okay, not as quickly as QuickBooks, but
you may be surprised by just how little setup is required to get the D365O system
up and running, because the default settings are so ingeniously devised.

REMEMBER

The ever shifting landscape of ERP is complex, to say the least. Both Oracle and
SAP have also come up with cloud strategies. In addition, literally hundreds of
other major players are in the game, such as Infor, Workday, UNIT4, Sage, Epicor,
and Deltek. Everybody claims to have simple-to-use-but-immensely-powerful
software. The truth is, of course, that you need to hire experts to help you decide
which system is the right fit for your organization, and you need experts with
experience and a good track record to design the solution and conduct the implementation. Also, you need to actively partner with the implementation team, not
simply sit back and wait for them to do it all. The users and management need to
participate in the design, training, and testing. Implementing ERP is a team effort
all the way around.

It's impossible to predict with any precision which ERP systems will prevail and
which will fall flat. It's safe to say that no single system will gain all the market
share. It's also safe to say that Microsoft has, in Dynamics 365 for Finance and
Operations, a winning product with a solid installed base that will continue to
capture a large chunk of the market, and that Microsoft is clearly committed to
providing world-class ERP solutions now and for the indefinite future.

WARNING

It's beyond the scope of this book to provide a comprehensive setup guide for any
of the more than a dozen modules of D365O. In this chapter, I provide a high-level
overview of the application, a bit of the history behind how it came to be, a practical guide for successful navigation, as well as a discussion of the general ledger
chart of accounts design features. Dynamics 365 for Finance and Operations is a
full-blown, heavy-duty, top-tier ERP system on the level of the SAP R3 and Oracle
EBS, so of course I am merely scratching the surface of all the powerful features
and myriad options you have in working with D365O. Implementing D365O
requires a careful study of the official Microsoft documentation and the assistance
of a trained team of certified Dynamics 365 ERP functional and technical
specialists.

Learning How to Get Around in D365O

Navigation is a breeze in D365O. You have many ways to navigate the system and find the exact screen you're looking for. When you sign in to D365O, you're greeted by the home page, as shown in Figure 13-1. Your home page in D365O is called your *dashboard*, which you can configure and tailor to your personal needs. The dashboard contains *tiles*, which can point to what is called a workspace. (A *workspace* is basically just another type of dashboard area, but one that's specific to a role or functional area.) In the workspace are more tiles, reports, graphs, and other links to give you instant information and help guide you to where you need to go.

Click here to extend the navigation pane.

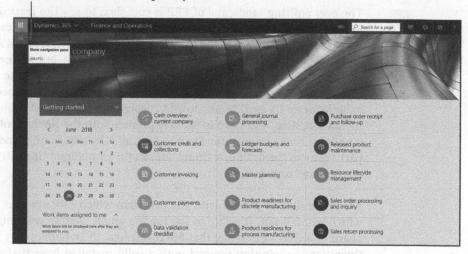

FIGURE 13-1:
The dashboard (home page), showing where to click to expand the navigation pane.

TIP

You can extend a navigation pane outward from the left side of the screen by pressing Alt+F1 on the keyboard or by clicking the button with three horizontal lines on it. You'll find it on the left side of the web page, toward the top of the page. (Again, see Figure 13-1 to see exactly where to click to extend the navigation pane.)

Figure 13-2 shows the navigation page fully extended. In Figure 13-2, the module section is expanded, and the Favorites, Recent, and Workspaces sections are collapsed. To extend a section, click the small Triangle icon to the left of the name of the section.

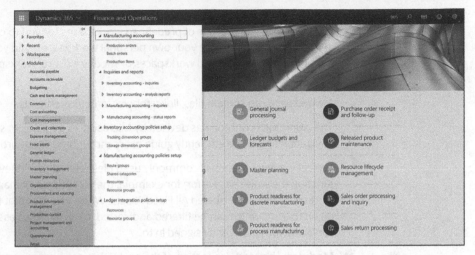

FIGURE 13-2:
Navigation
methods in
Dynamics 365 for
Finance and
Operations
(D365O).

As shown in Figure 13-2, D365O has these five major navigation sections:

>> **Favorites:** Favorites are the items you use most often, so they're listed at the top of the navigation menu.

When you start out, your default dashboard (home page) has no favorites on it.

You can add workspace menu items to your Favorites menu easily; to do so, click the small Star icon in the right corner of any Workspace menu item listed on the navigation pane in the Workspaces section.

TIP

To see the Workspace menu items, you may need to extend the Workspaces section by clicking the small Triangle icon to the left of the word *Workspaces*.

When you click the Star icon, the star becomes filled in to indicate that the workspace is now a favorite, and simultaneously a menu item for that workspace is added to your Favorites menu. Menu items appearing on the Recent menu area can be added as favorites in the same manner.

>> **Recent:** As you navigate the system and work with various screens, these locations are automatically added to the Recent menu by the system.

As with favorites, this menu area is personal; you see only the menu items for the screens that you yourself have visited, not the recent navigation of other users logged in to the system.

>> **Workspaces:** Workspaces are similar to dashboards; workspaces are like home pages that are focused on a particular role or function.

When you click a Workspace menu item on the navigation menu, your dashboard changes from your default dashboard (home page) to the Workspace dashboard.

D365O comes with dozens of predefined workspaces for you to choose from; in addition, you can create your own personal workspaces, and your system administrator can also add workspaces or modify existing workspaces for any user to take advantage of.

A workspace can contain tiles, links, reports, and filtered grids.

The workspace concept was devised by Microsoft as a means to speed up navigation and more efficiently guide users through business processes.

Typically, a workspace has commonly used tiles related to whatever role or function the workspace is for; for example, the Fixed Asset Management workspace has a tile labeled All Fixed Assets. When you click that tile, you're taken to a list, which can be filtered and sorted, of all the fixed assets in the company you're currently signed in to.

>> **Modules:** The Modules section of the navigation pane represents a more traditional, old-fashioned hierarchical menu system (the ones I like the best).

Fortunately, when Microsoft added the fancy new navigation features, such as tiles and dashboards, it kept the old-fashioned, straightforward menu navigation as well, so it's a best-of-both-worlds scenario.

As you can see in Figure 13-2, the Module menu item for cost management is selected. Selecting that menu item open the menu for that module immediately to the right of the navigation menu.

As you click modules on the navigation menu, the corresponding module menu appears to the right of the navigation menu; this is a convenient way to view the features contained in the module.

>> **Search for Page (navigation search):** Clicking the Magnifying Glass icon on the top of the web page, toward the right side on the black navigation bar, opens a Search text box.

Entering search criteria in the Search text box immediately causes a drop-down menu to appear beneath the Search text box. The search criteria apply to menu item names as well as to the menu path. (Figure 13-3 shows what happens if you enter the search criteria *bank* into the Search text box.)

This search feature looks for menu items, not for individual records — you can find the Customer screen, for example, but not a particular customer. (To search for a particular customer, you'd use the Customer screen itself.)

This navigation search feature gives you a quick way to find any menu in the system without having to fish for it in a maze of nested menus. Nice!

FIGURE 13-3:
An example of
the Search for a
Page feature in
D365O.

To quickly navigate back to your home page (your default dashboard), simply click the words *Finance and Operations* on the black navigation bar at the top of the web page or, alternatively, press Alt+Shift+Home on your computer keyboard.

Navigating with tiles

Tiles, which are an important navigation feature of D365O, are menu items that appear on the screen as squares or rectangles that you can click; they're sort of like oversized command buttons. Clicking a tile usually takes you to another screen. (The concept of tiles was introduced with the Windows 8 operating system.)

There are four types of tiles:

>> **Standard:** Standard tiles have a title (label) but show no additional information.

>> **Count:** Count tiles display a number that's updated by a query that refreshes periodically.

   For example, a count tile in the *Manage Customer Credit and Collections* workspace, called Sales Orders on Hold, shows the number of sales orders in the system that are in a Hold status. When you click the tile, you're taken to a list of those sales orders that are on hold.

>> **KPI:** *Key performance indicators* are metrics that you use to evaluate the status of important aspects of your operations.

For example, a key performance indicator for many companies is the number of orders shipped today or the total currency value of today's shipments or this week's sales, for example.

The KPI tile shows a summary or grand total for the metric it is tracking; for example, the total sales today KPI might read $25,000.

When you click a KPI tile, you're taken to an expanded view of the KPI report.

>> **Link:** Link tiles have a title (label) but, as with standard tiles, they don't convey any information; however, unlike standard tiles, link tiles map to a URL (website address).

When you click a link tile, your web browser launches a new web page, taking you to the URL specified by the tile; these links can take you to an external website outside of Dynamics 365 proper.

Setting user preferences

User options allow you to tailor your D365O experience to suit yourself. User options range from the "nice to have" variety such as color themes to the more crucial settings of language and time zone found under the User Preferences tab.

To set your user preferences in D365O, follow these steps:

1. **Click the Gear icon on the navigation bar at the top of the web page. It's on the right side of the page. (See Figure 13-4.)**

   A drop-down menu appears with the following choices: User Options, Task Recorder, and About.

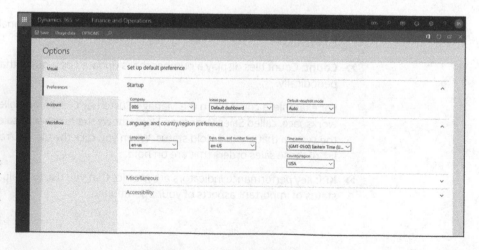

FIGURE 13-4:
Setting user preferences in Dynamics 365 for Finance and Operations.

2. Select User Options from the drop-down menu.

The Options window appears.

The navigation tab defaults to Visual; here, you can change the color scheme of the application.

3. Click the Preferences tab on the left side of the web page, under the word *Visual*.

The Setup Default Preference page appears.

4. In the Startup section, select the company that you want as your default company when you sign in from the Company drop-down list.

If your organization has multiple legal entities that are being accounted for in D365O, you can specify here which of these will be the default company that you're logged in to when you sign in to the system.

5. In the Startup section, choose the initial page you want from the Initial Page drop-down list.

Here's where you specify which dashboard appears when you initially sign in to the system; your initial dashboard acts as your home page in D365O.

6. In the Startup section, make a selection from the Default View/Edit Mode drop-down list.

Select View if you want pages to open records in Read-Only (unable to be edited) mode. Normally, you would set this to Auto, in which case the system determines whether the page is locked or editable.

7. In the Language and Country/Region section, select your preferred language from the Language drop-down list.

Language preference can be set at the individual user level, which is great because you can have two different users in the same company but have the screens displaying labels in different languages, to accommodate users' language abilities and preferences.

For example, after setting the language preference to Spanish, when I logged back in to the system the screens were automatically translated into Spanish. (Figure 13-5 shows the D365O dashboard in Spanish.)

8. In the Language and Country/Region section, select your preferred options from the Date, Time, and Number Format drop-down list.

9. In the Language and Country/Region section, select your local time zone from the Time drop-down list.

REMEMBER

Be sure to set your time zone so that you view scheduling information accurately; the system displays universal times stored in the database in your local time zone.

FIGURE 13-5:
The dashboard,
showing the
effect of setting
the language
preference to
Spanish.

10. In the Language and Country/Region section, make a selection from the Country/Region drop-down list.

11. Click the Save button.

The Save button is located in the top left corner of the web page.

Your preferences have been saved.

Harnessing the Power of Financial Dimensions

Dynamics 365 for Finance and Operations (D365O) is an ERP system, which means that it was designed (as its name suggests) to carry out enterprise resource planning, or ERP. ERP software used to be called accounting software, but those days are long past. The term *ERP* was coined because, as accounting software evolved over the years, most accounting software packages started to do more than simply act as a set of accounting ledgers. Nonetheless, the heart of any ERP system is still the general ledger. One of the best aspects of D365O is how well designed the general ledger is. The *accounting ledger* is where the debits and credits of the double-entry accounting system are recorded. The accounting ledger is what is called, in common parlance, "the books," or "the set of books," of the company.

Best practices dictate that each company that is a separate legal entity for tax reporting purposes should have its own separate set of books — its own separate general ledger. (In practical terms, that means you should never mix up the books of separate legal entities.) In D365O terminology, a legal entity is a company. Each legal entity also has a ledger for what is owed to vendors (the accounts payable subledger) and what is expected from customers (the accounts receivable subledger). The subledgers tie to the general ledger. The ledger is the source for the official financial statements (balance sheet and income statement) that are presented to tax authorities, investors, shareholders, and banks. The general ledger is therefore of utmost importance to any ERP system because all financial transactions that affect the company must flow into the general ledger. The general ledger tells you how profitable the company is, and this in turn has an effect on taxes owed, bonuses paid, dividends for shareholders, stock prices, and other such important matters.

The general ledger is a list of transactions recorded as lines of debits and credits called *journal entries*. Each journal entry in the general ledger consists of two or more lines that must balance perfectly before they can be *posted* (officially recorded to) the ledger. In other words, the sum total of debits for the journal entry must exactly equal the sum total of credits for the journal entry. Each journal entry always has a posting date and that date falls within an official accounting period (usually, a month). Each line of a journal entry is either a debit or a credit, and each line must hit one, and only one, account from the chart of accounts. The account is usually a 4-digit number that follows a commonly used convention for account numbering.

REMEMBER

The *chart of accounts* is simply the list of accounts. Accounts are either balance sheet accounts (permanent accounts that have a perpetual running balance) or profit-and-loss (P&L) accounts (temporary accounts that are cleared to retained earnings and thus zeroed out during the calculation of income or loss for the year) or unit accounts (non-financial accounts such as head count and square footage typically used in the calculation of allocation percentages).

Here are some examples of typical balance sheet account numbers from a chart of accounts:

>> 1000 Cash

>> 1200 Accounts Receivable

>> 2000 Accounts Payable

>> 3000 Retained Earnings

And here are some examples of typical P&L account numbers from a chart of accounts:

>> 4000 Sales Revenue

>> 5000 Cost of Goods Sold

>> 6010 Travel Expense

>> 6020 Rent Expense

>> 9000 Tax Expense

In the preceding example, the Sales Revenue account is 4000. The 4-digit number, 4000, is the *natural* account, or *main* account. In a typical accounting system, segments are used to denote important attributes for more granular reporting. For example, you may have a segment for division and a segment for region.

Here are some typical examples of divisional segments for a vehicle dealer:

>> 10 cars

>> 20 trucks

>> 30 motorcycles

And here are some examples of a regional segments for a vehicle dealer:

>> 1 north

>> 2 south

>> 2 east

>> 3 west

Here's a typical example of a journal entry to record the sale of trucks in the southern region:

>> **1200** Accounts Receivable $25,000 DEBIT

>> **4000-20-2** Sales Revenue – Trucks – East $25,000 CREDIT

Notice in the preceding example that the sales revenue account is *segmented* — there are financial dimensions that further describe the account. By contrast, the accounts receivable account isn't segmented — this company doesn't split out its receivable ledger by division or region or any other dimension. Its executives are comfortable with having one big communal accounts receivable balance on the company's books. It's common practice among many accountants to slice and dice certain main (natural) accounts by certain dimensions whereas other accounts may be split out in different ways. A good ERP system should have the flexibility to let its accountants define which accounts need to be split out with segments and which do not.

A flexible financial system should allow you to

>> Define your natural (main) accounts separately from your segments (not as a combined string).

>> Add segments (dimensions) that are custom entities of your own devising.

>> Define the valid choices for each custom segment (so that the user can choose a valid value from a drop-down list) or allow the user to enter any free-form text.

>> Add segments (dimensions) that are based on entities that exist in the system (such as a customer, vendor, project, or asset), and specify whether these will default from the transaction (such as, for example, the customer ID defaulting from a sales invoice header) and whether the user can override the default or whether it's fixed (not editable).

>> Create account rules that specify which segments (dimensions) are applicable to a natural (main) account; which are required; and which are optional as far as the user having to fill in that segment on a journal entry. These rules should also specify the order in which the segments are arranged. In the preceding example, the division segment comes before the region segment, and the sales account requires both a division and a region, whereas the accounts receivable account requires no segments.

That's pretty much all you need to know about how a flexible ERP system should work with regard to chart of account numbers and segmenting these accounts with custom and built-in dimensions. It's time to take a look at how D365O provides these all-important flexible features.

The key elements of the general ledger chart of accounts setup in D365O are described in this list:

>> **Main account:** The main account is the natural account number. (Account number 1000 might have a description of Cash-Checking-JPMorgan, for example.) The main account has an account number and an account description, among other fields.

>> **Main account categories:** Each main account should be categorized for ease of financial report creation. Typical account categories are cash, accounts receivable, loans receivable, furniture and fixtures, accounts payable, loans payable, retained earnings, operating expenses, and non-operating expenses. In D365O, you can define your own account categories.

Normally, several accounts fall into each category. In other words, there should be fewer main account categories than there are main accounts.

>> **Financial dimensions:** These are the additional attributes (sometimes described as additional account segments) that further qualify the account for reporting and analysis purposes.

The financial dimensions can be either entity-backed or custom.

Entity-backed dimensions are based on a system-defined entity such as project, inventory item, customer, or vendor. You're able to specify a different name for the dimension other than the system-defined name for that entity.

Custom dimensions are ones that you define yourself; you then specify the valid choices available to users. These are called the *dimension values.* Dimension values can be made active or inactive by using date ranges (effective dating).

>> **Account structures:** Account structures are, in effect, your account rules. They define which dimensions are to be applied to the main account, in which order they are to appear, whether they're required or optional, whether they are fixed or can be overridden, whether they will default with a value, and so forth.

As many as ten dimensions can be applied to an account in an account structure (which should be more than enough in most cases). You can also apply an account structure to more than one main account — in fact, that should be the case because you don't want to have a different account structure for every main account.

In a typical (simple and basic) scenario, you might have an account structure for balance sheet accounts, one for revenue accounts, and one for expense accounts; of course, you can get much more complex than that, if you need to.

REMEMBER

Different companies can use different account structures. This is handy in cases where a company is located in a foreign country and that country has financial reporting requirements that are different from your domestic companies.

To navigate to these key elements in D365O, follow these steps:

1. **Refer to Figure 13-1 to see where to click to expand the navigation pane (the button with three horizontal lines), or press Alt+F1 on the computer keyboard.**

   The navigation pane expands out from the left side of the web page.

2. **Choose Modules ➪ General Ledger ➪ Chart of Accounts ➪ Accounts ➪ Main Accounts from the navigation pane, as shown in Figure 13-6.**

   The Main Accounts window appears.

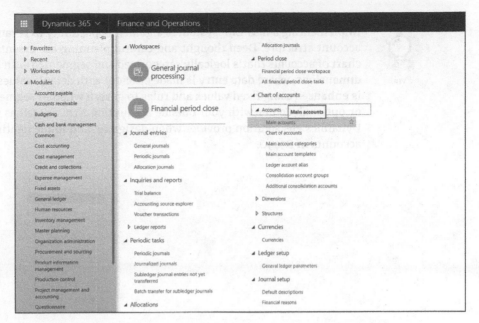

FIGURE 13-6:
Walking through
the steps of
adding a main
account in
D365O.

3. Complete the required information based on your organization's policies and procedures.

4. Modules ⇨ General Ledger ⇨ Chart of Accounts ⇨ Accounts ⇨ Main Account Categories from the navigation pane.

The Main Account Categories window appears.

5. Click New to add an account category.

6. Complete the required information based on your organization's policies and procedures.

7. Choose Modules ⇨ General Ledger ⇨ Chart of Accounts ⇨ Dimensions ⇨ Financial Dimensions from the navigation pane.

The Financial Dimensions window appears.

8. Click New to add a financial dimension.

9. Complete the required information based on your organization's policies and procedures.

10. Choose Modules ⇨ General Ledger ⇨ Structures ⇨ Configure Account Structures from the navigation pane.

The Account Structures window appears.

Complete the required information based on your design for your chart of accounts.

TIP

Implementing a new ERP system is a golden opportunity to revamp your chart of account structure. Deep thought and careful planning are essential to creating a chart of accounts that's logically categorized and segmented with useful reporting dimensions, where data entry is made efficient with default values, and validation is enhanced using fixed values and rules to govern whether segments are required or optional. Confer with your outside accounting firm as well as your authorized Dynamics 365 solution provider when designing and implementing your chart of accounts in D365O.

IN THIS CHAPTER

» Taking a look at capabilities by module in Dynamics 365 for Finance and Operations

» Surveying the master records maintenance screens for vendor, customer, and product

» Viewing keyboard shortcuts and switching between companies for faster navigation

» Sorting list pages, exporting rows to Excel, and applying filters with multiple fields

Chapter 14

Becoming a Smooth Operator with Operations

Dynamics 365 for Finance and Operations (D365O) is Microsoft's most full-featured enterprise resource planning (ERP) system. D365O has more modules than any other Microsoft ERP package, and each module has more features. Though the prowess of D365O is especially evident in the areas of global capabilities, warehouse management, manufacturing, inventory control, and product information management, it extends through pretty much every aspect of the software.

Microsoft's other ERP packages are Dynamics NAV (formerly, Navision, now Dynamics 365 Business Central), Dynamics SL (formerly Solomon), and Dynamics GP (formerly Great Plains). Dynamics SL and Dynamics GP aren't being made available as Software as a Service (SaaS) offerings in the Azure cloud environment, so they aren't part of Dynamics 365. Therefore, Dynamics 365 offers a choice of two ERP systems: Business Central for the small to midsize business ERP market, and D365O for the larger, mid-market enterprise ERP market. A broad overview of the D365O feature set is the main subject of this chapter.

Changing Companies

D365O was built to handle large organizations with multiple subsidiaries, many of which may be operating in foreign countries. D365O has features for sharing master records; for example, common reference tables such as the payment terms can be replicated across companies using the Cross-company Data Sharing feature. When working with D365O, it is common to navigate frequently between separate legal entities (companies). Switching between companies is easy and doesn't require you to sign in to the system again.

To switch the current company you're signed in to in D365O, follow these steps:

1. **Click the company code (number) displayed in the top right corner of the main navigation bar.**

Figure 14-1 shows where to click.

A drop-down list appears, which displays the companies in your instance of D365O.

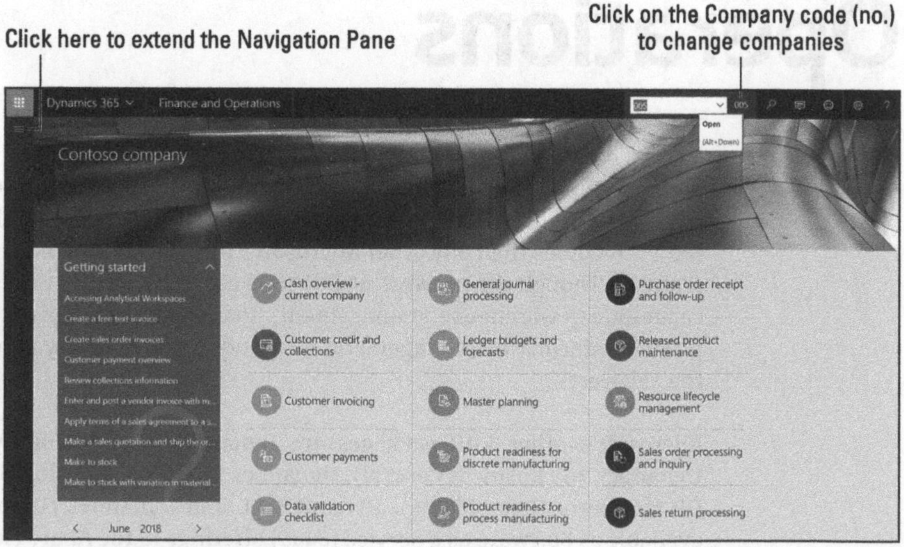

Click here to extend the Navigation Pane

Click on the Company code (no.) to change companies

FIGURE 14-1: Where to click to extend the navigation pane and to switch companies.

2. **Select the company you want to switch to from the drop-down list.**

The web page refreshes, taking you to the screen for the company you selected.

The company code of the selected company now appears on the top main navigation bar, showing you the current company; also, the company name shown in the top left corner of the web page refreshes to display the current company.

Navigating by Module

Figure 14-1 also shows you where to click to extend the navigation pane in D365O; the navigation pane has menus that can take you anywhere in the application.

To extend the navigation pane in D365O and access the Modules menu, follow these steps:

1. **Click the Black Square icon with three white horizontal lines in the top left corner of the web page.**

Refer to Figure 14-1 to see where to click.

The navigation pane extends out from the left side of the web page.

2. **Choose Modules in the navigation pane.**

The list of modules is displayed below, as shown in Figure 14-2.

FIGURE 14-2: Modules menu in Dynamics 365 for Finance and Operations.

3. **Click any module, such as Budgeting, Fixed Assets, or Inventory Management.**

The full module menu structure for that module extends immediately to the right of the navigation pane.

You're then able to navigate anywhere in the module by selecting the appropriate menu items from that module's menu choices.

The module's menu includes setup screens pertaining to that module, in addition to screens for master record maintenance, reports, inquiries, and entering and posting transactions.

REMEMBER

For ease of describing menu navigation in this chapter, in many cases I use the command arrow (⇨) between menu items as a quick and convenient notation.

For example, to describe how to navigate to the Item Charge Groups window, I could describe each click this way:

1. **Click the Black Square icon with three white horizontal lines in the top left corner of the web page to extend the navigation pane.**

2. **Choose Modules from the (extended) navigation pane.**

3. **Choose Inventory Management from the submenu that appears.**

4. **Choose Setup from the next submenu.**

5. **Choose Charges from the next submenu.**

6. **Choose Item Charge Groups from the final submenu, as shown in Figure 14-3.**

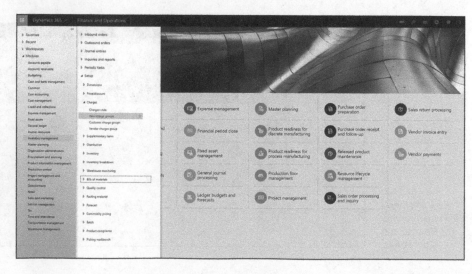

FIGURE 14-3:
Example of menu navigation notation from the Modules menu in D365O.

Alternatively, rather than list all those separate steps, I can simply write, from the Modules menu, "choose Inventory Management⇨Setup⇨Charges⇨Item Charge Groups."

Taking Advantage of Keyboard Shortcuts

To make navigation in D365O as efficient as possible, Microsoft provides keyboard shortcuts of many kinds. Depending on the web page you're viewing at the time, the list of available shortcuts varies. To view the list of available shortcuts at any time, follow these steps:

1. Right-click in any blank section of a D365O screen.

A pop-up menu appears.

2. Select View Shortcuts from the pop-up menu.

The Currently Available Shortcuts window appears, as shown in Figure 14-4.

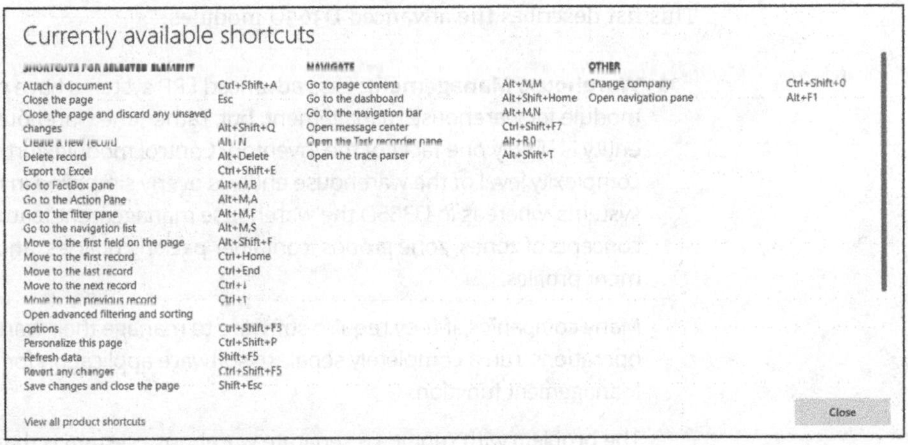

FIGURE 14-4: Viewing keyboard shortcuts in Dynamics 365 for Finance and Operations.

Currently available shortcuts

SHORTCUTS FOR SELECTED ELEMENT		NAVIGATE		OTHER	
Attach a document	Ctrl+Shift+A	Go to page content	Alt+M,M	Change company	Ctrl+Shift+O
Close the page	Esc	Go to the dashboard	Alt+Shift+Home	Open navigation pane	Alt+F1
Close the page and discard any unsaved		Go to the navigation bar	Alt+M,N		
changes	Alt+Shift+Q	Open message center	Ctrl+Shift+F7		
Create a new record	Alt+N	Open the Task recorder pane	Alt+R,0		
Delete record	Alt+Delete	Open the trace parser	Alt+Shift+T		
Export to Excel	Ctrl+Shift+E				
Go to FactBox pane	Alt+M,B				
Go to the Action Pane	Alt+M,A				
Go to the filter pane	Alt+M,F				
Go to the navigation list	Alt+M,S				
Move to the first field on the page	Alt+Shift+F				
Move to the first record	Ctrl+Home				
Move to the last record	Ctrl+End				
Move to the next record	Ctrl+↓				
Move to the previous record	Ctrl+↑				
Open advanced filtering and sorting					
options	Ctrl+Shift+F3				
Personalize this page	Ctrl+Shift+P				
Refresh data	Shift+F5				
Revert any changes	Ctrl+Shift+F5				
Save changes and close the page	Shift+Esc				

View all product shortcuts

Close

3. Take note of any shortcuts that you may find useful.

For example, Alt+S is a handy way to save a record.

4. Click the Close button.

Doing so exits you from the Currently Available Shortcuts window and you return to the window you right-clicked to access the pop-up menu.

Taking a Deeper Dive into D365O Capabilities by Module

A good way to get a feel for just how deep the feature sets go in D365O is to skim a list of the advanced capabilities in various modules. You should expect any ERP module to have the same basic features at a minimum, so in that sense all ERP applications are the same: If you've seen one, you've seen them all. For example, in any Accounts Receivable module, you should be able to create customers and enter credit memos; in any Accounts Payable module, you should be able to create vendors and enter vendor invoices; as another example, any decent ERP system will allow you to create multiple addresses per customer or per vendor. Truth to tell, any ERP system will have all the same basic common ERP modules, such as General Ledger, Budgeting, Accounts Receivable, Accounts Payable, and Inventory Control. What makes D365O stand out from the pack is that it offers advanced features in its common modules as well as special modules that not all ERP systems have. To see what I mean, all you need to do is check out some of these uncommon (in other words, more advanced) modules, as well as some of the advanced capabilities found in D365O's common modules.

This list describes the advanced D365O modules:

>> **Warehouse Management:** Less advanced ERP systems have no separate module for warehouse management, but, rather, the warehouse location entity is simply one facet of the Inventory Control module; furthermore, the complexity level of the warehouse entity is overly simplified in many ERP systems, whereas in D365O the warehouse management features include the concepts of zones, zone groups, container packing policies, and dock management profiles.

Many companies, if they require software to manage their warehouse operations, run a completely separate software application for the Warehouse Management function.

The problem with running a separate warehouse system is that you need to write and maintain custom integration programs between your Inventory Control module, Purchasing module, and Sales Order module in the base ERP package.

The D365O module for warehouse management is fully integrated with the other D365O modules, so no integration programs need be developed — which is a major advantage and cost savings. Unplanned disconnects between an external warehouse management system and the core ERP are all too common, and time-consuming troubleshooting of broken integrations is often an ongoing disruption to otherwise efficient operations.

REMEMBER

>> **Questionnaire:** A separate module for questionnaires isn't typically included in most ERP applications. However, the questionnaire is an important way for organizations to evaluate employee job performance as part of a human resources (HR) function.

Questionnaires can also be used for customer satisfaction surveys and to solicit feedback from customers for a variety of purposes.

Bear in mind that if your organization uses Dynamics 365 for Customer Engagement, a new module called Voice of the Customer also has survey functionality, so you may want to use it as well (or instead).

>> **Product Information Management:** Product information management (PIM) is a way to centralize information about your products so that all parts of the supply chain can speak the same language and have real-time access to changes in product descriptions, product images and diagrams, product specifications (specs), categorization of products, part numbers, and other attributes and identifiers related to the products your organization makes, distributes, and sells.

In recent years, stand-alone systems have sprung up that allow you to funnel information from your ERP system and other sources, such as suppliers' websites, into a centralized product information management hub. Of course, extensive custom integration programs are needed to accomplish this task, whereas with the D365O Product Information Management module, your PIM is embedded into your ERP system — a great advantage for your company because the product information is available in the Sales, Purchasing, and Inventory Control modules of the ERP with no need for custom integration programming.

TECHNICAL STUFF

D365O includes features to implement Kanban manufacturing. These features appear in the Production Control module and the Warehouse Management module. *Kanban* is a visual method for controlling production invented by Taiichi Ohno of Toyota, considered the father of lean manufacturing and the just-in-time (JIT) inventory replenishment method. The idea behind lean manufacturing is to make only as much product as you need based on the amount of product that has been pulled from the shelf by customers (known as *pull* manufacturing), rather than making product based on a forecast of what you hope the customers will buy (known as *push* manufacturing). In this way, you avoid making too much or not enough product because of inaccurate forecasts. However, to make JIT work, you need to respond quickly to fluctuations in inventory. D365O can help your organization adopt a Kanban manufacturing strategy.

The following listing of advanced features in D365O is meant to give you an overall feel for the depth of the D365O feature set. Providing detailed explanations and step-by-step instructions for all these advanced features is beyond the scope of this chapter. The Microsoft Docs website (`https://docs.microsoft.com/en-us`) provides a great deal of useful documentation regarding these features. Also confer with your authorized Dynamics 365 solution provider to learn more about how any of these advanced features can be implemented for your organization.

Here are some of the advanced features in the General Ledger module:

>> Consolidation of subsidiaries into a consolidated organizational entity

>> Forecasting of cash flow and currency requirements

>> Up to ten dimensional segments on a single account (Financial dimensions allow you to slice and dice your data for analysis and reporting purposes)

>> Automated allocation based on default templates defining percentages by dimension

>> Importing of currency exchange rates for exchange rate providers (no need to manually key in the exchange rates)

>> Settlement and revaluation of currency amounts

>> Compatible with the OpenXML format for electronic reporting for compliance with localization requirements of foreign governments

>> Mass financial period close, which can save you time by closing more than one financial period at a time

>> Posting restrictions by user group (helps with separation of duties)

And here are some of the advanced features in the Fixed Assets module:

>> Cross-company depreciation runs

>> Depreciation calculation using background processing

Advanced features in the Accounts Payable module include

>> Positive pay (an automated fraud detection tool specifically designed to deter check fraud)

>> Mobile invoice approval

>> Royalty management and broker contracts

>> A vendor collaboration invoicing workspace (lets vendors see the status of their own invoices using an online portal)

Advanced features in the Accounts Receivable module include

>> Electronic signature certificates

>> Trade agreement journals contracts you set up with your customers to specify pricing arrangements

>> Single Euro Payments Area (SEPA) direct debits

>> Customer pools for collections

>> Customer aging snapshots, which allow you to quickly view the accounts receivable aging of a customer without having to re-run the aging routine

>> Automation of nonsufficient funds (NSF) charges

Advanced features in the Cash and Bank Management module include

>> Letters of guarantee

>> Bank facility agreements (the terms and conditions a bank has agreed to extend to you for loans)

Advanced features in the Inventory Management module include

>> Consignment inventory

>> Commodity pricing

>> Forecast models

>> Product safety compliance (essentially help with tracking and reporting on restricted products and reported products such as creating product safety data sheets)

>> Warehouse load utilization reporting

>> Attribute-based pricing models

Advanced features in the Sales and Marketing (Sales Order) module include

>> Rebate agreements and rebate program types

>> Customer category hierarchy

>> Prospects, leads, and opportunities

>> Sales agreements

- » Shipment specifications

- » Shipping deviations (A handy way of viewing the differences between your actual ship dates and confirmed ship dates)

Advanced features in the Procurement and Sourcing (Purchase Order) module include

- » Purchase requisitions expenditure review

- » Intercompany order price discrepancies (A clean-up tool to help you synchronize prices and discounts for intercompany sales orders and purchase orders)

- » Legal entity-specific business rules and thresholds for fixed asset determination (Essentially this allows you to set different dollar thresholds in different companies for when the system will consider a purchase to be worthy of capitalizing it as a fixed asset.)

Mastering Master Data in D365O

In any ERP system, the master data records are a cornerstone of the application. A master data record (sometimes referred to as a *card*) isn't a transaction such as an invoice, purchase order, or journal entry, but rather it's part of the setup of the system. At the same time, however, it isn't a configuration setting, but rather acts more like a card you would have in a Rolodex of business cards. Three of the most basic and important master data records are the vendor, the customer, and the inventory item. You can get a good feel for how robust an ERP system is by surveying the maintenance screens of these main master data elements — namely, the Vendor Maintenance, Customer, and Inventory Item Setup windows.

Surveying the vendor record

The vendor record in D365O is extensive, to say the least. To navigate to the Vendor Maintenance window, follow these steps:

1. **Choose Modules ⇨ Accounts Payable ⇨ Vendors ⇨ All Vendors ⇨ New from the Finance and Operations navigation pane.**

   The New Record window appears for the vendor master data record, as shown in Figure 14-5.

FIGURE 14-5:
Vendor
Maintenance
window in
Dynamics 365 for
Finance and
Operations.

The New Record window is divided into the following sections/tabs:

REMEMBER

TIP

>> **General:** You can give the vendor not only a name but also a search name, a known-as name, and a phonetic name. Having all that information in the system means that there's now no excuse for a user not finding a vendor — which also means that no one will mistakenly add it again and create a duplicate vendor record.

The General tab is also where you put the vendor into a vendor group, set the vendor type, and activate vendor collaboration for automatic confirmation of purchase orders. (See Figure 14-6.)

>> **Addresses:** You can add unlimited addresses per vendor — just be sure to specify one address as the primary address for the vendor.

When you fill out the zip code, the city, state, and country automatically fill out.

>> **Contact Information:** Contact types include newer types of contact information such as Facebook, Twitter, and LinkedIn, in addition to the more traditional phone, fax, and telex.

>> **Miscellaneous Details:** Credit limit, rebate groups, hold status, and more are set in the Miscellaneous Details section.

>> **Vendor Profile:** The Vendor Profile section has several check boxes to capture important flags, such as minority owned, woman owned, veteran, and other attributes that are commonly required for reporting purposes with various government agencies.

>> **Purchasing Demographics:** In addition to setting the vendor's default currency for purchasing, you can set a responsible employee, the line of business, and market segment for reporting purposes.

>> **Invoice and Delivery:** Includes settings for sales tax, withholding tax, delivery methods, and more.

>> **Purchase Order Defaults:** There are 18 different fields just for PO defaults; that gives you an idea of just how robust the functionality is in this system!

>> **Payment:** This section is much more than simply setting your payment terms to net 30 days. This section has fields to handle bridging payments (where a third party is responsible for payment), payment schedules, cash discounts, payment day (vendors that pay on a specific day), and more.

>> **Tax 1099:** Most ERP systems have just a few fields for 1099 classification; typically, they have the 1099 yes/no flag and the 1099 type, such as miscellaneous income or royalty. D365O has 17 separate fields related to 1099 settings, including a yes/no slider control for W-9 Received. (It seems that the creators thought of everything.) This section is another example of how robust the system truly is.

>> **Retail:** The vendor retail product hierarchy is specified here, among other fields related to the Retail module.

>> **Financial Dimensions:** Here you can specify default values for financial dimensions for general ledger transactions related to this vendor; this is an important way to tag your general ledger detail with important reporting attributes accurately and automatically. For example, the vendor might be associated with a certain line of business, cost center, or business unit, and by tagging the vendor here, all transactions for that vendor can be likewise tagged by default with the proper dimensional values.

Click a section heading to expand a section.   Click here to toggle the Factbox pane.

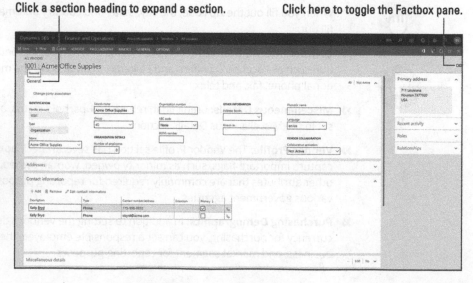

FIGURE 14-6:
The Vendor Maintenance window, with general and contact Information expanded.

TIP

A *factbox* in D365O is a graphical user interface (GUI) element that provides access to related information (facts) in a small area of the screen (box) that can be extended outward from the right side of the screen toward the middle of the screen. A factbox is available for many screens; for example, the vendor window has a factbox that shows the primary address, recent activity, roles, and relationships for the vendor you've currently navigated to. The Factbox feature was designed to help users work with records without having to keep opening additional windows. The idea is to have most of the pertinent information available at your fingertips on one screen. This is especially important in web applications where having multiple browser windows open requires multiple connections, and it becomes difficult to coordinate which records are being updated and in which order. You can toggle the factbox to make it visible by clicking the Factbox toggle button in the top right corner of the page. (Refer to Figure 14-6.)

Surveying the customer record

The customer record in D365O, like the vendor record, contains an extensive assortment of data elements.

To navigate to the Customer Maintenance window, follow these steps:

1. **Choose Modules ⇨ Accounts Receivable ⇨ Customers ⇨ All Customers from the Finance and Operations navigation pane.**

   The Customer List page appears, showing all customers.

2. **Click any customer ID in the Account column (the first data column in the list).**

   The Customer Maintenance window opens for the customer master data record (row) you clicked, as shown in Figure 14-7.

The tabs/sections in the customer maintenance window are described in this list:

>> **General:** The customer group, DUNS (*data universal numbering system*) number (used to gauge creditworthiness), number of employees, and classification group are among the fields on the General tab. Though most of these fields are optional and you might not use them right away, the point is that they are there if you need them; you won't need to create them as user-defined fields or, worse, repurpose another field to capture that information.

>> **Addresses:** You can add unlimited addresses per customer.

REMEMBER

A single address can have more than one purpose assigned to it; for example, an address can serve as both the delivery (where you send the goods) and invoice address (where you send the bill).

FIGURE 14-7:
Customer
Maintenance
window in
Dynamics 365 for
Finance and
Operations.

» **Contact Information:** This section isn't for contacts (people), but rather for contact information, such as email addresses, phone numbers, and URLs. (There's even a flag to denote that a phone number is a mobile number rather than a landline.) A great deal of attention was paid by the designers of D365O to including up-to-date commonly required information as an out-of-the-box feature, which isn't the case with many other more old-fashioned ERP systems.

» **Miscellaneous Details:** This tab includes several fields pertaining to inter-company setup, federal attributes, government identification, and more. Overall, this section alone has 20 fields!

» **Sales Demographics:** To better classify your customers, you can associate each one with a line of business, a sales district, a segment, or even a subsegment.

» **Credit and Collections:** You enter updates here about credit limits, credit rating, hold flags, and other information concerning the customer's creditworthiness.

» **Sales Order Defaults:** Being able to set the defaults for up to 20 fields on a sales order means that your billing process can be more accurate, efficient, and timely.

» **Payment Defaults:** This one is similar to the Payment section for vendors; in addition to payment terms, you can specify more advanced settings, such as payment schedules.

» **Financial dimensions:** As with vendors, being able to set the defaults in journal entries for the financial dimensions (segments) that are generated when posting transactions related to this customer improves accuracy and completeness and speeds up data entry. (You can always override the default values where appropriate and as necessary.)

>> **Warehouse:** Here you find customer settings related to the Warehouse Management module. Advance shipping note (ASN) functionality is included.

>> **Inventory and delivery:** Included here is a setting to send out electronic invoices. (Yeah, no more stuffing envelopes.)

>> **Transportation:** This is a small section with one field: Accepts Express Bill of Lading flag.

>> **Direct Debit Mandates:** Direct-debit mandates are important for putting your customers on autopay. Your organization then becomes authorized to directly debit the customer's bank account to collect future payments.

Functionality to support different types of direct debit mandate schemes is included.

>> **Retail:** Unless you're using the D365O Retail module, you can leave these settings blank.

Surveying the inventory item (released product) record

The inventory record in D365O is called a *released* product (to distinguish it from raw materials or component parts); remember that D365O is a manufacturing application, not just a wholesale distribution system. The inventory item's attributes are extensive indeed.

To navigate to the Released Product Maintenance window, follow these steps:

1. **Choose Modules ⇨ Product Information Management ⇨ Products ⇨ Released Products from the Finance and Operations navigation pane.**

   The list form showing released products appears.

2. **Click any item number in the Item Number column (the first column in the list).**

   The Released Product (Inventory Item) Maintenance window opens for the product master data record you selected, as shown in Figure 14-8.

FIGURE 14-8:
Released Product
(Inventory Item)
Maintenance
window in
D365O.

The tabs/sections in the Released Product Maintenance window are described in this list:

>> **General:** Here you find fields for the product name, a search name, and a long description, as well as an item number and a product number.

The storage dimension group is specified here as well; among other things, the storage dimension group can determine how prices are calculated based on which dimensions are included in the pricing matrix; for example, you can select whether a particular dimension, such as a site or warehouse, is included as a criterion in determining sales price as part of a sales agreement.

>> **Purchase:** Discounts, rebates, and taxation are among the 20 or so fields included in this section.

>> **Promote:** Here you can specify that you want to exclude coupons.

>> **Deliver:** Use this tab to specify which products ship alone as well as direct delivery and packing box options.

>> **Sell:** Sales prices, discounts, units of measure, and many more fields that affect how an item is treated on a sales order and sales invoice are specified here.

>> **Foreign Trade:** Dealing with companies overseas often means dealing with Intrastat, the system for collecting trade information and reporting statistics for the European Union (EU). This tab has fields for specifying the commodity that the item pertains to, as well as the country or region and the province of origin.

>> **Manage Inventory:** You can specify an item's weight and physical dimensions (depth, width, height, and volume) in this section.

To give you an idea of the robust nature of the feature set, you'll also find fields for yield, catch weight, and packing group, to name a few.

>> **Engineer:** This section is concerned with the bill of materials (BOM); if the item is something you manufacture, you specify what goes into creating it.

>> **Plan:** Specify the coverage group.

>> **Manage costs:** Here's where you update the item's cost group.

Cost groups define the segmentation for analyzing cost distributions in the calculated cost of an item; material, labor, and overhead may all be involved. (Cost group is sometimes referred to as costing breakdown, decomposition, or classification.)

>> **Manage Projects:** You can set a project category here for use of that item within the Project Accounting module.

>> **Financial Dimensions:** Here you can specify default values for financial dimensions for general ledger transactions related to this item; for example, the item may be associated with a certain line of business, cost center, or business unit, and by tagging the item here, all transactions with currency amounts pertaining to that item are tagged appropriately with the financial dimension values that you specify here; the default values can be overridden before posting.

>> **Warehouse:** The Warehouse section is extensive; how the inventory item is handled in the warehouse is defined here by the combined values of several settings, including minimum pick quantity, pack size, physical dimension group, and more.

TIP

Functionality for National Motor Freight Classification (NMFC) is also included.

>> **Retail:** D365O is quite powerful in terms of how it handles color, size, and style groups; this is a vital consideration in dealing with apparel and certain other goods. It's not enough to know, for example, how many units of a shirt or blouse you have on hand; you need to know the size, the color, and whether it's short-sleeved or long-sleeved.

Seasonality and date ranges for when the item is valid are also included.

>> **Transportation:** Here you can specify whether to use the Transportation Management processes.

REMEMBER

Turning on the Transportation Management functionality in D365O lets you specify vendor and routing solutions for inbound and outbound orders. With transportation management, for example, you can specify the fastest route to take or the least expensive rate available for a shipment.

>> **Product Variants:** Inventory item numbers for variants of an item (specific versions of that item) can be generated based on an item numbering convention that uses attributes of the product to generate a unique ID number; here you specify the configuration technology to use for the product variants.

TIP

The menus you see along the top of the window are called Action Pane tabs. For example, in Figure 14-9 you see that the Action Pane tab called "Sell" has been clicked, opening up a drop-down menu of menu items related to selling products, such as choices to view trade agreements and the commission calculation related to that inventory item. Also notice that lower on the screen is a section on the form called Sell and that clicking that section makes the fields that are included in that form section visible and accessible for editing.

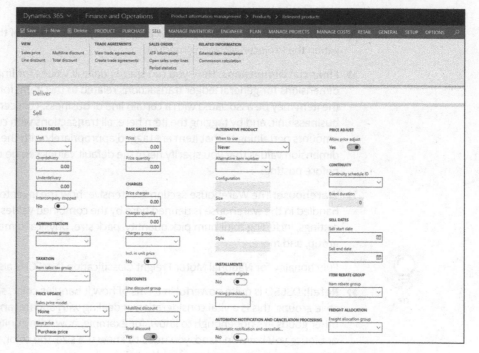

FIGURE 14-9:
The Sell menu
and the Sell
section of the
Released Product
Maintenance
window in
D365O.

REMEMBER

An Action Pane tab and a form section, even though they may have exactly the same name, aren't the same; the Action Pane tab displays menu items to open other windows or perform actions, whereas the section headings display fields on the form.

Using the More Options button

When working in master record maintenance forms in D365O, you may come across data grids, such as when you look at the addresses visible in the Addresses section of the Vendor Maintenance window. The data grid displays multiple records related to the one record you're working with; in the example, while working with a vendor, in the Addresses section you can see all addresses belonging to that vendor.

Knowing how to add an address isn't all that intuitive, unless you know the secret of the More Options button — the button with three dots (periods), which gives you (you guessed it) more options. When you click the button with the three dots (the More Options button), a drop-down menu appears; one choice on the drop-down menu is Add. To add an address record, start by choosing Add. (Figure 14-10 shows you where you need to click.)

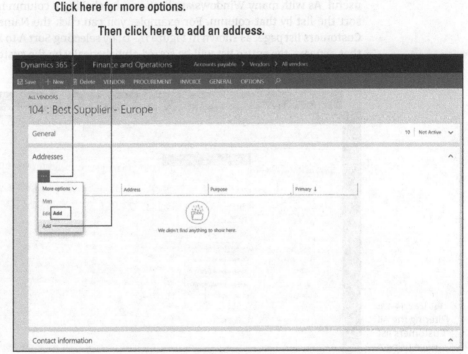

Click here for more options.

Then click here to add an address.

FIGURE 14-10:
Adding an address record in the Addresses section of the Vendor Maintenance window.

This list describes other options you can find on the More Options button in the Vendor Addresses section:

>> **Map:** This option launches a web page with a map that pinpoints the address you have selected.

>> **Edit:** Choosing this option opens on the right side of the page a form you can use to quickly edit the fields in the address record that you have selected in the grid of addresses.

> » **Set Defaults:** This option allows you to specify which address to use as the default address.

> » **Advanced:** Choosing this option opens a full-page form to manage the address, including fields to set the longitude and latitude of the address.

Working with List Pages

List pages are a common form in D365O, so knowing how to work with them is useful. As with many Windows applications, by clicking a column heading, you can sort the list by that column. For example, you can click the Name field in the All Customers list page, as shown in Figure 14-11; by selecting Sort A to Z from the menu that appears, the entire list will be sorted alphabetically by the customer name.

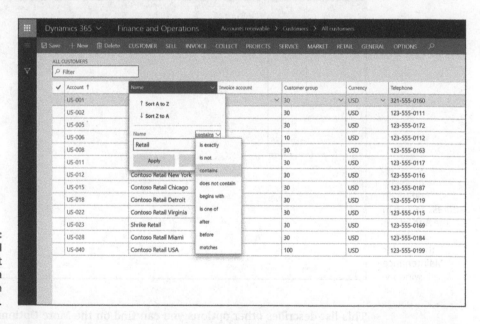

FIGURE 14-11:
Filtering the All Customers list page using a Contains filter in D365O.

You can also filter by an individual column by clicking the column heading. Notice in Figure 14-11 that a text box appears under the sorting options. In the example shown in Figure 14-11, the word *Retail* has been entered into the text box. To the right and above the text box is the word *contains*, which you can click to display a drop-down list of all filter options. When setting up the example, I changed the filter type from "begins with" to "contains." Then I typed the word *Retail* into the text box and clicked the Apply button. As you can see in Figure 14-11, the customers in the list have been filtered so as to display only customers whose name contains the word *Retail*.

You can also filter a list page (like the Released Products list page) by more than one field — by Item Number, Search Name, and Item Group, for example. Figure 14-12 shows what I mean. These are the search criteria I use there:

>> Item number begins with *D*

>> Search name contains *speaker*

>> Item group equals *Audio*

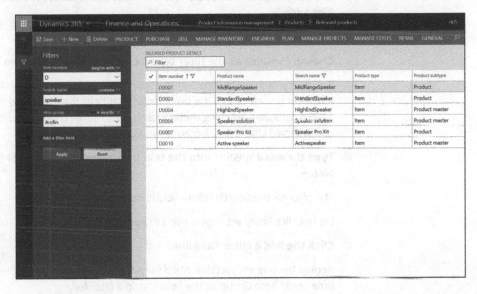

FIGURE 14-12:
Filtering the
Released
Products list page
using multiple
filter fields.

To create and apply a filter using multiple filter fields on the Released Products list page using the criteria listed in the preceding example, follow these steps:

1. Choose Modules ⇨ Product Information Management ⇨ Products ⇨ Released products from the Finance and Operations navigation pane.

The list page displaying all released products appears.

The list isn't yet filtered.

2. Click the Filter icon (which looks like a funnel) on the left side of the web page, toward the top.

The Filters Pane extends from the left side of the web page.

3. **Enter the letter** D **in the text box under the Item number label.**

The filter type you want for this field is "begins with," which is the default filter type, so you won't need to change it.

4. **Click the Filter pane's Add a Filter Field link, above the Apply button.**

A drop-down menu appears, listing all the various columns you can filter. This includes columns that aren't part of the list that's displayed on the list page but are part of the record (being fields in the underlying tables).

5. **Choose Search Name from the drop-down menu of filter fields to add.**

A new Filter Field text box appears below the previous Filter Field text box.

6. **Click the Begins With option (to the right of the label for the new field you just added).**

A drop-down menu appears and displays a list of filter types.

7. **Choose Contains as the filter type from the drop-down menu.**

The field you chose in Step 5 — the Search Name field — is now filtered by whatever you enter into the text box for that field. (Keep in mind that the search considers anything that contains your search criteria; you don't need to add wildcard characters, because the filter type is Contains.)

8. **Type the word** speaker **into the text box below the field label for Search Name.**

The filter for the Search Name field is now in place.

Do not click Apply yet — you need to add one more filter field.

9. **Click the Add a Filter Field link.**

Repeat the process just described for adding the Search Name filter, but this time select Item Group as the field to add a filter for.

Also, rather than choose Contains as the filter type, choose Is Exactly as the filter type.

10. **Select Audio as the item group from the drop-down menu.**

Notice that the text box for this newly added filter field has a small, downward-pointing arrow at the far right end of the text box.

The downward-pointing arrow — the one that looks like the letter *V* — lets you know that a drop-down list is available for that field. Some fields have drop-down lists because there's a reference table with a limited set of valid values for that field; others don't have a reference table because they're free-form text fields, free-form numerical, or date fields.

11. **Click the Apply button.**

The list is filtered based on the criteria and filter types of the three filter fields.

TIP

You can clear all filters by clicking the Reset button; doing so displays the full unfiltered list again.

Exporting List Pages to Excel Spreadsheets

After you have filtered a list page, you may want to export the results to Excel for further analysis or to share the data with an external party. You can select one or more rows by clicking in the far left column in any row. A check mark appears in the first column to indicate that the row is selected, as shown in Figure 14-13.

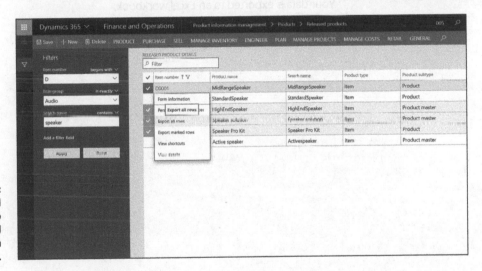

FIGURE 14-13:
Selecting and exporting rows to a Microsoft Excel workbook in D365O.

To export rows from a D365O list page to Excel, follow these steps:

1. **Choose Modules ⇨ Product Information Management ⇨ Products ⇨ Released Products from the Finance and Operations navigation pane.**

The list page displaying all released products appears.

No rows are selected, and none has been filtered (yet).

You may apply a filter using Steps 2 through 8 in the previous instructions and/or select individual rows.

2. Click in the leftmost column of any row to add a check mark to select that row for export.

Alternatively, you can filter the list and export all rows, or simply export all rows in the list and filter them later in Excel.

3. Right-click in any selected row in any field in the row.

A drop-down menu appears.

Refer to Figure 14-13.

4. Choose Export Marked Rows or Export All Rows, depending on your export preferences.

The Export to Excel pane appears on the right side of the screen.

5. Click the Download button.

Your data is exported to an Excel workbook.

Chapter **15**

Looking Under the Hood (Understanding the D365O Technology)

Upgrading from Dynamics AX to Dynamics 365 for Finance and Operations is not as simple as pushing a button; there's lots to consider. A closer look can help reveal the key factors that could make or break a migration from on-premise Dynamics AX to SaaS D365O.

How you see data arranged by the user interface is not necessarily how data is organized in the database. Sometimes it's helpful to understand what is going on under the hood, so to speak; for example, we'll take a look at the global address book which affects how addresses are created, stored, synchronized and refreshed for all sorts of entities such as customers, vendors, and contacts, to name a few.

We'll take a look at these topics as well as several other less-than-obvious ones that require a bit of a deeper dive to understand what is really going on, including personalizing the user interface, and leveraging the Microsoft Lifecycle Services website and the Talent and Expense Management modules.

Upgrading from Dynamics AX to Dynamics 365 for Finance and Operations

According to some estimates, Microsoft Dynamics AX is used by more than 20,000 companies throughout the world. Now that Dynamics AX has become Dynamics 365 for Finance and Operations (D365O), many, if not most, of these existing Dynamics AX sites need to be migrated to the Dynamics 365 cloud environment. To accommodate customers who aren't ready to move to the cloud, Microsoft is also supporting an on-premise version of D365O. Fortunately, an upgrade path is available for both cloud and on-premise D365O versions; you don't have to reimplement your ERP system and you will not lose your master data, transaction history, or system configuration settings. The entire database can be migrated and upgraded from AX to D365O. Of course, you need to be using a fairly recent version of AX. At the time of writing, AX 2012 R2 and R3 are supported for upgrade to D365O.

The reason a full upgrade path is possible is that the underlying database design hasn't changed much between Dynamics AX 2012 and D365O. The SQL tables are basically the same. For example, the design of the SQL tables as far as table names, column names, data types, primary keys, indexes and the like has not changed much between AX 2010 and D365O; in other words, this migration from AX to 365 did not include a total database overhaul, but rather, was more about re-doing the front-end user interface than the back-end database, taking AX from client/server application to a web-based app. Of course, there were changes to the database to allow it to operate in a multi-tenant SaaS environment, but those changes don't affect the entities such as customers or vendors, so much as how instances are partitioned and other SaaS related considerations.

REMEMBER

Dynamics AX was originally an application from Denmark called Axapta. Axapta was rebranded as Dynamics AX after it had been acquired by Microsoft along with another ERP system, Navision. Microsoft made a massive research-and-development (R&D) investment in improving Dynamics AX. The major changes came with the release of Dynamics AX 2012 R2. As part of the AX 2012 R2 overhaul, the underlying database design of AX was drastically revamped. Fortunately, that revamped AX 2012 R2 data model has been migrated into D365O, and improved even further.

The redesign of the Axapta database to Dynamics AX 2012 R2 included normalization. In a highly *normalized* database, the data is broken out into many separate tables so as to avoid storing redundant data and to organize the data in a more strictly logical manner. That makes a highly normalized database much more efficient and therefore more scalable, but it also means that it's difficult to query directly because the tables become fragmented and no longer human-readable. To overcome this issue, the trick is to query SQL *views* (which act as virtual tables); the views contain the SQL join statements that tie the tables together for you, and often will alias (rename) the physical column (field) names into more human-readable descriptive names. Furthermore, D365O includes *data entities* — higher-level abstractions of the underlying tables — which are used to create a denormalized view of the data. Through the D365O API (application programming interface), D365O exposes tables to other applications as data entities rather than directly as physical tables. Microsoft wanted to ensure that the underlying AX database would be able to handle many millions of records without performance problems so that this system could compete with rivals such as SAP and Oracle, whose ERP systems tend to handle larger client sites.

Migrating customizations from over-layering to extensions

If you have spent some time customizing your Dynamics AX screens, you can bring them with as you make the move to D365O, but the code migration needs to be carefully analyzed, and some programming may be required. In Dynamics AX, the method to create custom screens was to over-layer in different application code layers; the concept was that the code in each successive layer replaces the previous layer of code. In D365O, the concept of code layers has been abandoned in favor of code extensions. Code extensions don't replace underlying code; they just extend the official Microsoft code so that they're easier to cope with during an upgrade and are maintainable in a multi-tenant cloud environment, where all organizations subscribing to the software are running the same official Microsoft code (and therefore cannot be on an earlier or overlayered custom version of the code).

AX customizations should be migrated from programs that used the over-layering approach to programs that use the extensions approach. Microsoft is phasing out over-layering, but not all at once. The analysis of, and planning for, the migration of custom code from over-layering to extensions requires deep technical knowledge of Dynamics AX and Dynamics 365. Confer with your authorized Dynamics solution provider regarding this topic because, depending on the extent and nature of your customizations, you may be better off rewriting the customizations from scratch as extensions. Furthermore, rewriting the customizations from scratch can be an opportunity for business analysts to take a fresh look at your existing workflow and suggest process reengineering improvements, some of which may reduce or even avoid the need for the customizations.

Rewriting integrations created with AIF

The Dynamics AX Application Integration Framework (AIF) was designed as an infrastructure for coding custom integration programs (data feeds). Microsoft is abandoning the AIF in favor of newer, more generic integration technologies, as opposed to the AIF. (Microsoft realized that, although the AIF was geared specifically toward AX — a good thing — it had limited exposed touch points and weaker performance — not-so-good things.) If you have existing integration programs written using the AIF, these need to be redesigned and recoded for D3650.

WARNING

In the migration from Dynamics AX to D3650, not only has AIF been removed but the .NET Business Connector is also no longer available as an integration tool. If you have any integrations reliant on the .NET Business Connector, these are also an upgrade issue.

According to Microsoft, custom integration programs that interface with D3650 data should use one or more of these technologies:

>> **OData:** OData — short for Open Data Protocol — isn't a proprietary Microsoft technology, but rather a set of standards for describing and exchanging data between applications over the Internet adhering to HTML standards.

>> **Custom services:** A programmer can create a custom service that allows external applications to access Dynamics 365 functionality.

>> **SOAP:** SOAP — an acronym for Simple Object Access Protocol — is a protocol for applications running on different operating systems to send messages using HTTP (Hypertext Transfer Protocol) and XML (Extensible Markup Language).

>> **Batch data API:** A batch data API (*application programming interface*) can group multiple operations into a single HTTP request using a batch operation.

TECHNICAL STUFF

When talking about database operations, you may come across the term *CRUD*. You may wonder what CRUD means, or even mistake it for a derogatory comment, as in "This software is cruddy." CRUD stands for *create*, *read*, *update*, and *delete*. In SQL (*structured query language*) database programming syntax, these four main keywords are used to act on the data in a database table:

>> INSERT: Add a new record (row) to a table.

>> SELECT: View read-only data in a table without making changes to it.

>> UPDATE: Change the value of columns in an already existing row in a table.

>> DELETE: Remove and permanently get rid of a row in a table. You need to include the SQL keywords INSERT, SELECT, UPDATE, DELETE; those are programming language keywords, and they must be lined up with CRUD. C = insert, R = select, U = update, D = delete.

Full CRUD operations being supported means that you can set permissions and/or make API calls to execute database commands for INSERT, SELECT, UPDATE, and DELETE in the target application.

Tapping into technology for integrations and data conversions

Making data available for interaction with outside applications is easier and more efficient in D365O than it was in Dynamics AX. In fact, a common complaint about AX was that the data import features were limited and cumbersome to code and manage. Microsoft has fixed these issues with D365O. The big difference is that the focus is now on OData, which supports full CRUD operations.

The Dynamics AX Application Integration Framework (AIF) was SOAP based, but OData is a Representational State Transfer (RESTful) Web service, which relies on JavaScript Object Notation (JSON). JSON is a marked improvement over SOAP because it's more compact and clearly more efficient than XML, which the SOAP-based protocol makes use of. Here are a few more advantages of the OData framework over AIF:

- » **More secure authentication method:** The OAuth security protocol for OData endpoints include a 2-level authentication method for securing data against unauthorized access.

- » **Improved performance:** Performance has improved. (Everyone likes speedy integrations.)

- » **Increased number of access endpoints:** The number is vast, now numbering more than 1,800 Microsoft objects, so programmers can get at pretty much any kind of object in D365O — not just the most commonly used ones, such as the customer master record, vendor master record, or general ledger journal entry.

- » **Improved error messages:** Error messages returned by OData are more lengthy and cogent; you can understand better why something failed to integrate and then take steps to correct the error with less troubleshooting.

The following built-in operators are supported in D365O when using the OData to filter query results:

- » Addition
- » Subtraction
- » Multiplication
- » Division
- » Equals

- » Not equals
- » And
- » Or
- » Not
- » Greater than
- » Greater than or equal
- » Less than
- » Less than or equal

LEVERAGING DYNAMICS LIFECYCLE SERVICES

You can use the Microsoft Dynamics Lifecycle Services (LCS) web portal to plan, manage, and track your implementation of Dynamics 365 for Finance and Operations. The web portal, hosted by Microsoft on the Azure Cloud, is available to all customers of Dynamics 365. You simply sign in and use it, though you may need to create an account first. Speak to your Dynamics 365 system administrator to get your sign-in credentials and the correct URL path to the website for your organization's implementation project.

LCS is similar to SharePoint, in a way, because it's a place where you can share documents and collaborate with a project team to help organize and manage your IT project — in this case, the implementation of Dynamics 365. Your authorized Dynamics 365 solution provider may have a policy to use LCS for all its ERP implementation projects, or it may have its own methodologies, project management software, or web portal to use instead. Whoever you have engaged to implement D365O at your organization, whether they've used the LCS before or not, may be interested in learning what it has to offer.

ERP implementations can be tricky and complicated, and even become overwhelming. With the LCS, Microsoft provides a website loaded with information and tools to help your implementation team manage your D365O implementation project more efficiently. Project methodologies are available that have been designed especially for implementing Dynamics ERP systems. The methodology consists of a series of sequential steps that should be completed in order, all leading to a successful "go-live" — often referred to as an uneventful (or boring) go-live. Though a boring go-live may be the ideal x, most go-lives are anything but. Much can go wrong (and typically does) during the first few days or months of rolling out a new ERP system.

Though the LCS certainly isn't a silver bullet that can magically make a breeze of your D365O implementation, you definitely should check it out, take what you like, and leave the rest. That being said, the LCS is by no means a required part of a successful implementation strategy of D365O.

Using a comprehensive design document and a right-sized project plan

The cornerstone of any successful ERP project is the creation of a comprehensive and detailed design document (or documents) that acts as the main blueprint for building, testing, training, and deploying the system. A right-sized project plan that is kept up-to-date should also be a key ingredient in managing the project. The project plan should be detailed but not overly detailed, and neither the project plan nor the design document should be boilerplate. In other words, the documents should be highly tailored for your organization's unique situation.

Too many times, consultants cut corners by reusing the same old tired documents from previous implementations, simply swapping in the name of your company and replacing the previous client's name by using the Find and Replace function in Microsoft Word. The text of these boilerplate documents is generic hogwash that serves no purpose other than to confuse and befuddle those paying for the document, and to give the appearance that the design is well thought out; however, there's really no proof of concept — no vetting of the design — if all you get is a boilerplate document, scattered emails, and random meeting notes that the implementers fail to methodically organize and carefully edit into a coherent blueprint for the new system.

The design of your ERP new system needs to be put in writing with clear diagrams, charts, and code lists, and explanations of naming conventions, key design decisions, and important setup parameters and the like. There's no need to laboriously list in a Word document every single setup option in the entire ERP system — that would be a grand waste of time. However, the solution architect needs to use common sense to ascertain which topics to include and then document only the salient and critical settings, schemes, conventions, and strategies that significantly impact the project. What these things are exactly varies from implementation to implementation, so a cookie-cutter methodology won't work.

WARNING

If the consultants you have engaged for your D365O implementation project aren't providing good design documents — such as a project blueprint that's highly tailored, detailed, and comprehensive yet readable by a layman — along with a right-sized project plan and weekly status reports on the progress of the project, that's a red flag. Speak up and demand proper documentation, and then take the time to carefully read it. ERP implementations is a team sport; the consultants and the clients both need to be active participants.

Personalizing the User Interface

One of the best aspects of D365O from a user perspective is that you can modify screen layouts without doing any computer programming — you can do this yourself without having to contact your IT department or system administrator. Your personalized screen layouts affect how data appears on the screen for you. Now, if you've personalized your screen in a neat way and you want other users to also have the nifty new layout, you can export your personalized page by creating a personalization file. The personalization file can be imported by another user, thereby giving that person the screen layout you created.

You can even add new fields (create user-defined fields, in essence) without computer programming or IT involvement. Your Dynamics 365 system administrator has to grant you permissions to personalize your forms (screens). You need a separate, higher-level permission to allow you to add custom fields, which may not be so easy, given that most system administrators tightly control who gets to add custom fields.

REMEMBER

Adding custom (user-defined) fields is a big deal. You can easily imagine how that situation can get out of hand. If everybody is adding their own fields to the database via the user interface in a willy-nilly manner with no centralized coordination, you can end up with fields that are only haphazardly updated and that are missing from key reports. Even the more basic type of screen personalizations (ones that don't involve adding custom fields) can get out of hand; if every user has a different screen layout, it can cause confusion or outright chaos.

Fortunately, D365O provides a way for the Dynamics 365 system administrator to centrally control personalization. D365O has a Personalization page with the following tabs:

>> **Apply:** Personalization files can be imported and then applied to multiple users by selecting a role and the users who are assigned to that role.

Also, an existing personalization can be applied to multiple users.

>> **Clear:** Personalizations can be cleared (removed) for one or more users and from a page or a workspace.

>> **Manage per User:** Here's where the administrator can control who is allowed to create personalizations, either for specific pages or as a global system setting for that user.

The administrator can also see which pages the users have personalized and then enable or disable those personalizations.

>> **System:** In this clean-up utility area, the administrator can delete all personal-ization and start over if it gotten a little out of hand.

Another option is to disable all personalizations rather than delete them. In this way, the administrator can easily enable them again later.

WARNING

Deleting a personalization in the System area of the Personalization page is permanent. You should export any personalizations that you may want to reuse later. You have no way to recover a deleted personalization, other than to import a saved personalization file. These personalization files are generated for you by the system in XML format during export.

A personalization that a user makes to modify the appearance of a user interface form (page) — such as moving fields around, adding existing available fields, changing field labels, or hiding fields — is an *explicit* personalization. An explicit personalization is made by putting the form (page) into Interactive Personaliza-tion mode.

For example, the Vendor Maintenance window can be personalized to add the Federal Tax ID field to the General section; doing so makes that field more visible to the user and easier to access quickly. For example, perhaps this field in your system gets lost in the confusion of having so many fields and the accounts payable manager insists that the field be considered when creating or editing a vendor record.

To add the field in this example, follow these steps:

1. Choose Modules ⇨ Accounts Payable ⇨ Vendors ⇨ All Vendors from the Finance and Operations navigation pane.

The Vendor List page appears, displaying all vendors.

2. Click any vendor ID in the Vendor Account column (the first data column in the list).

The Vendor Maintenance window opens (by default) to the General section of the vendor master data record (row) you clicked.

3. Click the General section heading to toggle that section, first hiding and then showing the fields in that section.

The General section collapses, hiding the fields in that section.

When you click General again, the section expands, displaying the fields, such as Vendor Account, Name, Search Name, and Group.

4. Right-click anywhere in the General section.

The Form drop-down menu appears, displaying choices such as Form Information, Collapse All, and Expand All.

TIP

5. Select Personalize: General from the drop-down menu.

If you don't see this choice on the drop-down menu, right-click directly on the word *General* or on other sections of the screen in the General section.

The Personalize: General pop-up menu appears, as shown in Figure 15-1.

The color of the General section changes to indicate that you're now in Personalization mode.

You can change the name of the section by overwriting the text in the text box under the word *Personalize;* as you type, you see the section name change on the screen.

On the Personalize: General pop-up menu, you also have choices to hide the section, skip it when you tab through it, disallow editing, and add a field.

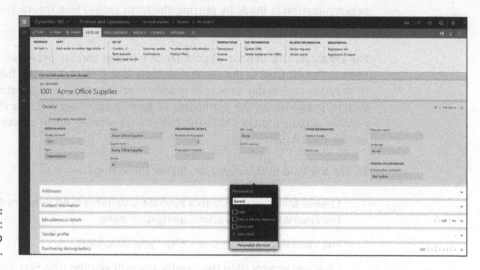

FIGURE 15-1:
The Personalize:
General pop-up
menu.

6. Choose Add a Field from the Personalize pop-up menu.

The list of existing available fields you can add to the page appears on the right side of the web page, as shown in Figure 15-2.

This list of fields can be sorted by any column by clicking the column header.

To add one or more fields to be inserted on the form, simply click the check box in the far left column next to the field(s) of your choice.

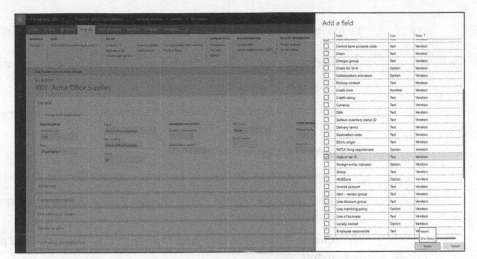

FIGURE 15-2:
Adding a field to the General section.

7. **Click Table (the column heading for the rightmost column in the list of fields), and then select Sort A to Z.**

The list of fields is sorted by the Table column.

You can see that you can insert fields from tables that are related to the vendor table, in addition to fields in the vendor table itself.

8. **Press Page Down on the keyboard, or use the scroll wheel or slider bar to scroll down the list.**

The fields in the Vendor table are toward the bottom of the list.

Look for the field labeled Federal Tax ID. (This is an important field that it would be nice to see in the General section of the form.)

9. **Select the check box for Federal Tax ID.**

You're now ready to insert the Federal Tax ID into the General section.

10. **Click the Insert button.**

The field you selected is visible on the form, and the screen changes back to the normal color to indicate that you're no longer in Personalization mode.

You can add fields using the Personalize pop-up menu, but moving a field to a better position onscreen involves using the Personalization toolbar. To display the Personalization toolbar, choose the Personalize This Form option at the bottom of the Personalization menu. (Refer to Figure 15-1.)

To move, for example, the Federal Tax ID field you just added, follow these steps:

1. Right-click the Vendor Maintenance window's General section.

The Form drop-down menu appears.

You have choices, for example, to see form information, collapse all, or expand all.

2. Select Personalize: General.

The Personalize: General pop-up menu appears. (Refer to Figure 15-1.)

The color of the General section changes to indicate that you're now in Personalization mode.

3. Choose Personalize This Form from the Personalize: General pop-up menu.

The Personalize toolbar appears.

4. Click the Move button. (the second button from the left on the Personalization toolbar; see Figure 15-3.)

The screen is now in Move mode.

Click the Move button.

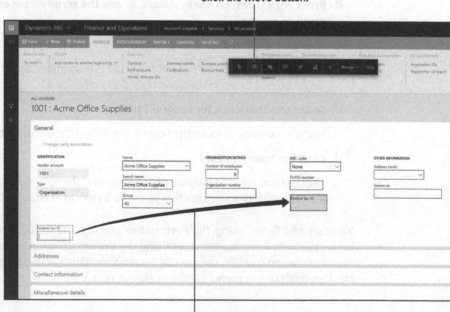

FIGURE 15-3:
Moving a field in the General section.

Drag a field to place it elsewhere on the screen.

5. Click the label of the field you want to move.

In this example, click the Federal Tax ID field.

The field becomes surrounded by a gray dashed line to indicate that it's ready for repositioning. (Again, refer to Figure 15-3.)

6. Click to select the Federal Tax ID field, and then, while holding down the left mouse button, drag-and-drop the field to another position in that section of the form.

The screen automatically adjusts to fit the field, automatically shuffling other fields around in the process.

You can always move the field again, as many times as you need to, to position it where you want.

7. Click the Close button on the Personalization Toolbar.

The field is moved, and your personalization changes are saved.

REMEMBER

You can export the personalization from the Manage button menu, to ensure that you have a backup copy of your personalization.

The Personalization toolbar has nine buttons you can use to help modify the screen in various ways. (See Figure 15-4.) When you hover the cursor over each button, a balloon Help message pops up to remind you of the function of each button.

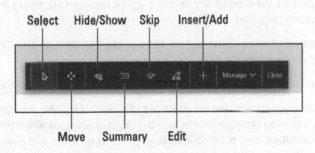

FIGURE 15-4: The Personalization toolbar in Dynamics 365 for Finance and Operations.

From left to right, the nine buttons on the Personalization toolbar are described in this list:

>> **Select:** Clicking the Select button activates Select mode. When in Select mode, clicking an element onscreen brings up the Properties window for that element, allowing you to change the field label, hide it, include it in the FastTab summary, skip it in the tab sequence, or lock it so that it cannot be edited.

You're unable to hide a required field (and for good reason), so sometimes that option isn't available; in fact, the properties you can change may differ, depending on the element you have selected.

» **Move:** Clicking the Move button activates Move mode. Now whenever you click a screen element, such as a field, a dashed gray line appears around the element, indicating that it's now ready to move.

Click it, and then drag-and-drop the element to another location. You cannot precisely position the field; instead, the screen adapts to wherever you drop the element and readjusts itself to fit it in with other elements.

» **Hide/Show:** Clicking the Hide/Show button gets you to Hide/Show mode, which, as its name suggests, lets you choose whether to hide or show an element onscreen.

In Hide/Show mode, hidden fields appear in a different color, to distinguish them from visible fields.

Simply click the label of any field to toggle it between Hidden and Shown (Regular).

When you click the Close button, the hidden fields disappear from the screen.

» **Summary:** Clicking the Summary button activates Set Summary mode.

In Set Summary mode, summary fields appear in a different color to distinguish them from nonsummary fields.

Simply click the label of any field to toggle it between Summary and Nonsummary (Regular).

When you click the Close button, the summary fields start appearing in the FastTab summary.

» **Skip:** The Skip function is for making a field skip the tab sequence.

If your organization doesn't make use of a particular field, you can save the user's time by skipping that field in the tab sequence, so when the user tabs to the next field, they don't have to keep pressing tab over and over again to tab through unused fields.

This tool works like the Show/Hide and Summary tools.

You click the label of the field to set the field as skipped; the color changes to indicate that it's no longer to be included in the tab sequence.

» **Edit:** The default here is for Editing to be enabled, but you can toggle it off to lock an element.

This tool works like the Show/Hide, Summary, and Skip tools.

You click the label of the field to set the field as locked; the color changes to indicate that it's no longer allowed to be edited.

After clicking the Close button, and later going back into that screen, you notice that the field is grayed out (disabled for editing); any data in that field is visible, but you cannot make changes.

>> **Insert/Add:** This tool allows you to add fields.

Click the Insert/Add (+) button, and then click a section of the screen. Doing so opens a list of fields that you can add; the list pops up on the right side of the screen.

>> **Manage:** Clicking the Manage button causes a drop-down menu to appear with these choices:

- *Clear* removes (deletes) your personalization from the page section you're personalizing. This acts as a reset button, in essence — if you have messed up the personalization beyond salvaging, use this.

- *Import* allows you to load a personalization file that you or someone else has previously exported. This is a way to share a personalization that another user has created.

- *Export* allows you to save your personalization to a file.

Personalization files are in XML format and are downloaded to your Download folder on export.

Close: Click the Close button to exit the Personalization toolbar, thereby saving your personalization changes.

Reload the page to see all your changes take effect; you may need to close the window and then navigate back to it later to see your personalization take effect.

REMEMBER

Configuring the Global Address Book

The way addresses and contacts are organized in D365O is quite ingenious — after you get used to it. D365O is a flexible system as far as addresses and contacts go, but there's no getting around the fact that it can seem a bit complicated for the uninitiated. Everything centers around the concept of a party. Think of a party as in the legal term for a participant (not as in a fiesta or a celebration). A party is the core element in the global address book. A party can be either an individual person or an organization (such as a privately held or publicly traded company, a government agency, or an institution). A party can have one or more locations, and those locations are either postal addresses or contact information, such as email addresses.

Another separate element, the party role, lines up with its role as a prospect, customer, vendor, or worker (employee), for example. Each party role is then associated with a party — just keep in mind that you can associate the same party to more than one party role. Suppose that you work with a company that sells you items *and* buys them from you. In this example, the same company is sometimes a customer and sometimes a supplier (vendor). The beauty of this Global Address Book feature is that both the customer and the vendor record can be associated with (related to) the same party record. Now, if you update an address record for the party, both the customer and vendor get the change instantly because the address is a global party address, not an address that's stored specifically in the Customer table or the Vendor table.

This system of organizing addresses allows for a fluid and flexible approach toward updating and entering address and contact information, because the party isn't tied to any particular type of master record (party role); rather, it's a generic contact person or company (organization) along with the sites (branch locations) for that person or company. After you set up all the location addresses and contact information for a party, you can associate that party with one or more particular record types (party roles), such as a customer, prospect, vendor, user, or applicant.

For example, when adding a new customer, you enter that person's name in the Name field, and when you do so, the system checks the global address book and pops up a list of names matching what you keyed in. This is a handy way to avoid creating duplicates, and it lets you take advantage of party record information already in the global address book, saving keystrokes as well.

A key advantage of this kind of organization is that, as roles change, the address doesn't need to be rekeyed. You simply associate the party with the other party role. For example, if an applicant is hired by your organization and later becomes both a user (someone who uses the D3650 application) and a worker (employee), the address information for that person is already in the system attached to the generic party record for that individual person. It can then simply be associated with the new party role records for the user and worker. Likewise, if a prospect (a prospective customer) eventually makes their first purchase and becomes a full-fledged customer, their address and contact information is already in the system as well — you simply relate the party record that was associated with the prospect party role with the new customer party role.

The following list spells out the party role categories available in D3650:

>> **Prospect:** An individual person or organization that you're trying to sell to but that has not yet made a purchase

>> **Customer:** An individual person or organization that you definitely are selling, have sold, or will sell goods or services to

- » **Vendor:** An individual person or organization from which you make purchases of goods or services, such as a supplier or trade vendor

- » **Applicant:** An individual person who has filled out an application to work at your organization

- » **Worker:** An individual employee of your organization or a contractor working on behalf of your organization

- » **User:** An individual person who has a license under a subscription plan to sign in to the D365O application and use the system (in other words, an ERP user)

- » **Competitor:** An individual person or organization that offers goods and/or services similar to the ones your organization offers and is in competition with you

- » **Contact:** An individual person inside or outside your organization

Creating additional address books

Every address can be stored in the global address book, and the global address book spans multiple companies (legal entities/sets of books) that you have within your instance of D365O. To make things even more flexible, D365O has the concept of additional address books. An example of why you might want to create additional address books is to have the addresses isolated by company. You can also create separate address books by line of business, division, region, or what-have-you. Additional address books make address lookups easier because you have fewer records to search. Of course, you aren't required to create any additional address books. Another reason you may want to create additional address books is for security purposes. For example, you may have users who are supposed to work only in certain companies in D365O. You can set security privileges to party records by limiting or granting access to the additional address book. You can add a new party record directly in the global address book, and when you do so, you can specify one or more additional address books in which to include that party record. In other words, the Address Books drop-down menu on the Party Record screen is a multiselect drop-down menu, so you can make more than one selection.

Setting global address book default values

To complete part of the D365O setup, you must decide on default values (settings) for the global address book. Those default values are also used for any additional address books you may create.

REMEMBER

Normally, your Dynamics 365 authorized solution provider updates these default values for your organization during the configuration of the global address book.

>> **Person Naming Sequence:** Defines the order of last name, first name, and middle initial.

>> **Cascading Delete:** Determines whether a party role record (such as a customer or vendor) is deleted when the party record (the record associated with it in the global address book) is deleted.

>> **Notification for Duplicates:** If a duplicate is found in the global address book, determines whether a Duplicate Record message is displayed to users when creating a new record.

>> **DUNS Inclusion:** Concerns the Data Universal Numbering System (DUNS). You must decide whether to include the DUNS number as part of the data you capture in the global address book. The DUNS number, which is regulated by Dun & Bradstreet, is a way to uniquely identify a business or another legal entity. DUNS is normally associated with credit ratings, but can also be used as a unique numbering sequence, to avoid adding duplicate records for organizations — similar to how you would use a Social Security number to uniquely identify individual persons.

>> **DUNS Uniqueness:** Another DUNS-related setting, where you decide whether D365O will perform a uniqueness check when a DUNS number is entered.

>> **Default Type:** Determines whether a party record is always either a person or an organization. You should decide which type of party record your organization tends to use more often and then make that type the default; otherwise, during data entry, users will have to keep changing it from person to organization or vice versa.

>> **Security for Private Information:** Lets you limit which user roles have access to the private addresses and contact information of party records.

Creating new party records

Normally when you create a party record, you know the party role. It's unlikely that you're adding an address while not knowing specifically what it's for or related to. However, the system is flexible enough that you can go directly to the global address book and add the party record there. The party record will then exist in the global address book and not yet be assigned to any party roles. Typically, party records are added automatically to the global address book behind the scenes by the system when you're creating a party role, such as a customer, vendor, or worker. For example, if you're adding a vendor, go to the Vendor list and click the New button to open the vendor maintenance form, as shown in Figure 15-5.

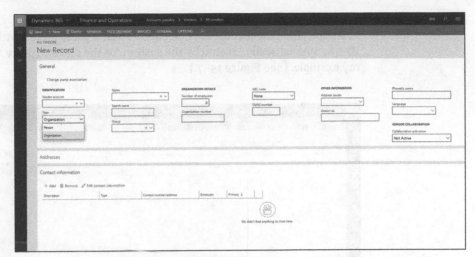

FIGURE 15-5:
Selecting a type
while adding a
new vendor.

REMEMBER

When you create a new vendor record, the Type drop-down box gives you two choices: Person or Organization. The reason (as I mention in the previous section) is that a party record must be either an individual person or an organization (a company, institution, or other legal entity).

Figure 15-6 shows how to add a new vendor. When you click the Add button in the Addresses section, the New Address pane appears on the right side of the screen. After you fill in the needed information and click the pane's OK button, the address is added to the vendor. You then click the Save button to save the vendor. When you add this vendor and an address for the vendor, the global address book is automatically updated.

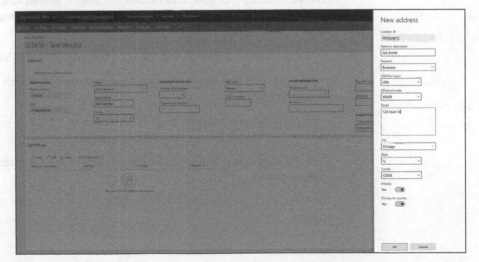

FIGURE 15-6:
Adding a new
vendor with a
new address.

I can open the global address book and see that a party record with a unique party ID was automatically created by the system for the vendor (party role) I created in my example. (See Figure 15-7.)

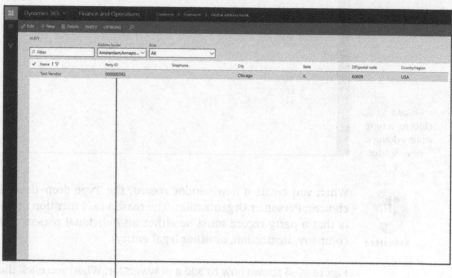

FIGURE 15-7:
Looking up a party record in the global address book.

A unique party ID was automatically created by the system.

To look up a party record in the global address book, follow these steps from the Modules menu:

1. **Choose Modules ⇨ Organization Administration ⇨ Global Address Book ⇨ Global Address Book from the Finance and Operations navigation pane.**

    The Global Address Book list view appears, as shown in Figure 15-8.

2. **In the Filter text box above the Name column, enter a search string to locate the record.**

    In my example (refer to Figure 15-7), I entered the search string *Test Vendor* because that was the name of the vendor I created.

3. **Click the Magnifying Glass icon on the left side of the Filter text box to apply the filter.**

    The list is filtered to show the party records matching the search string you applied.

Alternatively, you can click the Filter icon (the one that looks like a funnel) on the black bar on the far left side of the web page to extend the Filters pane.

A more complex search involving multiple fields can be performed using the Filters pane.

Notice that each party record in the global address book has a sequence party ID number that was system-generated.

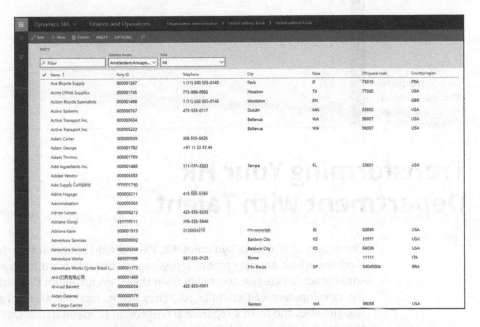

FIGURE 15-8:
Global Address
Book list view.

4. **Click the link in the Name column; in other words, click the name of the party record that you want to look at in more detail, and possibly edit.**

The Party page (Maintenance window) appears, as shown in Figure 15-9.

REMEMBER

The Party ID field isn't editable, because that field is a system-generated unique identifier, not a free-form text field.

On this page, you can edit the party address in the Addresses section; doing so changes the address for the vendor party role record that is associated with this party record. The records are automatically synchronized by the system, saving you time and avoiding confusion.

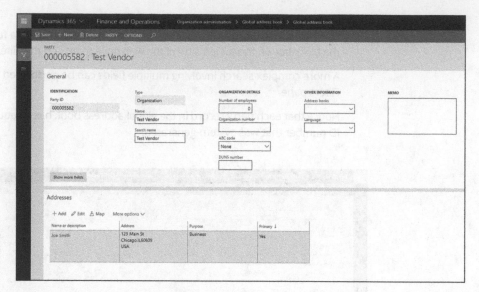

FIGURE 15-9:
The Party
Record screen in
the Global
Address Book.

Transforming Your HR Department with Talent

The origin of D365O is Dynamics AX. I've talked about many of the Dynamics AX modules which are now part of D365O and accessible from the module menu, but some modules are not accessible from there, even though they originated during the development of Dynamics AX. They are in fact accessed through a separate website URL and from a separate arrangement of menu items. One such module is Human Resources, which is now called Talent.

The URL for Talent is: https://attract.talent.dynamics.com

Microsoft Dynamics 365 for Talent is a human capital management application consisting of three modules (or experiences):

>> **Human Resources:** Streamlines the human resource function

>> **Attract:** Improves the hiring process

>> **Onboard:** Manages new-hire orientation

Configuring the Human Resources module involves defining departments, jobs, and positions — the main organizational elements of the HR module. A *department* is a functional area of your organization; departments can be cost centers, profit centers, or business units, as well as the traditional departmental areas such as accounting, sales, marketing, and customer service. A *job* is a collection of tasks and responsibilities that define the role of an employee.

These are the four HR job types:

>> Hourly

>> Salary

>> Full-time

>> Part-time

A *position* is an instance of a job. A job can have more than one position, but not the other way around. In other words, you post an open position for a person to perform a certain job (role). Positions exist within a department and are eventually assigned to workers (employees) when a person is hired to take the position. Position additions and changes can be workflow enabled, and an audit trail history can be kept to show who has made changes and when. Positions can have a set duration, and effective dating is available for both jobs and positions.

REMEMBER

Effective dating allows you to set a start and an end date for the job or position to be active or valid. Effective dating also allows you to future-date position changes; for example, you can assign a worker to a position that somebody has already filled using a future date because you know that the person who has that position now will be leaving the company in a few weeks or months.

In the Attract module, an applicant for a position is called a *candidate.* After a person applies for a job, they receive an email, generated by the system, that invites them to sign in, where they can see the status of the job hiring process, review their job application, and respond to any task requests assigned to them.

This list describes the main features of the Attract module:

>> **The Attract dashboard:** The hiring managers at your organization or the internal recruiters in your HR department can use this feature to post open positions for jobs.

>> **The Jobs tab:** Assign interviewers to interview the candidate; you can see the job description here as well.

>> **The Candidates tab:** Add and maintain information about the candidate; if the candidate has a LinkedIn profile, it may be visible here.

>> **Stages of the hiring process:** Track the hiring stages in the process: Apply, Screen, Interview, and Offer, in that order. A candidate starts in the Apply stage and may or may not be advanced to the subsequent stages, depending on the discretion of the hiring manager and HR staff. Interviews are scheduled and feedback is gathered.

>> **The Candidate app:** After a candidate is added to a job and receives an email containing a link to download this app, that person can communicate with the hiring manager and HR staff, including notifying them when they're available for interviews.

REMEMBER

Having a proper onboarding program lets your organization help employees hit the ground running on their first day on the job. (Too many organizations don't start the onboarding process, a hot topic in the HR world, until the employee's first day at work; then everyone makes a mad rush to get the new person up to speed.) As soon as the employee has accepted the offer letter and a start date has been agreed on, the onboarding should begin.

The Dynamics 365 for Talent Onboard module has a handy feature called Onboarding Plan for creating emails and adding documents, links, and maps that can be sent to the new hire before they begin work. You use this feature to instruct and inform the person about your organization and their new role in it.

With the addition of the Talent application, Dynamics 365 now has a full-featured HR solution for your organization.

Filing Expense Reports with Expense Management

Employees are always eager to be reimbursed for the expenses they incur on behalf of their employers. Sales reps and executives usually who incur most of the expenses, because of the amount of traveling they do, but if your organization is a service-based business, you may also have technicians and consultants of various kinds who regularly incur significant business-related expenses. If employees rack up credit charges on their personal credit cards and don't get reimbursed in a timely manner, you can create a stressful situation. It's a challenge for the accounting department to quickly (but *accurately*) process expense reports to get the employee reimbursed and also to distribute expenses to the proper general ledger account numbers for financial statement purposes and tax reporting.

Long ago, expense reports were paper based. Receipts were photocopied and then stapled together, inserted in large manila envelopes, and sent by postal carrier to an administrative staff who would laboriously review the stack of paper receipts, run a tape on a printing calculator, and then, at long last, key the information into an accounting (ERP) system. Eventually, the employee would receive a paper check from the Accounts Payable department, necessitating a trip to their local bank to deposit it. Companies have come a long way since then. Employees can attach PDF files as receipts, key their expense information into a web page, and then submit it all to the accounting department so that the data is already keyed into the system when it's first reviewed. A manager who needs to approve the expense report can be out and about, maybe playing golf or attending a Little League baseball game, and approve the report using only a smartphone.

The advent of paperless, online, mobile-enabled, and workflow-enabled expense report solutions has greatly improved and streamlined the employee expense report processing function for many organizations. However, most of these solutions sit outside of your ERP system — separate systems that require a separate user license, in other words, and some of them are expensive. Then there's the need to develop and maintain integration programs to import data and synchronize data with the ERP system. Many of these systems need to interface with not only the ERP system but also an outsourced payroll provider because employees often prefer to be reimbursed by direct deposit as part of their regular payroll cycle rather than receive a separate check.

The Expense Management module is a full-featured expense report system embedded within the Dynamics 365 for Finance and Operations ERP system, so it's fully integrated with the general ledger module and requires no custom integration programs. Also, it has mobile capability, workflow features, and the ability to go paperless. Advanced features for per diems, credit cards, cash advances, and tax recovery are also included in the module.

As you can see in Figure 15-10, the menu choices for the Expense Management module are quite extensive; this is a full-featured module.

The Expense Management mobile workspace is an especially slick feature that you should be sure to evaluate. This mobile workspace is accessed with the Microsoft Dynamics 365 for Unified Operations mobile app.

Here are some of the tasks you can perform in this mobile workspace:

>> File a new expense report.

>> Attach credit card transactions, receipts, images, and files to your expense report.

>> Submit your expense report for approval and reimbursement.

>> Approve or reject other employees' expense reports that you've been assigned to approve.

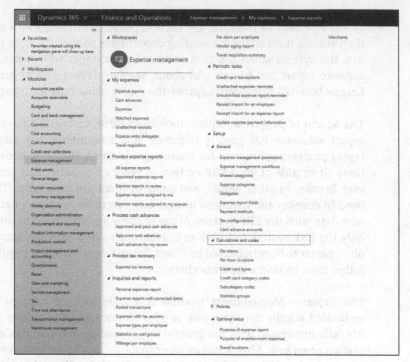

FIGURE 15-10:
The Expense
Management
menu in
Dynamics 365 for
Finance and
Operations.

The Microsoft Dynamics 365 for Unified Operations mobile app not only handles expense reports — your system administrator can also publish workspaces for other purposes, such as for working with sales orders, on-hand inventory, and project timesheet entry and approval.

We live in an increasingly wired world where everybody is connected to the Internet most of the time. With Dynamics 365 for Finance and Operations, Microsoft has created an ERP system that is ready to meet the requirements of today's Internet-centric workplace and, indeed, to help shape a future where workers are more focused on serving customers than wrestling with rigid and disconnected ERP systems.

5

The Part of Tens

Chapter **16**

The Ten Most Exciting Capabilities of Dynamics 365

With the release of Dynamics 365, Microsoft has transformed the ERP and CRM cloud computing landscape with a well thought-out mix of applications, modules, technologies, and standards that provide exciting capabilities for revamping your organization's front-office and back-office information technology. Let's take a look at some of these important capabilities.

Supercomprehensive Coverage

Dynamics 365 is a truly outstanding array of software capabilities that work together to digitally transform your organization toward new heights of efficiency, accuracy, and productivity. Only Microsoft has the widespread adoption, the breadth and depth of technical knowledge, the financial resources, and the creative talent to bring together so much functionality into one interconnected cloud service. Microsoft's leadership at so many different levels of software engineering gives Dynamics 365 a unique advantage among competing choices for ERP or CRM. No other company can provide so many pieces of the pie itself without having to rely on outside organizations to develop the underlying operating and database systems, or without having to worry about strategic shifts made by other computer companies that may negatively impact their own R&D roadmap. For the most part, Microsoft sets the agenda for others to follow. Even if the technology trend is something the company didn't initiate, before long it tends to dominate that new technology anyway.

REMEMBER

Microsoft is not entirely free of internal squabbles, as is the case with any giant corporation; nonetheless, no other ERP or CRM developer can deliver all the pieces of a world-class ERP or CRM Software as a Service (SaaS) solution by itself as part of a cloud service you can license with a month-by-month subscription at a reasonable price.

Just take a look at the components of Dynamics 365:

>> **Computing power: Microsoft is a leader in cloud computing.**

The Azure Cloud is a planet-scale public cloud that rivals any other provider's cloud services as far as coverage, security, resources, and capabilities go. Dynamics 365 runs on Azure. Competing products often must rely on another company's cloud infrastructure.

>> **Database: Microsoft is a leader in database technology.**

The Azure SQL Database is essentially the same as the Microsoft SQL Server relational database management system (RDBMS), the leading database product that has become a widely adopted standard for business applications. SQL Server is the same database that Dynamics has run on for many years, but now the Azure SQL version is optimized for the cloud; it has elasticity that allows it to grow as your business grows. Dynamics 365 runs on Azure SQL. Most competing ERP and CRM products also run on Microsoft's SQL Server database; so they must rely on Microsoft, but not the other way around.

>> **Customer engagement: Microsoft is a leader in CRM.**

Dynamics CRM Online is now Dynamics 365 for Customer Engagement; this is the same popular and very widely adopted leading CRM package, but now with more connectivity to the Dynamics ERP offerings (AX and NAV), standard reporting tools (such as Power BI), point-and-click customization tools (such as PowerApps), and more connections to other cloud services (such as Google, Amazon, and others). Dynamics 365 for Customer Engagement (CRM) has expanded the traditional CRM capability of organizing and tracking communications with contacts and prospects to automate the sales cycle, to include applications for not only sales force automation but also customer service, marketing automation, field services, project service automation, and HR talent (applicant tracking and on-boarding).

» Finance and operations: Microsoft is a leader in ERP.

With two cloud ERP applications to choose from, Microsoft has your SaaS accounting software requirements covered with Dynamics 365. For larger (enterprise or midmarket) organizations with more extensive requirements, there is Finance and Operations (formerly Dynamics AX), and for midsize to small organizations, there is Business Central (formerly Dynamics NAV). Both Finance and Operations and Business Central are full-featured, full-blown ERP systems with modules like General Ledger, Budgeting, Accounts Receivable, Accounts Payable, Inventory Control, Sales Order Processing, Purchase Order Processing, Manufacturing, and more.

» Common Data Model: Microsoft is a leader in business intelligence.

The Dynamics 365 applications are built on the Microsoft Common Data Model. This means your development efforts for data integrations, custom reporting, and custom applications can leverage a shared data architecture. You can extend Dynamics 365 in innumerable ways, but all the extensions will point to a shared set of standard entities so that a change to one of the entities (such as adding a new field to the Inventory record) will be automatically reflected everywhere. The code inheritance and code reuse that are inherent in using a common data architecture can speed up development *and* reduce the cost of maintaining your customizations.

» Office 365: Microsoft is the standard in office suite software.

Microsoft is the standard for spreadsheets (Excel), word processing (Word), email (Outlook), presentations (PowerPoint), and more. Office 365 integration in Dynamics 365 is extensive and *bidirectional* (moving seamlessly from Dynamics 365 to Outlook and from Outlook to Dynamics 365). You can receive emails in Outlook and see the sender's information from Dynamics 365 for Customer Engagement (CRM) on a pane that appears to the right of the email you're reading. This kind of convenience saves you from having to toggle between applications or cut-and-paste data or laboriously attach and reattach files. What you do in Outlook is reflected in Dynamics 365 applications and vice versa. Dynamics 365 includes an unprecedented level of integration with not only Outlook but also Excel and other Office 365 applications.

» SharePoint: Microsoft is a leader in document management.

Chances are good that organizing your documents on SharePoint is already an established way to collaborate on projects at your organization or to distribute marketing collateral, knowledge base articles, periodic reports, and other items to teams inside and, sometimes, outside of your organization. Dynamics 365 is connected to Office 365 SharePoint, making it easy to distribute Dynamics 365 reports and other information on SharePoint.

>> **LinkedIn: Microsoft is a leader in professional networking.**

Microsoft's LinkedIn is the number-one professional networking website in the world. LinkedIn has become the de facto way for business professionals to reach out to one another, find opportunities, and match requirements with people.

Scalability with Azure

One of the most exciting facets of Dynamics 365 is that it runs on a true multi-tenant cloud SaaS architecture. With Dynamics 365, your ERP and CRM are in the cloud, not on-premise. What this means to you and your IT department is that you don't have to worry about all this stuff:

>> The operating system (patches, updates, and upgrades)

>> The SQL databases (upgrades, backup maintenance plans, query optimization, having a full-time database administrator, and so forth)

>> File system backups

>> Computer virus and malware protection on the servers

>> Adding memory to servers

>> Swapping out failed hardware

>> Resizing, reallocating, and reapportioning servers as your business grows

>> Installing, patching, and upgrading your ERP or CRM software

Scalability with Azure means that as your organization grows over the years, you don't have to worry about the infrastructure of the application servers or the database servers for your ERP or CRM, because the elasticity of SQL Azure will handle whatever growth you can throw at it. The volume of transactions that your ERP and CRM can handle will scale with no need to purchase, design, or maintain additional hardware or virtual servers on the part of your IT department. The Microsoft Azure cloud service is designed to accommodate growth in transactional volume, database size, user counts, and reporting requirements.

TIP

Though the advent of virtualization for computer servers has made it much easier to spin up a server than in the bad old days when a new server meant new hardware, maintaining a purely on-premise network is still a lot of work. Private cloud (as opposed to public cloud) services provide the best of both worlds in giving you your own network but having it in the cloud. Private cloud services also tend to be in a position to offer more specialized attention, especially if you purchase services from a smaller provider, who may respond to your organization's needs more readily due to your being a more important customer to it, relatively speaking. Microsoft considers all its customers important, but because the company is so enormous, you can sometimes feel like a number or have the sense that you're getting lost in the crowd. But even if you go with a smaller cloud provider, you can still run your ERP and CRM on Dynamics 365, because that smaller cloud provider will be able to give you access to the Microsoft Dynamics 365 cloud service.

Mobile Computing

As with biology, technology evolves over time, though it evolves much more rapidly and somewhat more unpredictably. The telephone evolved into the cellphone (which was still primarily a telephone), but then the cellphone evolved into the smartphone, which is so much more than a phone that the term *phone* no longer describes the device adequately. A smartphone is not actually a telephone, but rather a portable personal computer that acts as a magazine, a newspaper, a dime store novel, a television set, a map, a kind stranger giving accurate directions, a pen and notepad, a perfectly precise watch that needs no winding and remembers to adjust to daylight savings time all by itself, a tape recorder, a color camera that needs no film, and a video recorder and player, all while being constantly connected to a global computer network (the Internet and the cellphone carrier network), which in a very real sense turns it into your own, unique node within the collective consciousness of humanity. This personal portable computer allows you to communicate 24/7/365 with just about anybody in the world.

These days, practically everyone has a smartphone with them at all times and they rarely take their eyes off the tiny screen for more than a few minutes. The smartphone already does almost everything. So why can't the smartphone be your CRM and ERP system as well? Why do you have to wait to get into the office, or back home to your basement to boot up your desktop PC or unpack your laptop to catch up on approving employee expense reports, sending out quotes to customers, resolving customer service issues, reviewing the quarterly profit-and-loss statements or ordering inventory? Hey, get your work done now. Just use your phone while waiting in line at Starbucks for your tall mocaccino.

Dynamics 365 has added mobility features to align with Microsoft chief executive officer Satya Nadella's declaration of a mobile-first, cloud-first strategy. In addition to PowerApps — the cloud service that allows you to create and distribute custom mobile apps that can access any data, including Dynamics 365 data — Microsoft has a front-end graphical user interface (GUI) specifically for Dynamics 365. The Dynamics 365 mobile app is a mobile-ready user interface for Dynamics 365.

The Dynamics 365 mobile app is available for any mobile device, including Android (Samsung Galaxy) and iOS (Apple). You can download the Dynamics 365 mobile app from

>> Windows Store

>> Google Play

>> App Store (Apple)

Here are a few examples of things you can do with the Dynamics 365 Mobile App:

>> Email a sales quote to a customer.

>> View key performance indicators on a dashboard.

>> Search for a customer account and view the invoice history.

TIP

Dynamics 365 has separate mobile apps for field service and operations because the Field Service offering evolved from the FieldOne Field Service Management application, which already had its own highly specialized mobile features. Mobility is especially important and needs to be robust in field services because technicians are rarely in the office, but rather are out in the field, servicing equipment for customers. If you use the Field Service application, you'll want to download the Field Service mobile app in addition to the Dynamics 365 mobile app.

Localization Features

Dynamics 365 for Finance and Operations (formerly Dynamics AX) was designed as a true global ERP solution, which means that it has robust localization features. Many computer programs have a feature whereby the labels that appear on the screens can switch to another language by means of a global language setting. This translation feature can even be set at the individual user level, so, depending on which user is logged in to the system, a different language can display on the screens. However, localization is so much more than merely language translation.

Localization includes the language settings, but goes beyond that to provide specific features for a country or region to more closely adhere to local business customs, governmental requirements, tax compliance, and other considerations related to operating within that particular region or country.

Dynamics 365 for Finance and Operations has localization features available for these countries:

>> Australia

>> Austria

>> Belgium

>> Brazil

>> Canada

>> China

>> Czech Republic

>> Denmark

>> Estonia

>> Finland

>> France

>> Germany

>> Hungary

>> Iceland

>> India

>> Ireland

>> Italy

>> Japan

>> Latvia

>> Lithuania

>> Malaysia

>> Mexico

>> New Zealand

>> Norway

- » Poland
- » Russia
- » Saudi Arabia
- » Singapore
- » South Africa
- » Spain
- » Sweden
- » Switzerland
- » Thailand
- » The Netherlands
- » United Kingdom
- » United States

TIP

If you don't see your country listed here, be aware that more localizations are provided by Dynamics 365 channel partners and independent software vendors (ISVs). Be sure to consult with your authorized Dynamics 365 solution provider to determine whether a localization exists or can be developed to meet your requirements.

Employee Self-Service

Most people like to pump their own gas, drive through the automated toll lanes without stopping their car, and pay bills online without having to write out checks, lick stamps, or walk to the mailbox. If they can avoid waiting in line, they do so. If they can avoid being put on hold, they do so. (After all, who among us enjoys listening to a repeating loop of distorted Mozart or warped smooth jazz?) Self-service is a benefit to the person trying to get something done as well as to overburdened workers who are busy helping other employees.

Microsoft Dynamics 365 Employee Self-Service (ESS) Portal is a knowledge management tool. This tool leverages the Knowledge Base capability in Dynamics 365 for Service. The challenge to getting the most benefit out of this tool is to make sure your organization loads up enough relevant Knowledge Base articles, keeps them current, and tags them in such a way as to increase the likelihood of a match.

To install the Dynamics 365 Employee Self-Service (ESS) Portal, follow these steps:

1. **Point your browser to the Office 365 Admin Center at** https://portal. office.com/AdminPortal/Home#/homepage.

   You can expand or collapse the navigation menu — the black menu to the left on the web page — by clicking the left arrow (<) to collapse it and clicking the right arrow (>) to expand it.

2. **Choose Admin Centers from the bottom of the menu.**

   A pull-out menu appears, displaying all the other admin-related sites that you can go to in order to configure various settings for applications that fall under the Office 365 umbrella.

3. **Choose Dynamics 365 from the navigation menu on the left side of the web page.**

   Doing so launches another tab on your web browser, which takes you to the Dynamics 365 Admin Center.

   The URL is https://port.crm.dynamics.com.

4. **Click the Instances tab on the navigation bar along the top of the page and then select the instance you want to add the portal for from the options displayed.**

   Information about that instance is displayed in a gray pane to the right of the instance you have selected.

5. **Click the blue circle to the right of the word** *Solutions,* **which appears toward the bottom of the gray pane.**

   The Manage Your Solutions window appears.

6. **Click the Dynamics 365 Portals — Employee Self-Service row in the list of solutions you are managing.**

   The information in the gray pane to the right of the solution changes to display a description of the solution you have selected — in this case, Employee Self-Service. (See Figure 16-1.)

7. **Click the Install button (the blue circle with the pencil icon) to install the portal.**

   A wizard guides you through the process.

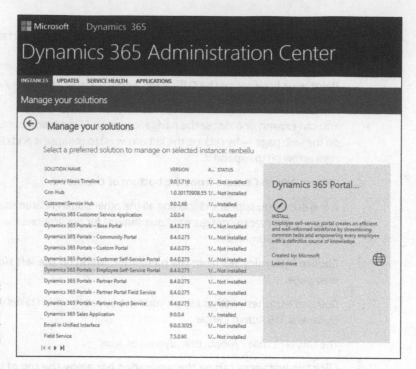

FIGURE 16-1:
Installing the
Dynamics 365
Portal for
Employee
Self-Service.

Microsoft has created other portals, which are preconfigured for different purposes:

>> Customer Self-Service

>> Partner Portal

>> Partner Portal for Field Service

>> Partner Portal for Project Service

>> Custom Portal

These portals are only as good as what you put into them, as far as loading them with pertinent information. However, this feature provides a quick and handy way to set up a website that can be accessed by your own employees or people outside your organization, such as customers or partner organizations. For example, with the Customer Self-Service Portal, you can give customers the ability to submit, view, and update a customer service case (for example, a support ticket) online, rather than have to call in to a call center. On this portal, you can provide Knowledge Base articles that relate to the issue they're trying to resolve, in the hope that they will get the answer they need by themselves from a Frequently Asked Questions (FAQ) document or other information you have loaded to the portal.

Common Data Model

The Common Data Model doesn't sound like a particularly sexy feature. I guess you have to be quite a nerd to get excited about these kind of things, but if you're passionate about your organization having an efficient and reliable computer system, the Common Data Model is a topic you should be thrilled about. Rather than your IT department having to design its own data warehouse, Microsoft is, in a sense, spinning up a prebuilt data warehouse architecture for you, an architecture that contains standard schemas (similar to the concept of file layouts or a SQL table designs) for common entities (such as customers, vendors, inventory items, and invoices). You can then base your custom reports and custom apps on these standard schemas. When you need to extend the standard schema (such as adding a user-defined field to the customer record), all your custom reports and custom apps will get that new field automatically. It saves you time and money to make a change in one place and have all your custom reports and custom screens recognize that something changed, without having to recode everything. This kind of code inheritance makes it possible to change your system much more easily to adapt to new user demands.

Microsoft has taken the trouble to create prebuilt data analysis objects combining data from SQL tables from various Dynamics 365 applications to save you a tremendous amount of development time. In other words, Microsoft has already created mappings of commonly used and important fields from the Dynamics 365 family of applications into the Common Data Model. It's all about saving you time and getting your system working as quickly as possible.

Another important consideration is that Microsoft Power BI (the custom reporting tool) along with Power BI Insights (preconfigured Power BI apps for Dynamics 365 modules), Microsoft PowerApps (the custom app creation tool), and Microsoft Flow (the custom workflow creation tool) are all built to work with the Common Data Model. So the combination of a common data architecture and standard tools for custom reports, apps, and workflows is what really makes it all come together as a powerful integrated technology. (Figure 16-2 gives a schematic view of how these pieces fit together.)

The Common Data Model technology allows for code reuse and code inheritance, which is advantageous. The amount of time you can save in software development and maintenance along with the ability to quickly adapt your ERP and CRM systems to changing business requirements is the thrilling part. Wouldn't you love to tell your staff, "Yeah, no problem. We can add a drop-down box to tag those special orders, and all the reports will automatically reflect it." That sounds a lot better than this: "Sorry. You'll just have to keep track of it on a spreadsheet, because it will take at least a year to consider adding any new features to the system, due to all the re-programming it would require to existing screens and reports."

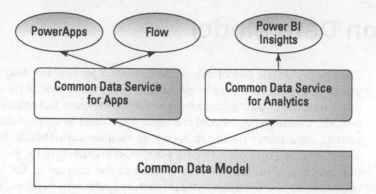

FIGURE 16-2:
Microsoft's
Common Data
Model
architecture.

Now, to be realistic, Microsoft is stretching the truth a bit if it is indeed claiming that all of Dynamics 365's applications are built on a *communal* data model (the SQL tables used by all the applications are shared and consistent across applications). The truth is that Customer Engagement (CRM), Finance and Operations (AX), and Business Central (NAV) were three separate products with their own separate SQL tables, originally designed by completely separate development teams many years ago (before these products were acquired by Microsoft). Nonetheless, these three applications, as well as several others, were successfully ported to the cloud by Microsoft developers and given a snazzy new web-based graphical user interface (GUI) — or, as it's sometimes called, web front-end. The porting of these applications to the cloud is great news, and migrating these complex applications must have taken an enormous development effort on the part of Microsoft's software engineers. So it will take some time for the underlying SQL tables to become increasingly communal. Each of these applications still has its own data model to some extent, but Microsoft is moving toward more and more commonality within the Dynamics 365 family of applications.

The important thing to know is that Microsoft has seen the need to help organizations move in the direction of a common data architecture for standard entities (think of standard layouts across applications and reporting systems for customers, vendors, purchase orders, and so forth), and has created a data warehouse repository, so to speak, and provided integration connectors that allow you to easily load data into it and keep that data synchronized to the various Dynamics 365 applications as well as other applications (if you so choose to incorporate those in the Common Data Model).

WARNING

You will most likely need the help of a qualified Dynamics 365 solution provider to get the most out of the Common Data Service and Common Data Model. Working with the Common Data Model intelligently so that it will work properly isn't for the light-hearted, but it's worth doing. Microsoft has made some powerful tools available, but those tools need to be artfully and expertly configured to provide the most value to your organization.

Team Member License

With Dynamics 365, Microsoft has created a supercomprehensive cloud ERP and CRM solution, and, as you might expect, it's not the cheapest system out there. Less expensive alternatives are available. Of course, as the saying goes, "You get what you pay for" with some of those cheapo systems. Actually, Microsoft's prices for Dynamics 365 are competitive with services offering similar capabilities.

Furthermore, you should be aware that Microsoft also offers a much less expensive license. This Team Member license allows for read-only access to all modules and update access (in other words, write access) to several commonly used entities. A user who is assigned a Team Member license can update the following entities in Dynamics 365 Customer Engagement:

>> Accounts (customers)

>> Contacts

>> Activities

>> Tasks

>> Notes

>> Custom entities that your organization creates

The Dynamics 365 for Team Member subscription also allows users to record their own time and expenses for Dynamics 365 for Project Service Automation and to update their personal information.

TIP

When the time comes to get serious about buying a Dynamics 365 subscription or adding more licenses or subscriptions, download the Microsoft Dynamics 365 Licensing Guide — an Adobe PDF file that Microsoft creates and periodically updates with the latest rules about which functionality is covered under each subscription type. (you can get it at `https://mbs.microsoft.com/Files/public/365/Dynamics365EnterpriseEditionLicensingGuide.pdf`) This licensing info can get mighty complex, so review the guide and confer with your authorized Dynamics 365 solution provider to help you understand your options.

General Data Protection Regulation

The European Union (EU) has passed a law to protect the privacy of its citizens, called General Data Protection Regulation (GDPR). If you have subscribed to the Microsoft Dynamics 365 cloud service, you may be concerned about how the strict

GDPR privacy requirements (and the steep penalties for failure to comply) may put your organization at risk.

The Microsoft Trust Center provides detailed information on how Microsoft is prepared to help organizations with GDPR compliance.

The URL for the Microsoft Trust Center is

>> www.microsoft.com/en-us/trustcenter/default.aspx

Microsoft has gone on record to state that it is committed to ensuring GDPR compliance in its products and cloud services — and, of course, Microsoft Azure, Microsoft Office 365, and Microsoft Dynamics 365 are major services that Microsoft is focused on with regard to GDPR compliance. Choosing Dynamics 365 for your ERP or CRM application can potentially help your organization become more compliant with GDPR requirements.

Unified Interface

Dynamics 365 is a family of applications, not just one app. It has Customer Engagement (formerly Dynamics CRM), Finance and Operations (formerly Dynamics AX), Business Central (formerly Dynamics NAV), and so much more. Porting all these applications over to the cloud has been a monumental task for Microsoft, and it has done an amazing job. In addition to getting the existing screens to work in the cloud, Microsoft has introduced a new user interface that uses its new model-driven apps technology it developed for PowerApps. This new user interface is called Unified Interface. However, not all screens are yet available in Unified Interface. Furthermore, on a screen that is available in Unified Interface, not all functionality from the old screen is available. Nonetheless, many screens are available, especially in the Customer Engagement (CRM) applications.

One big benefit of using Unified Interface is that the same app can run on a web browser or on a smartphone as a mobile app. The app automatically resizes to fit the device using a technique called *reflow*, where the controls on the screen are not fixed to a form but, rather, flow into spaces available on the screen, even if you rotate the device. With PowerApps, you can also create your own apps that conform to the Unified Interface.

The following are examples of Dynamics 365 apps, created by Microsoft, that conform to the new Dynamics Unified Interface:

>> Sales Hub

>> Customer Service Hub

>> Field Resource Hub

>> Project Resource Hub

Categorized and Relevance Search

Let's face it: People are so used to using Google to search for things that old-style searches that look in only one field or search only one type of record and find only exact matches are simply no longer sufficient. That old-style search is becoming more and more passé. Fortunately, Dynamics 365 has introduced a search-engine-style capability more like Bing or Google, called the *categorized*, or *global*, search. The global search allows users to enter a search string in the navigation bar and conduct a global search of as many as ten entities (types of records, such as customers, vendors, or cases) at a time. You can use the asterisk character (*) as a wildcard to specify *begins with*, *ends with*, or *contains*.

For example, I ran a search for the top navigation bar in Customer Engagement (see Figure 16-3) using the following search string:

wood

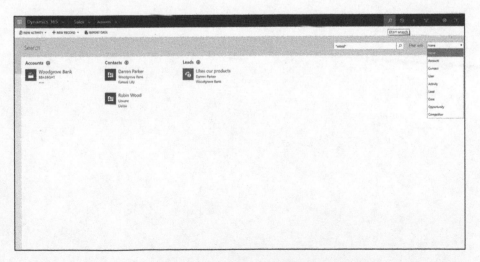

FIGURE 16-3:
Example of a global search result in Customer Engagement.

The search looked at accounts, contacts, leads, cases, activities, and other items. The intelligent search capability scanned all these different types of records and looked in several fields within each record, and it then applied the wildcard to search for anything containing the word *wood*. The search came back with one account, two contacts, and one lead. One contact that was found had the last name Wood. The other records were found from being associated with an account (in other words, customer) called Woodgrove Bank.

TIP

You can adjust which ten *entities* (types of records) are included in the global search, as long as you have the appropriate privileges to alter that setting. Ask your system administrator if you want to change which entities are to be included in the categorized global search setting in Dynamics 365.

For Dynamics 365, you also have the option of enabling another feature known as *relevance search.* The results of the relevance search are sorted by relevance in a similar fashion to an online search engine such as Bing or Google, which tries to place the most relevant matches at the top of the results list rather than alphabetically. The relevance search is powered by an Azure search service. Unlike the categorized search, the relevance search has no limit on the number of entities (types of records) that can be included in the search.

For old-timers who are attached to the earlier versions of Dynamics, the Advanced Find features are still available. In Customer Engagement, for example, if you need to create a more complex and precise search, you can still access the Advanced Find feature by creating a personal view. You can do this when viewing entities such as accounts, leads, and contacts. Simply click the View name, and then click on Create Personal View, found toward the bottom of the list of view names. Doing so opens the Advanced Find window. That window allows you to create a view and name it; thereafter, that new view name will appear in the list of view names.

Chapter **17**

Ten Dynamic 365 Myths to Dispel

Unicorns and mermaids are mythical creatures that have a place in children's literature, but when it comes to the getting down to business and investing large sums of money in information technology, myths should be dispelled straight away. Because cloud computing is a new trend, many myths and misunderstandings still surround it, especially as it pertains to ERP and CRM systems. Let's take a look at some common myths that may be shrouding your appreciation of the benefits that Dynamics 365 can bring to your organization.

Myth 1: Investing in ERP Doesn't Pay

Over the years, I have attended many meetings with business executives who were evaluating whether to purchase and implement new back-office accounting software packages for their organizations. These software systems — referred to as *enterprise resource planning* (ERP) systems — typically handle general ledger, financial reporting, budgeting, accounts payable, accounts receivable, inventory control, supply chain, and other mission-critical finance and operations functions. I was often surprised to note that the chief executive officer (CEO) was rarely in attendance, and in fact, quite often the chief financial officer (CFO) also failed to make an appearance. Apparently, the CEO and CFO had more important things to do that day, or any day when ERP was being discussed.

Many business leaders don't consider an ERP system to be anything more than a necessary evil — an expense you must endure as a cost of doing business; they do not regard ERP as a driver of success and overall profitability for their organizations. They regard the ERP system in the same way they regard the HVAC (heating, ventilation, and air conditioning) system in their office buildings: You need an HVAC system to heat or cool the buildings. The HVAC system costs money, and if it breaks down, you need to pay to get it fixed right away, but as long as it continues to run, just don't touch it. "If it ain't broke, don't fix it" is their motto for HVAC, and for ERP.

Certainly, implementing a new ERP system is perilous and painful because you can't stop paying vendors, billing customers, releasing financial statements, shipping products, and the like for even one week, much less for six months (or as much as two years) while you design, build, test, and deploy a new ERP system. You have to keep up with the day-by-day operations, right up until the moment when you're ready to cut over to the new system, all without missing a beat. Your organization's ERP users, who have been using your existing ERP system for a dozen years or more, have to be trained in the new system. You will have to teach some old dogs new tricks, and some of those old dogs bite: They're often stubborn, averse to change, and skeptical about the new system, especially if previous attempts to migrate to a new ERP system have failed and been scrapped. Furthermore, ERP implementations tend to get quite expensive because you need to hire consulting firms who are experts in the ERP software package you're implementing, and the longer the project takes, the more it ends up costing, as the project scope tends to expand as you keep discovering additional drop-dead requirements. Lastly, there's the enormous business risk of serious disruption to operations or, worse, complete operational standstill, during cutover or soon after going live.

When you consider all the expense and risk and the enormous amount of energy you need to muster to overcome the natural tendency to stick to the status quo, it's easy to understand why business leaders dislike the idea of implementing a new ERP system, and why they tend to feel about it the same way most people feel about going to the dentist or getting a colonoscopy. Business leaders tend to delay ERP projects, year after year, as their ERP systems grow more obsolete, antiquated, unreliable, and unsustainable. It's a sad sight, but it's all too common to see a green screen, character-based application being emulated on a color monitor. The advent of virtual servers has allowed IT departments to run old software on virtual servers capable of running obsolete operating systems that support the obsolete applications. It used to be that the hardware would fail, thus forcing the organization to upgrade the ERP applications, but with virtualization the IT departments can continue to run old operating systems on new hardware, so much so that the obsolescence of hardware no longer acts as an impetus to modernize ERP systems.

Furthermore, it's difficult and, some might argue, even impossible to measure the true return on investment (ROI) of an ERP implementation. Many of the gains are quite nebulous. Something that you could measure is, for example, salary reduction from the new ERP system's reduced requirement for clerical workers. However, rarely can you reduce your clerical workforce by going live with a new ERP system. Typically, it's just the opposite: The new ERP system demands more ERP users to capture the data that used to be outside the system, so your payroll expense may actually go up.

Sadly, it appears to be common sense that implementing a new ERP system is a task you should put off for as long as possible and avoid at all costs. However, nothing is further from the truth. Your ERP system is the electronic brain of your organization; that brain needs new blood, more connections, and better neural pathways.

Business leaders are too often blind to the costs of running antiquated ERP systems. They don't weigh the costs of delaying ERP projects, because those costs are typically ephemeral, indirect, and non-obvious. However, just because you cannot precisely quantify a cost in terms of dollars and cents doesn't mean that it's not a harmful cost. Likewise for benefits, an investment that pays for itself may not be precisely or easily measurable.

Revamping your organization's ERP system by migrating from an obsolete, on-premise monolithic application to a cloud-based interconnected ecosystem of Internet- and mobile-enabled cloud services can provide critical and game-changing benefits for your organization. ERP modernization is an opportunity to improve bottom-line performance, and represents an investment that should be made without delay.

A newly implemented modern and effective ERP system yields all these benefits and more:

>> **Better search capability:** Users are able to look up information much more rapidly as well as find information they wouldn't have been able to find previously. In many cases, these new search capabilities provide timely information that can be the difference between losing or retaining a customer.

>> **More integration possibilities:** The key to gaining operational efficiency in information systems is extensive use of integration programs. These integration programs eliminate the rekeying of data; in other words, data that has already been captured in electronic form previously in a related system is imported or synchronized in the ERP system automatically and without human intervention. Obsolete ERP systems lack entry points for data integration such as web services, XML compatibility, message queuing, REST API, and the like.

>> **Tighter coupling to Internet services:** On-premise ERP applications that were initially designed before the advent of not only cloud computing but also the Internet in general are hardly sufficient to stay connected to an Internet-centric ecosystem of suppliers, customers, couriers, tax calculation services, and so on.

>> **Less data entry, more data analysis:** Reducing the data entry burden on your employees lets them spend their time analyzing data rather than keying data. It's impossible to overemphasize the dramatic effect of freeing employees from the grind of data entry and enabling them to use their minds rather than their mitts.

>> **Ad hoc reporting:** Dynamics 365 is a perfect example of a cutting-edge ERP system that is all about empowering users to report on, extract, and manipulate data without having to rely on and wait for their IT department to respond to their request for a new report or data dump. Quite often, the already overburdened IT department declines to provide the requested report or, if it does agree to do it, the report may take many months to be delivered. Dynamics 365 includes predefined and configurable dashboards, the ability to save and name your filtered views of data, push button export functions to Excel and PDF, and, finally, access to powerful ad hoc report writers such as Microsoft Power BI. When users are able to access information in more and better ways using self-service reporting tools, the entire organization benefits in ways that are hard to measure but that make a huge impact on the profitability and sustainability of the organization.

Myth 2: Our ERP Is Too Entrenched

The barriers to migrating from an obsolete on-premise legacy ERP package to a modern SaaS (Software as a Service) cloud offering may seem overwhelming. Most likely, your legacy ERP system is an octopus with many tentacles, including

>> **Custom reports:** Custom reporting systems may contain hundreds of mission-critical reports, such as contracts, invoices, packing slips, picking tickets, financial allocation distribution amounts, bonus calculations, and commission calculations.

Replacing your custom reports is too often seen as an impossible undertaking, largely due to the sheer volume. However, after you perform an in-depth and comprehensive analysis of your legacy custom reports, you typically find that most of the reports are no longer used, many were ill-conceived in the first place, some are inaccurate, and others can be replaced with either workflow features or electronic distribution of documents to outside parties, such as billing to customers using emailed PDF files, instead of printing hard copies, stuffing them in envelopes, and mailing them.

Your custom reports may appear as an insurmountable barrier to a new ERP system, but they're probably instead a fertile ground for harvesting efficiency gains.

» **Existing integrations:** Your legacy ERP system may already have innumerable touch points with other systems inside and outside of your organization. If the integrations were poorly designed, you may be regarding the integration middleware as a rat's nest of tangled spaghetti code; if you change one thing, the entire process (which isn't well documented and which nobody fully understands) will be hopelessly scrambled. You don't dare touch it. You are stuck; the ERP system is entrenched due to its tenuous connections to other systems. You feel you're better off just leaving everything as it is.

What you may be leaving out of the equation, though, is the IT cost of administering a broken integration platform as well as the cost in time, lost customers, missed orders, system down time, and squandered productivity. Your ERP integrations should have been well documented, written using a widely adopted standard technology and designed to be flexible by working with standard schemas in a middleware that will allow for the repointing of interfaces from an old system to a new system without the need to recode the entire works. Again, entrenched integrations are most likely an excellent opportunity to gain efficiency.

» **Technophobic users:** If you're running an ERP system that has been in place for 10, 15, or as much as 20 years or so, you're likely to have ERP users who have been with your organization from the time the ERP was first installed. That system is all they know, and they're comfortable with it. The users don't want to undergo the painful process of learning a new system; such an endeavor will be traumatic for many of them. Clerical ERP workers are typically change-adverse and risk-adverse individuals who prefer set routines that follow predictable steps and fixed schedules. Furthermore, many of them are afraid of new technology; they're technophobic.

Here is a case where you need to apply tough love. Don't let the reluctance of your ERP users — whether they're clerical workers or accounting managers, controllers, or even the chief financial officer — determine the rate at which you modernize your ERP system. In the end, the ERP users will be glad that they're off the antiquated technology and running a cutting-edge system that provides countless benefits as far as Internet, mobile, and search capabilities go, and includes ease of data extraction, superior ad hoc reporting, as well as an intuitive and customizable user interface.

Myth 3: ERP Is Too Complex for the Cloud

Cloud-based ERP services are much newer than on-premise ERP packages, which have been around for nearly 50 years. SAP (the big daddy of ERP systems) was first released back in 1973, and JD Edwards, another major player in the on-premise ERP world, was founded in 1977. The first cloud-based ERP of note was NetSuite, founded in 1998 and backed by Larry Ellison, the founder of Oracle Corporation. However, NetSuite did not gain widespread popularity until more recently, as it has slowly added more modules, features, and capabilities. On-premise ERP developers have been incrementally adding features to their software for several decades, before the advent of cloud ERP software, so of course on-premise ERP is much more feature rich. There's also the added advantage that on-premise ERP has an ecosystem of independent software vendors (ISVs) who have created add-on products for the major on-premise ERP packages. Many of these on-premise add-on products address industry-specific requirements that are rarely addressed within the base package and are thus now unavailable for cloud ERP systems.

Cloud ERP, where ERP is offered as SaaS, is the future of ERP. The research-and-development effort of all major ERP vendors is clearly focused on the cloud. More features will be added to the cloud versions, and the on-premise ERP software packages will become *sunset* products that will be slowly phased out. Though it's true that on-premise ERP has more features and modules than cloud ERP, it isn't true that this situation will last. Cloud features and modules will eventually surpass on-premise. But the advantage of cloud computing isn't limited to modules and features, because there are benefits to it that are fundamental to the way the software is installed, maintained, upgraded, and interconnected that cannot be matched by on-premise software right now.

Cloud ERP software can be extended. For example, Dynamics 365 can be extended with PowerApps as well as with customization features that are native to the applications. (One example of the latter is Dynamics 365 for Customer Engagement, which has the ability to create custom entities and easily modify forms without low-level coding.) Cloud ERP is not only ready to tackle complex enterprise requirements today but can also position your organization for future growth on a highly scalable, highly adaptable platform.

Myth 4: Integrations Are Not Worth It — Just Rekey the Data

Automated data integration programs are the most powerful means by which one can help organizations become more efficient in processing information. However, integration programs are complex to devise and tricky to get working. After they're working, they can often run for years on end with little or no maintenance. I have written integration programs that have run for ten years or more without my being called back in to fix them even once. The integration programs tend to settle down and become stable after a few months of operation, but integration programs can be difficult and costly to set up. It's often the path of least resistance to simply keep banging the data into the system by brute force using a data entry screen, even as the volume of data may be increasing year after year, or month after month. So managers and clerical workers tend to keep quiet and keep keying.

REMEMBER

Some workers may fear that they will lose their jobs and be replaced by an automated integration program that enters the data for them, rendering them obsolete. The idea of integration programs isn't to steal jobs from humans; rather, the idea is to free up the humans so that they can use their brains to analyze information and respond to vendors, customers, co-workers, and agents, rather than be bound to their cubicles with a ball-and-chain of data entry for eight hours a day.

Automated data integration is the key to increasing the efficiency of business software; this is why Microsoft has stressed the tight coupling of Office 365 with Dynamics 365, and why so many connectors are being made available for Microsoft PowerApps to connect Dynamics 365 with services throughout the Internet. Microsoft SQL Server has had SQL Server Integration Services (SSIS) and SQL Agent as a scheduler to run SSIS packages as steps in SQL Agent jobs as a standard integration platform for decades, but with Dynamics 365, integration technology is taking another giant leap forward.

Microsoft's Common Data Service — a service that uses the Common Data Model to organize and make available data from throughout the Office 365 and Dynamics 365 family of applications in one central place for easy accessibility — is a cornerstone of Microsoft's new data integration strategy. Data made available in one central place and accessed by standard means makes integrations easier to develop and maintain.

TECHNICAL STUFF

Representational state transfer (REST) application programming interfaces (APIs) with JavaScript Object Notation (JSON) are now a preferred method of updating, deleting, inserting, and reading records from databases in web apps using the HTTP protocol. Widespread use of REST API with JSON as a standard will make it easier for varied special-purpose web applications to share the same data set, thereby avoiding discrepancies inherent in data storage duplication and redundancy.

Myth 5: Software as a Service Is More Expensive than On-Premise

If you purchase something outright for cash, as a rule of thumb it's cheaper in the long run than renting it month by month. Think of credit cards or 7-year auto loans — the interest charges are painful. Ouch! It may seem obvious that you can save money in the long run if you choose to purchase on-premise software rather than pay a per-user charge month after month with no end in sight, even though you will have to cough up the full purchase price on day one. However, deciding on the right ERP system for your organization is a much more complex issue than, for example, buying a used car.

The complexity of the decision is due to a plethora of factors, such as these:

» **The cost of purchasing and maintaining your own on-premise hardware (or cost charged by your parent company for apportioning servers):** It's not just the cost of the software that must be considered; the hardware as well is a major factor.

» **The cost of the annual software maintenance premium:** Even if you purchase on-premise accounting software outright, and even if you pay cash so that you have no debt and no interest expense, you still have to pay approximately 20 percent of the purchase price (or sometimes the list price) of the software each year as an annual maintenance plan in order to stay on the upgrade path and to remain authorized to receive technical support, patches, and software updates from the software developer. Yes, even on-premise ERP packages require you to pay a recurring amount. Refusing to pay it is perfectly legal, but that leaves you unsupported and unable to upgrade to never versions as they become available, so it's generally most unwise to refuse to pay the annual software maintenance premium.

» **The efficiency and productivity gains of using the cloud software:** It's probably fair to offset costs by considering these gains; however, these benefits are difficult, if not impossible, to precisely quantify or even grossly estimate.

>> **Implementation costs:** These costs are supposedly lower with cloud ERP, but it depends on the extent of scope creep during the implementation and on who is doing the implementation — in other words, how good the implementers are. The often heralded claim that cloud implementations, cloud upgrades, and cloud customizations are always cheaper than on-premise is overblown. The costs for customizations and upgrades will be more affected by how much customization was done, how well designed the customizations were, and how extensively and clearly they were documented. You may end up customizing more in the cloud (due to lack of features in the SaaS offering) than you would have if you had purchased an old-school, on-premise ERP that was loaded with prebuilt features. It's truly impossible to know how everything will play out in the long run.

The reality is that it isn't easy to know whether the on-premise or SaaS solution will be cheaper in the long run. What is clear is that the ERP industry is moving quickly and totally in the direction of SaaS, and there is likely to come a time when on-premise solutions from the top vendors, such as Microsoft, will no longer be available anyway, so the choice will be made for you; you may want to adopt SaaS now so as to not get left behind. Also, it's a great relief to most chief financial officers and business owners to not need to come up with a huge chunk of money to buy a new ERP system; most are happy to simply pay for SaaS by the month, just like they do for their telephone and electricity bills.

TIP

If you're interested in analyzing cloud versus on-premise costs, you may want to use a calculation tool available on Microsoft Azure. Microsoft has released a tool to help you calculate the total cost of ownership (TCO) comparing cloud cost to on-premise cost for similar capabilities.

The URL for this TOC calculator is `https://azure.microsoft.com/en-us/pricing/tco`.

Myth 6: The Cloud Is Not Secure Enough for ERP

Data security is a major concern. Hackers are working day and night to compromise systems, gain unauthorized access to information, and conduct illegal activities, including stealing your trade secrets or your money. The fight against hackers will continue and will, no doubt, evolve in unpredictable ways. As the good guys create a defense, the bad guys will figure out a way around it, and the cat-and-mouse game will proceed endlessly and with a fearsome intensity.

In the meantime, you have a business to conduct or an organization to run, and you need software applications to manage your operations and report on your results. You can keep all your software on your own on-premise hardware, or you can use SaaS cloud services for some of these applications, such as ERP and CRM. To shy away from selecting cloud services based on a fear of hackers is wholly unwarranted. After all, what is to stop hackers from attacking your own local on-premise servers? Don't you think that Microsoft and other major cloud providers (such as Amazon and IBM) have the most sophisticated hacker defenses in place — defenses that are being constantly updated and enhanced to stay one step ahead of the latest computer hacking techniques? Do you think that your IT department is as sophisticated as Microsoft, IBM, or Amazon in guarding data against unauthorized access?

Well, now, you may not trust the cloud provider corporations themselves, but that is another issue (one beyond the scope of this book). Every time you make a cell-phone call or send an email, you're sending your personal and private communication out into a cloud of unknowing, where your government or a foreign government or a megacorporation may have access to (or attain access to) your data. Perhaps such entities may in fact have the desire to spy on you without your consent or knowledge, but this is a wider issue about personal privacy, not a decision point about whether to go with cloud or on-premise solutions for ERP and CRM. How much of these privacy concerns are instead paranoia versus genuine concerns is another debate entirely. The point is that you aren't going to stop writing emails or making cellphone calls, so if those privacy issues aren't affecting your choice of wireless carrier or email provider, why would they be a concern about selecting an ERP or CRM system?

It took years for the average shopper to feel comfortable about using a credit card to make online purchases. Likewise, it has taken business executives and IT directors years to feel comfortable with cloud-based SaaS ERP and CRM solutions. The success of Salesforce.com is evidence of the earlier willingness of executives to embrace the cloud for CRM as opposed to ERP; this is because CRM systems contain mostly correspondence information regarding prospective customers, rather than more sensitive information like financial transactions (disbursements of cash to vendors or payroll checks to employees, for example). ERP in the cloud has had a slower adoption rate, for two reasons: First, the ERP data is more sensitive, and second, the ERP requirements are more complicated, which means that they require more robust features, which were more difficult to port to the cloud.

REMEMBER

Security concerns exist regardless of whether you're in the cloud or on-premise, so I wouldn't reject SaaS based on data security concerns. The exception is if your business is conducted within an industry or government sector that necessitates special-purpose, ultrasecure networks to guard some kind of highly sensitive transactions or knowledge such as trade secrets or top secret classified information.

Myth 7: What If the Internet Goes Down

If the Internet goes down, it will be catastrophic, but the catastrophe will be widespread, not limited to your organization. So worrying about the reliability of the Internet is like worrying about the reliability of the international banking system: You have to assume that it will be there daily. Also, can you remember a day when the Internet was broken and you couldn't even get on the Internet? Power outages can knock out your computers, but that can be a problem for on-premise computers as well as for SaaS services. The human race is now past the point where the Internet is considered anything less than an absolute necessity for survival of the species. In a sense, the Internet has become the collective mind of humanity. It makes perfect sense to have your business software connected and embedded in the Internet, because that is where business is most likely to be conducted in the foreseeable future.

Myth 8: I'll Lose My Data in the Cloud

I have worked at client sites where the physical hardware (the database and application servers) are all located within the corporate headquarters office building, yet the ERP users had little access to their own data. The data was trapped in the databases of applications that had poor reporting capabilities and even worse data extract and integration options. The users were doing things like printing reports to text files and trying to parse them in Excel manually. Yuck! Where the data resides physically makes no difference whatsoever if you don't have user-friendly ad hoc query tools that can connect to the data and allow you to mine it.

The Microsoft Power BI business intelligence reporting tool works hand in hand with Dynamics 365 and can empower users to retrieve and analyze data by themselves. Users can create visual representations of data, such as graphs, charts, and lists that they can share on dashboards or as links within SharePoint with colleagues within the organization, as well as parties outside the organization, such as vendors, customers, and government agents. In all likelihood, migrating your ERP to the cloud will actually give your users more access to your data.

Dynamics 365 is a tenant-based cloud service. Microsoft partitions your own tenant area within its server farm environment, so, virtually speaking, your organization does have its own servers, and therefore its own private area of data. Your data stays separate from other organizations, and you have 24/7/365 access to it (although, to be realistic about it, there may be some brief periods where Microsoft has planned or unexpected outages, but such is the case with on-premise networks as well). The application software is shared, but that's the good news.

You don't have to install your own software; instead, you sign in to a website that runs communal software. Upgrades, enhancements, and patches to the software are instantly delivered to all clients using the service, with no work on your part. This is the beauty of the SaaS architecture.

Myth 9: You Won't Have Control of Your Data

It is true that, from an IT infrastructure perspective, you have more direct control of your data if your data is stored in a database located on a computer database server that is physically located in a building you have access to. For example, if your data is stored on your own physical computer server in your offices, you can physically walk up to the machine and reboot it. You cannot do this kind of direct manipulation of a virtual tenant instance that is located in a Microsoft Azure data center. You aren't even allowed to walk into that building. You're not authorized to do so, and asking permission to do so is pointless. For security reasons, you will be kept out, and, in any case, the data center may be located hundreds of miles away from where you are. You will be at the mercy of the cloud provider to manipulate hardware. You will have to initiate a support ticket and wait for the technical support staff to assist you. You won't even know if there is a hardware problem or if the problem is purely software related.

When your data is in the cloud, you may not know where it is physically, what hardware it's running on, what the backup and disaster recovery plan is, and how it's partitioned and sectioned off from other client's data. But do you want to know any of that? Do you want that much control? Do you need it? Do you want to have to worry about the details of the hardware infrastructure? Wouldn't you rather let the cloud provider handle all the technical minutia concerning data storage, backups, security, redundancy, latency, and so forth, so that you can focus on your core business, which may be something completely unrelated to computer technology, such as baking cupcakes, making bicycles, or providing home healthcare to seniors? When you get electricity from a utility, do you care that you cannot directly manipulate the turbine in the power plant or manipulate the uranium rods in a nuclear reactor?

What you want is the power; in the case of an ERP or CRM system, you want computing power. You don't want or need to have to deal with all the technical details involved in generating the computing power. With cloud computing, you can use the computing power to run your business more efficiently. Microsoft's strategy to move its flagship ERP and CRM offerings to a true multi-tenant cloud architecture by releasing Dynamics 365 makes perfect sense because you gain control of your information, which is what counts, even though you don't have direct control to manipulate the underlying hardware and software infrastructure.

Myth 10: Cloud Apps Are Not Customizable

In true cloud computing architectures (as opposed to hosted old-school client/server applications that some people may mistake as cloud computing), all companies using the service are running the same software application so that you're freed from having to install and patch your own software. You won't lag behind in the upgrade cycle, because the cloud provider is regularly upgrading the entire system and because every company using the service receives the latest version of the software automatically. Because of this communal approach to the application software in true cloud computing, it isn't possible for you to run your own modified version of the application. Because of this lack of independence in the software your organization is running on, some people believe that cloud applications are rigid, lacking in customization and modification tools. Though that is an understandable conclusion to reach, it isn't accurate.

For example, Dynamics 365 for Customer Engagement (CRM) is highly customizable because the application itself (including the original on-premise version) has built-in features for customization that don't require you to run a different version of the application to have unique master record types (entities) or unique form (screen) layouts or unique command buttons available on a form. To understand how this is possible, take a look at the different ways that customization can be accomplished in software applications.

The main methods used to customize computer applications are described in this list:

>> **Layering custom application code on top of the out-of-the-box application code to override the base code:** With layering, you're overriding the official base source code developed by the software developer with your own custom code. Doing so gives you the ability to make precise and powerful customizations, but it takes you off the upgrade path because now your organization is, in essence, running a different application than everybody else. When the developer upgrades the base code, your customization may no longer be compatible. The code overlay and override method of application customization isn't compatible with a true multi-tenant cloud computing architecture because, in cloud computing, every tenant should be running the same version of the software.

Dynamics 365 for Finance and Operations (AX) uses layering, but Microsoft is moving away from this approach and will end up phasing it out completely as Finance and Operations becomes a pure cloud-based application.

If code overlay and override were the only method of customizing software applications, it would be true that cloud services are not very customizable when it comes to tailoring them to a user's unique requirements, but, fortunately, this isn't the only method.

REMEMBER

» **Point-and-click customization features:** A point-and-click customization feature allows users to create objects, screens, command buttons, lookup lists, and other items, all without having to do any computer programming. The user is able to drag and drop controls from a toolbox onto a blank or existing form.

What you can customize and how much you can customize are limited to what the modification feature allows you to change, so this method isn't as flexible or powerful as code override, by any means; however, this method is fully upgradable because you're changing the data in the database, not the code that runs the application.

At runtime, the application code interprets the settings you made and stored in the database using the customization feature, and the screens are rendered at that moment to include your customized preferences. This method of customization is perfectly compatible with true cloud-based computing.

Dynamics 365 for Customer Engagement (CRM) has extensive point-and-click customization features as a native aspect of the application; these features actually predate the migration of CRM to the online version.

» **Separate applications that extend functionality:** Another method to customize applications is to kick off completely separate special-purpose apps that don't live within the main application. They communicate with the main application via connectors, but they're not a problem when you upgrade the main application, because they do not override or modify any of the computer code within the main application.

Microsoft PowerApps uses this method of customization. You don't use PowerApps to modify Dynamics 365 applications; instead, you create separate mobile or web apps using PowerApps that can interact and extend the power of Dynamics 365, often by creating a bridge between Dynamics 365 and other applications or teams of people such as suppliers or third-party agents. The apps you create with PowerApps may depend on data that is native to the Dynamics 365 application and may be able to invoke processes within the Dynamics 365 application, but they do so by connecting to Dynamics 365 and interacting with data schemas, events, and actions that are exposed by the connector, not by overriding core application code.

REMEMBER

It's the responsibility of Microsoft to keep the connector compatible with future versions of the core application, so, as Microsoft continues to upgrade, update, patch, and enhance the Dynamics 365 core application, your PowerApps code will continue to be compatible because it's connecting using a connector that Microsoft will ensure is still compatible with each iteration of the core application.

Index

M

T

tablets, Skype click-to-call, 46

tabs

  Action Pane (Finance and Operations), 276

  Candidates (Talent), 305

  Jobs (Talent), 305

Talent, 14, 15, 240, 304–306

tasks (App for Outlook), 36

Tasks component (Customer Service), 118, 121–122

taxes, general ledger records for, 252

Team Member license, 323

Technical Stuff icon, 4

Technician Scheduling, 15

templates

  for Business Central from Microsoft Flow, 92

  Marketing, 157–158

  for Microsoft Flow, 86

tenant, 8, 18

Teradata, 56

Tesla, Nicola (inventor), 7

tiers, 18

Tile Selector (Customer Engagement), 104

Tile Selector menu (Field Service), 172

Tile Selector menu (Project Service), 145

tiles

  Customer Quick Navigation (Business Central), 206

  Finance and Operations, 246

  navigating with (Finance and Operations), 249–250

time-and-billing system, 139–140

time-and-materials project, 141

time entries (Project Service), 147

time-off request (Field Service), 173

time units (Project Service), 150

timesheet (Project Service), 147

Tip icon, 4

tools, upgrade analyzer, 23

total cost of ownership (TCO) tool (website), 335

tracked, 35

transaction categories (Project Service), 150

transactions (Business Central), 197

transitioning to cloud computing, 16–24

Trello (PowerApp connection), 76

Triangle icon (Finance and Operations), 247

Twilio, workflow notifications from, 90

Twitter, 76, 85

U

Unified Interface for Apps, 242, 324–325

Unified Operations mobile app (Finance and Operations), 308

upgrade analyzer, 23

Upgrade AX 2012 to Dynamics 365 for Finance and Operations, 23

User Acceptance Testing (UAT), 19, 22

user-centric design, 220–221

user dashboards, 164

User Groups button (Business Central), 233

user interface (Finance and Operations), 290–297

user post (Customer Service), 129

user preferences (Finance and Operations), 250–252

users

  managing (Admin Center), 25–27

  managing (Business Central), 230–233

  working with (Customer Service), 119–120

Users (Customer Service), 118

V

value-added reseller (VAR), 28

vendor item numbers (Business Central), 208

Vendor Maintenance window (Finance and Operations), 268–269, 270, 277

vendors (Business Central), 207–209

Vendors screen (Business Central), 209

view definition, 123

View list (Customer Service), 125

View Records button (Customer Service), 136

view(s)

  assigned leads in Customer Engagement, 108–109

  contacts (Customer Engagement), 111–112

About the Author

Renato Bellu hails from New York city, where he graduated from Stuyvesant High School in Manhattan. Ren, as he is known, received his Bachelor of Science in Accounting from the University of Delaware, and went on to work for Pricewater-houseCoopers, Avanade (a joint venture of Microsoft and Accenture) and RSM McGladrey, among other notable CPA and IT consulting firms. Ren is an ERP solutions architect as well as a hands-on computer programmer specializing in data conversions and integrations. Ren's vision and focus has always been on bridging the gap between accounting and computer technology. Ren has been a vocal proponent of Microsoft's business software solutions from the beginning, when Microsoft acquired Great Plains and rebranded it as Dynamics GP. Ren is the author of *Microsoft Dynamics GP for Dummies* from John Wiley & Sons.

As an ERP consultant, Ren has architected and managed some of the largest and most complex ERP implementations ever successfully completed with Dynamics GP, as well as completing many other IT projects involving Dynamics AX, CRM and other applications.

Ren is also a Microsoft Dynamics author for Lynda.com and LinkedIn Learning, having created several well received video courses. Ren holds certifications for Dynamics AX, and is experienced in CRM, ECM, business intelligence and other technologies related to ERP and cloud computing. Ren lives in the historic town of Haddonfield, New Jersey near the great city of Philadelphia with his wife, Marie, and daughter, Clare.

Dedication

This book is dedicated to my darling wife, Marie, and lovely daughter, Clare, who have loved, cared, and encouraged me throughout this arduous and rewarding journey.

Author's Acknowledgments

I wish to acknowledge the following people:

My parents, Dr. Renato R. Bellu and Elena Bellu, whose guidance, support, and loving devotion has made my career possible.

Matt Wagner of Fresh Books, my literary agent, for making this project a reality.

Matthew Campana for overall moral support as well as technical contributions to select chapters.

Chris LoPiccolo of Reiger Consulting, Inc., who served as technical editor.

The acquisitions team of Amy Fandrei, Steve Hayes, and Ashley Barth for getting the project off the ground and keeping it moving.

Paul Levesque (Project Editor) and Becky Whitney (Copy Editor) for ensuring that my writing was as clear as it could possibly be.

The entire Wiley team, including the graphics team, for their adept work in bringing the text to life with their superb presentation skills.

Our wonderful bunny, Dakota, and dapper goldfish, Jefferey for all their demanding scratching and encouraging splashing during the course of writing this book.

Publisher's Acknowledgments

Acquisitions Editor: Amy Fandrei, Steve Hayes, Ashley Barth

Senior Project Editor: Paul Levesque

Copy Editor: Becky Whitney

Technical Editor: Chris LoPiccolo

Editorial Assistant: Matthew Lowe

Sr. Editorial Assistant: Cherie Case

Production Editor: G. Vasanth Koilraj

Cover Image: © Kalawin/iStockphoto

Leverage the power

Dummies is the global leader in the reference category and one of the most trusted and highly regarded brands in the world. No longer just focused on books, customers now have access to the dummies content they need in the format they want. Together we'll craft a solution that engages your customers, stands out from the competition, and helps you meet your goals.

Advertising & Sponsorships

Connect with an engaged audience on a powerful multimedia site, and position your message alongside expert how-to content. Dummies.com is a one-stop shop for free, online information and know-how curated by a team of experts.

- Targeted ads
- Video
- Email Marketing
- Microsites
- Sweepstakes sponsorship

20 MILLION PAGE VIEWS EVERY SINGLE MONTH

15 MILLION UNIQUE VISITORS PER MONTH

43% OF ALL VISITORS ACCESS THE SITE VIA THEIR MOBILE DEVICES

700,000 NEWSLETTER SUBSCRIPTIONS TO THE INBOXES OF

300,000 UNIQUE INDIVIDUALS EVERY WEEK

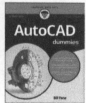